The New England Village

CREATING THE NORTH AMERICAN LANDSCAPE

Gregory Conniff
Bonnie Loyd
Edward K. Muller
David Schuyler
Consulting Editors

Published in cooperation with the Center for
American Places, Harrisonburg, Virginia

THE
New England Village

Joseph S. Wood

with a contribution by Michael P. Steinitz

THE JOHNS HOPKINS UNIVERSITY PRESS
BALTIMORE AND LONDON

For Diane, and many more good years

© 1997 The Johns Hopkins University Press
All rights reserved. Published 1997
Printed in the United States of America on acid-free paper
06 05 04 03 02 01 00 99 98 97   5 4 3 2 1

The Johns Hopkins University Press
2715 North Charles Street
Baltimore, Maryland 21218-4319
The Johns Hopkins Press Ltd., London

Library of Congress Cataloging-in-Publication Data
will be found at the end of this book.

A catalog record for this book is available from the British Library.

ISBN 0-8018-5454-7

Contents

Figures

Preface

~: WHAT GOES AROUND COMES AROUND. IN THE 1880s, THE JOHNS HOP-
kins University published a number of studies on the origins of New
England's towns and villages and its town-meeting government, and in
so doing universalized an invented Romantic tradition. The tradition—
of New England colonists establishing compact agricultural villages and
thereby sustaining religious and community orthodoxy while providing
for common defense—is embedded as collective memory in picturesque villages today. The tradition has endured because ensembles of
houses, commons, and villages endure and because New Englanders are
proud of the history such village landscapes mirror. This book, which
Johns Hopkins University Press publishes, now challenges that tradition. It tells a different story about the human shaping and reshaping of
New England village landscapes, both on the ground and in our minds.
Even as it challenges historical understanding, however, the book, like
its predecessors a century ago, celebrates New England villages as important cultural icons in American memory.

The book began two decades ago as a question: How did the compact
agricultural villages of the seventeenth century become the commercial villages of the nineteenth century? The question engaged Martyn Bowden at
Clark University and several researchers at Old Sturbridge Village, as well as
Michael Steinitz and myself, both of us graduate students at the time. The
answer was not immediately apparent, although we can find much of what
we have to say in this book in preliminary statements from the early and
mid-1970s. When in the late 1970s I undertook to publish my dissertation

on colonial New England villages, an external reviewer nevertheless said the work was nonsense, that of course New England villages had been like fried eggs—settlements, or yolks, in the middle surrounded by resources, or whites. So I proceeded systematically to reresearch, rework, and publish incrementally the elements of the original argument. Time has been good to the argument. Michael's work has come to complement my own, which I have been able to refine substantially. And scholars now accept the argument. What the passage of time has especially allowed, however, is an opportunity to conceptualize findings. In particular, time has allowed us to frame findings in the context of ideas about collective memory and tradition. In large measure, then, the book reflects development of the argument as much as it relates the argument.

In this work we make no claim of comprehensiveness. The study is limited in scope to what Michael Steinitz and I have previously published—a series of complementary essays on a common topic developed over time. It has not been our purpose to rewrite the articles republished here. At the same time, the articles necessarily employed some redundancy in order to link them to the larger argument about invention of the village and the village tradition. We have done our best to reduce this redundancy, but some inevitably remains. Certain portions of the republished work reflect some correction and refinement as well. We have especially added substantially to maps and illustrations, which enrich our visual understanding of villages. All notes, subtitles, and captions have been reworked for consistency. We have retained spelling, punctuation, and capitalization in quotations as completely as possible.

A Note on Sources

When I first undertook this study many years ago it was to determine how the New England landscape had been transformed from one of agricultural villages into one of commercial villages. My reading of geographical location theory told me that commercial villages probably arose during the Federal period—the first time that sufficient and widespread economic activity was present in rural New England to allow nonfarmers to gather together. To prove my point, I turned to the histories of hundreds of towns for descriptions of villages at any given time period. What I found, of course, was that most New England villages had indeed emerged in the Federal period, but not from agricultural villages. These center villages emerged from town centers that had been adorned with little more than meetinghouses during the colonial period. As I mapped the distribution of colonial villages, I realized that conventional wisdom was wrong, and so I found I had to address the premises upon which convention was based as well. The interpretation here focuses on the New England village that I have reconstructed not from premises, but from great stores of historical evidence.

My primary source of evidence has been town histories. Boosterish and idiosyncratic as they may be, town histories are mines of information. Town historians have, of course, always tried to shed favorable light on their subject. Considerable attention is given to the events leading up to the founding and chartering of the town, to the town's role in Indian wars and the American Revolution, to the history of the church and the meetinghouse, to genealogy, and to the town's leading citizens. For this reason, for their "blatant filiopietism," and because they are "most singularly lacking in understanding larger historical movements," some researchers consider town histories less than admirable sources.[1] Such criticism, however, is not relevant to this research. Historians may have lied about the virtues of their fellow townspeople, but they had no reason to lie about the morphology of settlement and the size and location of dwellings. Town historians also provide little enlightenment on town planning, because so few town plans were followed. Nor did it necessarily occur to town historians to interlard their writing with broader historical interpretation, including any reference to tradition or scholarly convention.[2] Rather, town historians collected and reproduced, along with all a town's anecdotes, land records, village and townscape descriptions, early surveys, and, not uncommonly, maps.

Maps have proved to be especially important sources of evidence, and care has been taken in reproducing a number of them here. Not many maps drawn before the nineteenth century show dwelling locations. Commonly they depict physical features—attractive brooks and meadows or obstacles like steep hills; they show lot lines and other property boundaries; they show mills and meetinghouses; and they show principal roads leading to the site of the meetinghouse. The first systematic mapping of towns took place after the Revolution. Massachusetts, for instance, required towns to submit surveys to the legislature in the early 1790s and again in the early 1830s. The 1830s maps are far more detailed than the 1790s maps, often showing center villages and mill villages, but, too, by then villages had emerged across New England. Cultural symbols like meetinghouses and mills on seventeenth- and eighteenth-century maps, including Massachusetts's 1790s series, were intended to suggest settled land. Often exaggerated in size, however, such symbols thereby implied nucleated settlement to unwary readers. Moreover, and too frequently, maps of nineteenth-century settlement patterns have been used to detail colonial settlement patterns, and though settlement patterns tend to persist over time, such analysis is fraught with danger.[3] Still, enough readable maps and reconstructions are available to get a reasonable picture of settlement patterns throughout much of the history of New England, which we have tried to present here.

Woven throughout this book is the overriding premise that humans make geography, both on the ground and in their heads. If this premise is at all correct, then this book is hardly the last word. And that is as it should be, as each generation also writes its own past.

Acknowledgments

~: I WISH TO ACKNOWLEDGE A NUMBER OF PEOPLE WHO HAVE PROVIDED intellectual support for this project over many years. Mark Worthen introduced me to historiography, and then during long and fruitful retirement years in Jamaica, Vermont, followed my scholarly development. I hope I brought him some pleasure in watching his student do well. Rowland Illick and Vincent Malmstrom at Middlebury College introduced me to fieldwork in geography in the Champlain Valley. Ted Miles at the University of Vermont insisted that I meld the two, history and geography, while Peirce Lewis at Penn State insisted that I write it correctly, thoughtfully, and well. Martyn Bowden at Clark University first goaded me into thinking seriously about New England villages — and in the same fashion he spurred Michael Steinitz into studying common houses. He has been a staunch supporter of our work ever since. To all of these fine mentors we owe a very special debt of gratitude.

The work republished here, I have noted, is to my mind more mature and more sophisticated than the original argument, in part due to the substantial intellectual contribution of many colleagues. Those who have contributed to my thinking on villages include John Allen, Richard Candee, Christopher Collier, John Conron, Jere Daniels, Bob Gross, David Jaffee, Terry Jordan, Jack Larkin, Don Meinig, Bob Mitchell, Ted Muller, Michael Steinitz, Kevin Sweeney, Bill Wallace, and Wilbur Zelinsky. Jim Lemon especially has been my strong intellectual supporter over many years with historians. Michael also wishes to acknowledge the intellectual contribution to his work of members of the Vernacular Architecture Forum, especially Claire Dempsey, Bernie

Introduction: "As a City upon a Hill"

No one who has ever lived or travelled at the North, can forget a New England village. In many respects it is unlike every other place where human beings congregate. Its broad streets; its gravelled side-walks; its neat white houses, with their green venetians and pretty porticos; its fine old elms at the corners, and shrubbery in the court-yards, and rich meadows all about it; make it worthy of the fame it has acquired, the world over. Take the pleasantest country town elsewhere, and it lacks something of coming up to the standard of a New England village. There may be more elegance and more wealth in many a hamlet at the South, and the Middle States boast numbers of towns of great taste and beauty; yet there is wanting that air of neatness, and that true independence of manhood, which the mountain breezes give to the population of her valleys, which associates with a New England village, all that we love in nature, with all that we admire in humanity.

JOHN CARVER, 1842

~: THE NEW ENGLAND VILLAGE IS ONE OF ANGLO-AMERICA'S GREAT historic landscape icons—the object of an enduring collective memory. Who does not find sentimentality and cultural meaning in John Carver's evocative village description of 1842 or in Charles Louis Heyde's richly textured view of Arlington, Vermont, about 1852 (FIG. I.1)? Such literary and visual images of New England villages repeat generation after generation. These images provide a tableau upon which Americans have written a substantial cultural history about houses, commons, and villages. The purpose of this book is to characterize how the New England village evolved as a vernacular settlement

1

form as well as how cultural meaning associated with village landscape evolved—how Americans wrote this substantial cultural history.

A recurring theme intertwines these collected articles: The common New England village landscape is burdened by an invented tradition, both popular and scholarly, which has become universalized. In the collective American mind the New England village is a nucleated agricultural settlement encircling a green and standing for community forbearance in a period of societal discipline and economic stability—"as a city upon a hill," to use John Winthrop's oft-cited characterization of his goal for New England settlement. Towns, in short, were planted and perpetuated by compact settlement. In time, tradition asserts, such forbearance and attachment to compact settlement declined—the transition from puritan to yankee—but the village remained.

Understanding the New England village, however, requires investigation of the suspect geography located between the landscape we have shaped and the ideologies we have shared. Not only did the colonial village rarely exist in nucleated or compact form, but in this first of its several guises it fostered highly independent, community-sanctioned, individual landholding. Center villages arose in the early nineteenth century as proto-urban places, not puritan agricultural settlements. And nineteenth-century villagers themselves invented the tradition.

Village tradition is based on what historians and geographers have identified as centripetal forces acting on colonial settlement form: requirements of defense and mutual protection, puritan tenets about how community should be spatially organized, and open- or common-field systems of land division. Because compact settlement was prescribed by centripetal forces, a corollary notion asserts that planned, compact villages were the basis of new towns and settlement expansion during colonial times.[1] This book challenges tradition and tells a different story.

The story, in brief, unfolds this way: New England settlers brought with them cultural baggage that included a predisposition toward dispersed settlement on freehold farms, which they located in relationship to grasslands to support cattle. To early colonial New Englanders, spaces called towns and villages, the latter secondary to the former, had the function of providing land for a community. Villages took on the meaning of community but were not necessarily nor commonly compact in form. By the early nineteenth century, town centers—commonly a meetinghouse and burying ground around a meetinghouse lot—had changed considerably, had acquired central-place

FIG. I.1 Arlington, Vermont, c. 1852. A painter or illustrator would have an exceptional, and Romantic, view of a nineteenth-century New England center village, as landscapes were cleared far more then than now. (Painting attributed to Charles Louis Heyde. Courtesy, Russell Vermontiana Collection, Martha Canfield Memorial Free Library, Arlington, Vt.)

functions, and generally had come to reflect thriving commerce. They had become center villages (FIG. I.2).

Meanwhile, nineteenth-century Romantics, not satisfied with associating the meaning of the place with its contemporary function, larded new meaning on center villages. In particular, they attributed the form of the place and its commercial success to community function and meaning in the early colonial period. So successful has this elaborated meaning become in attracting residents and tourists in the present century, that the tradition associating nucleated form and community has pervaded academic and popular culture alike.

The story employs a variety of approaches and methodologies, including cultural ecology; field-based interpretation of houses and landscapes; archival work with primary sources, such as colonial records, maps, and the 1798 Direct Tax Census; close reading of hundreds of individual New England town histories; and application of geographic location theory. Employing

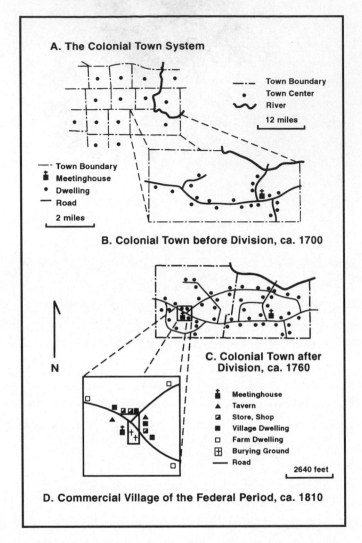

A. The Colonial Town System

Town Boundary
Town Center
River

12 miles

Town Boundary
Meetinghouse
Dwelling
Road

2 miles

B. Colonial Town before Division, ca. 1700

N

C. Colonial Town after Division, ca. 1760

Meetinghouse
Tavern
Store, Shop
Village Dwelling
Farm Dwelling
Burying Ground
Road

2640 feet

D. Commercial Village of the Federal Period, ca. 1810

FIG. I.2 Origin of the New England Village. The New England village evolved from a space to plant community into a place to support commerce. During the colonial period a mosaic of towns, each with its own town center, formed across New England (A). If the town center proved to be poorly located for a portion of the congregation (B), townspeople often requested division. Division led to establishment of new villages or parishes, which were secondary to towns until formally incorporated as towns in their own right (C). The center villages we recognize today arose about town centers in the early nineteenth century (D).

these methodologies, we assess how English settlement of New England was preadapted to particular settlement sites and dispersed settlement forms. We analyze how community functioned in dispersed settlements. We illustrate how the common New England village geography we know today developed and took shape in the Federal or Early National period, looking at both construction of houses and configurations of houses and other buildings. We investigate the idea of the village and link that idea to issues of nineteenth-century Romantic culture and contemporary suburban developments. Finally, we lay out an argument for how American landscape traditions get invented and elaborated. Several important and original conclusions follow.

The conventional, diachronic narrative, that puritan settlers brought communal forms of religion, society, agriculture, and settlement to a wilderness, which they tamed, and that over time these communal forms declined into those of individualism as puritans became yankees, misses key synchronic variations and complexities of early settlement. In particular, New England's settlers were well preadapted to settlement and from the start employed particularly rich agricultural resources located in a set of regionally specific ecological zones.

Within key local ecological zones, colonial villages, like the towns for which they were secondary settlements, were pieces of territory laid out for settlement by an incorporated community of freehold farmers on dispersed farmsteads that would form a corporation and an ecclesiastical parish. Indeed, this colonial New England village was not as much a deviant or exceptional form of settlement as it was an early American manifestation of English antecedents that ultimately came to characterize the form of much of the agricultural settlement expansion of the United States in the nineteenth century.

Likewise, at the end of the colonial period, most houses in eastern and central Massachusetts in particular and New England as a whole were smaller, had fewer stories and less ornamentation, and were more dispersed about the settled landscape than we have commonly believed. Late-eighteenth-century houses that we locate in the landscape today were often products of a rebuilding accompanying substantial post-Revolutionary economic change.

Center villages, the ones we recognize today, also arose in the late eighteenth and early nineteenth centuries from economic change and related growing interaction as measured by increases in trade, transportation, and communication. They were town centers that evolved into central places. Center villages

grew by accretion of activities about meetinghouse lots—town land that remained open in the center to form a new, proto-urban form with few colonial
antecedents. By midcentury, many were thriving places, while others had already succumbed to continuing economic change (FIG. I.3).

Meanwhile, nineteenth-century elites who lived in these new center villages also invented a geographical past and appealing settlement ideal in their
rendition of the colonial village. The contemporary village ensemble of substantial houses and village greens became the historical tableau upon which
the Romantic myth was played out. Village-improvement, architectural-
preservation, and local-historical societies self-consciously carved out a landscape of relict features. Scholars of town origins and of the roots of vernacular building traditions assumed the tradition and converted it to conventional
scholarly wisdom.

As a consequence, the postcard-perfect town and village landscape we observe in New England today—Stowe, Vermont, for instance—with white-
painted, black-shuttered, classical-revival dwellings, churches, and stores
abutting a tree-shaded village green has come ironically to reflect more continuity with the past than change in the past. For the first century and a half of
New England settlement, the Europeanized landscape of towns and villages
filled with single-family farms linked to town and village centers formed a
pre-urban space. Center villages that epitomize this landscape today mark
New England's nineteenth-century commercial ascendancy. They were proto-
urban places. That center villages remain in the landscape today suggests the
passing not of New England's colonial past but of its commercial past. Indeed, as one observer noted romantically in 1868,

> In the days when numerous teams wended their way over the hill,
> and the tavern was haunted by the quidnuncs of the town, as well as
> by travelers, when two stores attracted purchasers, and all the cattle
> and horses were taken by turn to the blacksmith; when the room of
> the Justice of the Peace was thronged by the crowd who often met at
> the trial of some petty malefactor, and the doctor and minister, and
> even the lawyer, were sought by those needing advice and counsel,
> the old Centre was quite a busy place. But this is all changed now,
> and the quiet of a perpetual sabbath reigns there. Yet it is a pleasant,
> healthful spot, and the time may come when men doing business
> in the [mill] village will choose it for their home, and as a suitable
> place for the rearing of their children.[2]

FIG. I.3 View in Sterling Centre, Massachusetts, 1856. This midcentury illustration shows a lively center village that was both a commercial place and a cultural center marked by stylish architecture. (Courtesy, American Antiquarian Society.)

FIG. I.4 Stowe, Vermont. Today the center village is a cultural commodity of great appeal. (Courtesy, Stowe Area Association.)

And so, ironically, what most marks the majority of center villages in the twentieth century is the fairly complete absence of the kind of commercial quickening that created and shaped them in the nineteenth century. They are now largely places of residence for people never engaged in or purposefully disengaged from urban society. Villages, once the sites of trading in commodities, have themselves become commodities (FIG. I.4).

All of this is meant to be provocative—to make us all, scholars and intelligent lay readers alike, think critically about landscapes. Lessons of this story are important for the present. Intellectually, the story illustrates that we create human geographies as much on the ground as in our minds. Cartographic abstractions and symbols, like sketches of meetinghouses marking town centers on 1790s maps, became metaphors interpreted as more than they represented. Meanings attributed to places are inventions—images of what functions places serve and how successfully they serve these functions. Meanings make places attractive or unattractive, even if meanings are abstract or inaccurate. As changes in relationships give rise to changes in places, so human beings invent new meanings as well. The present forms the past. Cultural hegemony and critical inheritance occur in which the modern world, consciously or not, invents its past in its own image—as nineteenth-century villagers did quite literally and as contemporary suburban developers do now, undertaking historical reconstitution of a geographical image of the past as a culturally meaningful entity for shaping contemporary forms of community. In practical terms, this understanding has importance for historic preservation, as well as implications for development of tourism, living museums, and even new places and settings for community, commerce, and recreation. But, then, as with any amenity, too much of a good thing can lead to ruin. Finding a place for tradition in landscapes and landscape in traditions is the work of cultural geographers for years to come.

1 · The Colonial Encounter with the Land

~: This chapter offers a cultural-ecology approach to understanding the process of seventeenth-century settlement in New England, thought to be driven by religious dissent and population growth. In it I challenge the conventional narrative of settlement in which puritan settlers brought communal forms of religion, society, agriculture, and settlement to a wilderness, which they tamed, and that over time these communal forms declined into those of individualism as puritans became yankees. I argue that this diachronic version of the story misses key synchronic variations and complexities of early settlement. In particular, I argue that New England's settlers were well prepared to employ New England's grasslands—you can see these salt marshes and freshwater meadows when flying over New England today. Furthermore, it was division of grasslands more than it was covenanted community, puritan ideology, or defensive precautions that shaped human geographical patterns and forms of agricultural settlement. New Englanders built New England villages on the human geographical foundations established by the first settlers raising cattle. :~

THE NEW ENGLAND VILLAGE

~: IN THE NEW ENGLAND EXCEPTIONALIST TRADITION, PIONEERS IN A wonder-working providence converted "howling desert wilderness" to garden. Puritan settlers had it in mind to create a new, purer England, one built upon an idealized vision of a past England. Political order, religious conviction, moral righteousness, literacy, commerce, and community relations in villages and towns were to prevail. Considerable recent historical scholarship, however, has revealed how great was the gap between ideal and real, rhetoric and action.[1] Collectively, such scholarship has challenged the conventional, diachronic narrative of early New England in which communal forms and their material manifestations declined into those of individualism as puritans became yankees. Because of the incompatibility of what histories we have been told and what histories we now write, it is time as well to rethink the geographical spread of communities driven across New England by population growth and religious dissent and in which settlement form declines from compact to linear to dispersed as puritans became yankees.[2] That narrative fails to account for the settlers' encounter with the land and the degree to which attractive sites for settlement drew settlers inland.

I propose here a new narrative of the geographical spread of settlement, one that addresses recent historical scholarship, draws on a synthesis of hundreds of settlement experiences, and treats settlement synchronically. In doing so, I employ a cultural-ecology approach that celebrates the preadaptive nature of English settlers in encounter with the land in colonial New England. I suggest that New England's settlers from the start employed particularly rich agricultural resources, grasslands, located in a set of regionally specific ecological zones (FIG. 1.1). New England was in many respects already a garden.[3]

Cultural ecology provides explanatory power for what geographical notions of migration and diffusion, as well as of cultural landscape and region, describe. It views culture as an adaptive system, serving thereby to facilitate long-term, successful, nonorganic human adaptation to the environment, a new environment, or a changed environment. Adaptation implies a process of perceiving possibilities and acting on choices, leading to a simplification of complex sets of traits. Preadaptation involves trait complexes that cultures possess prior to advancing into new environments or experiencing environmental change that give them a competitive advantage in occupying that new or changed environment. We might view cultural transfer, therefore, as an adaptive strategy in which diffusion and simplification are processes of weeding out maladaptive traits and encouraging survival of preadapted traits.[4] In

FIG. 1.1 Intervale in Eastern Massachusetts. English settlers found fresh meadows, what New Englanders called intervales, and salt marshes attractive agricultural resources for raising cattle. (Photo by J. S. Wood.)

the New England context, a cultural-ecology approach reveals how a new English culture came about when a postfeudal, capitalistic, family-based, puritan people came to employ overseas lands, and in so doing reduced old world diversity brought with them. We can observe what took hold and what withered among imported traits, what indigenous traits settlers adopted in the new environment, and what landscapes they thus produced.

The production of landscapes is the gist of this chapter's narrative of the interaction of English settlers with the cultural environments and ecological contexts they encountered in southern New England. Thus, I focus on land types, land uses, and landscapes. I argue that the geographical patterns of settlement reflect in large measure preadaptation of English settlers to particular environmental circumstances that attracted them to specific sites in certain ecological zones. In particular, I argue that the colonial New England landscape was from the 1620s one of single-family farms and that settlement forms resulted largely from an attachment to grassland sites by settlers raising cattle and employing rectangular land division. It was division of marsh and meadows, as much or more than covenanted community or puritan ideology or defensive precautions, which shaped geographical patterns of agricultural settlement.

Finally, in rethinking the New England encounter with the land from a cultural-ecology approach, I find little to support the New England exceptionalist tradition of puritans converting wilderness to garden. New England was in many respects already a garden encountered by preadapted English settlers. I do not mean to understate how terrifying New England's cultural and physical environment could be to colonists. Nor do I suggest New Englanders could or should have made more of their opportunity. I do mean to note that despite much hardship in a cruel environment, English settlers intent on recovering an old England were well prepared to construct their new England.

The Exceptionalist Tradition

Tradition derives from a need to establish some aspect of social life as continuous and unchanging in the face of innovation and change in the modern world. It writes an uncomplicated narrative of social development. It obscures historical disorder and discontinuity. It reduces both diachronic complexity and synchronic richness. It produces a comprehensible ensemble of a few key elements, a historical image of selected elements of the past. In the New England, indeed American, case, tradition builds from and reinforces a sense of the providential.[5]

In the exceptionalist tradition, puritans confronted an "ignoble savage" in a *vacuum domicilium*, a "desart [sic] wilderness" that they converted to a garden. For over a century and a half, introspective and self-contained townspeople carved out their garden landscape. They erased evidence of the non-European humanized landscape they had first encountered and then the early implanted English subregional differences exemplified in architectural form and building practice, field systems and crop and animal preferences, settlement forms, and governance and economy. They looked to meetinghouses at town centers to symbolize their community, perambulated their bounds to insure proper land division, and warned off strangers to protect their exclusivity. Through incorporation of towns and settlement of villages, New Englanders sustained their principles, formed their character, promoted their industry and economy, provided for their education, and secured independence for the country as a whole.

The New England settlement ensemble of center villages, town commons, and substantial dwelling houses has become the symbol of this colonial past across a generic New England landscape. In cultural-geographical terms, the village was a direct cultural transfer of the English manorial village, and it served as the material basis for covenanted community. Close proximity sustained community, enhanced puritan tenets, and provided defense. Puritans had converted wilderness to garden. Only the transition from puritan to yankee challenged the pillars of colonial New England conformity and caused dissolution of religious and community life, increased commercialism, modification of architectural forms and styles, division of common fields, and dispersal of settlement from initial house lots and compact agricultural villages. Despite decline in puritan virtues and ways, the New England settlement landscape still sustains continuity with its founders and their ideals. New England villages, after all, survive. But the New England experience, as this book details, was quite different from what the tradition suggests. That New England experience begins with the colonial encounter with the land.

Cultural Context

What were the English ways that preadapted emigrants to success in their encounter with New England? Land division and tenure practices, field patterns, crop and animal systems, village forms and functions, occupational skills, household and family forms, and social values and attitudes were all reflected in an English worldview. But although English colonists shared a common English heritage, England's regional cultures varied considerably in cultural habits and material forms, producing distinctive cultural-geographic regions and local ways. Within English village bounds, local custom dictated the particular shape of the landscape, pattern of settlement, mode of landholding, and rituals of agrarian activity. No single model of how an agricultural community was to operate or how a settlement was to be formed prevailed. Not all English shared the same experience, and not all wished to replicate the same English ways. Nor was England static. A mix of English ways in a context of cultural change tempered by puritan ideology and the experience of New England settlement would inevitably shape a new England.

The old English methods and forms of using open fields in common had several virtues. This adaptive strategy was particularly appropriate to very fertile agricultural areas, such as the plains of northwestern Europe or the English Midlands, where its deepest roots and classic form could be found in England. Common herding on undivided land and common cultivation in rectangular strips on divided but still open fields unbroken by hedges allowed sharing of labor and implements and considerably minimized the need for fencing. Common rights to woodlots and meadowlands for fodder provided equal quality of land, if not necessarily the same amount for every farmer. All was regulated by an assembly of cultivators or a manor court, and villagers set farmsteads in close proximity to one another, which produced several disadvantages. Fragmented fields might lie at some distance from the settlement and from one another; open fields depended upon a communal calendar, encouraging inefficiencies and low productivity. Yet "open field" is perhaps a misnomer, as many were technically subdivided. "Common field," likewise, denoted common rights, including to open fields, but not necessarily communal farming. Common rights might entail intensive, even communal, farming of infields near a settlement, and access to pasture, woodlot, and individually farmed outfields. Moreover, the reclaimed fens (large swampy areas) of the southeast and the artificial watermarshes of the south and southwest of England produced common lands, but not commonly worked lands. Diking of marshes, reclamation of fens, or construction of watermeadows did require, however, corporate enterprise, large lot sizes, and division of land by lottery among individuals, all characteristics of settlement in New England. Moreover, adaptive strategies devoted more to pasturing livestock and less to growing grain tended especially toward enclosed land and dispersed settlement, as in the more agriculturally marginal highland areas of Wales or Scotland and the foothills of southeastern England.[6]

Significant parts of England, then, had never fully developed common fields. In Kent, in the southeast of England, for instance, there is no evidence of the Midlands fielden system, and the successful cultivation of closes had long encouraged others in the southeast to undertake voluntary enclosure of their fields. With prolonged decline in population, decay of long-standing village life and husbandry, and, in some regions and some periods, the action of landlords with an increasing interest in sheep production, enclosure was under way several centuries before settlement at Plymouth. Especially where there was an abundance of pasture or meadow or arable land, there was no compelling reason for adherence to the system of fragmented fields held in common. Indeed, tenants had exchanged strips, amalgamated small closes, and engrossed land with purchases of adjacent fields from as early as the thirteenth century in some regions. By 1550, although more than half of English fields remained open, open fields were concentrated in the Midlands and

; previous vil-
red in neigh-
onstitute the

s also in flux.
: were experi-
ommon fields
es and tended
highlands re-
s altering the
ting force for
n century "less
ave believed,"
revolution of
dlands as me-
years by the

, the English
and farming
nclosure, and
culture. And,
reclamation,
lish were be-
n agriculture
id social and
rough which
communities
ndeed, migra-
f a society in
sion of culti-
rants, figura-

grants them-
ury England,
ure, it seems,
of disposses-

1 as Essex, Suffolk, and Kent in the

tury of convertible husbandry and
:d the quality and productivity of
vertible husbandry employed grain
alternate husbandry was the alter-
istead of fallow in the same fields,
elation to one another. Small sown
reater manuring, leaving more land
ecially attractive on the lighter soils
e husbandry was probably used on
ds as well. Wood-pasture farming
emphasis on cattle and pigs on de-
erienced recent clearance. Pioneer-
Although weakly manored, wood-
d and paid attention to markets.
od-pasture farming would prove an
ion, wherever it went.[8]
Villages functioned to provide eco-
of moral economy of interconnected
classes—and its inhabitants shared
lish village was not necessarily a nu-
ings adjacent to a church and manor
English did live in the countryside,
: primary territorial unit of English
of the parish. Here, interdependent
d agriculture, the economic basis of

many villages, but not all villages had
variety of forms. Where community
nd village organization were virtually
forms had evolved, with nucleated
n regions. Nucleated forms included
g a road; compact, green villages with
or some mix of all of these. Many of
th centuries, depopulated by plague
urch remaining. Village space, which
esponded with the parish, which was

focused geographically on the church building and retained th
lage name. Where farmsteads were dispersed or loosely clust
borhoods or hamlets, several communities of farmers might
parish, whose church might stand alone.[11]

The society that colonists would leave behind in England w
Significant portions of sixteenth-century England's countrysid
encing slow but steady change in which increasingly large c
were converted to smaller individual holdings bordered by hedg
by tenant families living on detached farmsteads. Peripheral
tained their long-standing social organization, but change wa
populated countryside and proving to be an important motiv
puritan migration. England had become in the early seventeent
peasant, static, closed, cohesive, corporate, and settled than we l
notes Jack Greene. England was experiencing an agricultural
sorts, its greatest transformation ultimately to occur in the Mi
dieval open fields came to be replaced over several hundred
hedged, enclosed fields one sees today in England.[12]

Thus, by the late sixteenth and early seventeenth centurie
were accustomed to seeing old customs of land division, tenure
crumble in the face of innovations like alternate husbandry, e
increasing commercialization and regional specialization of agr
despite expansion of cultivated areas (via forest clearance, fer
and cultivation of marginal soils), increasing numbers of Eng
coming economic dependents employed by others, whether
or trades. Commercialization fed competition and fostered raj
geographic mobility. Villages and parishes became areas th
people moved rather than places of familial rootedness, and
lost their cohesiveness as English life became more transitory. I
tion to America may be viewed as a response to the stresses
flux, as an extension of a wholesale population shift and expar
vated areas in a context of considerable cultural upheaval. Emi
tively, were leaping from a passing train.[13]

Emigrants

All of this is not to say, argues Virginia Anderson, that m
selves, responding to the unsettledness of early-seventeenth-cen
were necessarily dispossessed. But they were land hungry. Enclo
was for many of the English as much a cultural habit as a cause

sion or economic depression. They held the strong notion that land owner-ship was a necessary adjunct to competency—the ability, notes Daniel Vick-ers, "to absorb the labors of a single family while providing it with something more than mere subsistence." At the same time, however, they were not nec-essarily betterment migrants, those seeking to improve materially the quality of their lives. Elimination of feudal forms of economic dependency and com-mercialization of agriculture "provoked both ambitions and anxieties, en-couraging Englishmen to secure a situation whereby they could provide for one's family." [14]

The rhetoric of the period about New England, John Canup argues, inad-vertently conveyed a picture of American nature as "deeply alien and antago-nistic to English culture, [to the point] that there was a disparity so great be-tween the natural environment of the new world and the familiar landscape of England that a fully successful transplantation would be unlikely and per-haps impossible." Hence, the "'call' to migrate coincided with private spiritual crises, employment change, family problems, or debt," concludes David Cressy. Emigration seems to have "had much to do with private hopes and frustra-tions, and opportunities of the moment," even the novelty of the idea—all themselves shaped by unsettling circumstances—than by any rational com-parison of religious or economic prospects in New England. [15]

Those who came to New England were largely of "middling" English soci-ety—few aristocrats or gentry, or lower classes either. They were "an upper-class of peasantry"—a "landed" middle class of tenants and copyholders, produced over several centuries of voluntary enclosure, engrossing land, and lease-hold tenure. Neither destitute nor especially prosperous, heads of household represented relative class homogeneity. On the other hand, they also represented a great variety of backgrounds and occupations. They were yeomen, husbandmen, artisans, craftsmen, merchants, and tradesmen, people of skill and endeavor, including those who had made a living in the cloth industry. They were literate but not unmindful of folk beliefs. Many were urban. Fewer than a third were agriculturalists prior to migrating. Fully 60 percent of one sample of emigrants came from market towns, at least most recently. Hardly urban as we might think of them, market towns were still qualitatively different from neighboring agricultural communities, from manorial villages to separate farmsteads. Given the mobility of the early-seventeenth-century English, one's last abode and recorded occupation might well, then, mask one's abilities, skills, experiences, predilections, and motiva-tions. Still, most would of necessity come in New England to be farmers.

Despite their variety of occupational experiences, there would not be a sufficiently diversified economy in New England for generations to support many in nonfarm pursuits.[16]

A common emigrant denominator was the nuclear family, which averaged over six persons. Families were the building blocks of society, upon which values and skills were transmitted and communities organized. Worldviews were shaped by family contexts, and families would bear the burden of transfer of culture to New England. The English family was long organized as a patriarchy in which the conjugal unit was the nucleus of a broad community of kinship and neighborhood. Yet this extended family was, in the early modern period of which we speak, already lost. Reconstitution of the family as a private social unit separate from the community had been a significant consequence of enclosure of fields and replacement of cooperative farming. At the same time, households were extended to include servants, who migrated with families to be artisans or work the land.[17] These mature nuclear families, with accumulated resources and servants who were coming to establish farms, had an immediate need for land.

This need was compounded by an expansive individualism in society, economy, and politics, a fertile ground for ideas that had grown and developed in sixteenth- and seventeenth-century England. Improvement of the individual through acquisition of wealth and social and material status was especially well embedded in English society in the seventeenth century. This drive for personal independence—competence—and the pursuit of happiness were closely associated with promotion and perpetuation of the welfare of the lineal family and land. "The pursuit of self was equated with the fulfillment of family obligation" but "emphatically did not diminish institutions" of social order—church and community. Indeed, "competence"—the desire to support a family on property—"and spirit of community were necessary opposites," the tension between which produced, as we will see, an economically stable society.[18]

Ultimately, well over half of all New England colonists came from southern and eastern England, where emigrants had known many different forms of social organization, agricultural practice, industrial development, and local government. In the early seventeenth century, East Anglia was the most densely settled, urbanized, and commercialized portion of England. Its flat, open country mixed good soil and bad. Farming was comparatively advanced, the commercialization of agriculture having gotten an early foothold here. Mixed crop and livestock farms marketed food and wool in the numerous small ports and market towns. Here, in the east and south of England, where enclosure for individual use had long been under way and many villages enveloped dispersed farms, settlement was varied in form and a middle class of farmers had emerged. Commercialization of agriculture, population growth, straightness of land, and industrial underemployment were intertwined. And East Anglians in particular, whether from the countryside, market towns, or urban places, tended to be puritans. The proportion of emigrants from southeastern England was larger than that region's share of the total population of England. Puritanism especially found favor among middle-class families located in urban areas and in those portions of the weakly manored English countryside where dispersed farmsteads dominated settlement form. The puritan elite, especially from East Anglia, were those who would most shape New England's society and material culture.[19]

Puritanism

Puritanism provided the rhetorical justification to emigrate—words to shape an image of a new England—and the common thread among most emigrants. The cosmology of English Calvinism beheld a world of organic unity, in which New England would offer an expectation of economic competence in a land of laws. Yet puritan emigrants were no monolithic group of dour, gray Calvinists fleeing religious persecution to become devout fanatics in New England. Their religious impulse was deeply felt and extensively expressed. For most nonconformists, inner lives fused formal theology, rationalized belief, and structured ritual with superstition in a world of multiple meanings. Popular religion, for that is what it was, was embedded in the fabric of daily life and accommodated a diversity of religious opinion, while a high level of literacy enabled individuals to interpret religion directly. Thus, personal piety was nourished through the collective public commitment to a redemptive community that each member of a church made, and it was presided over by a standing clerical order. In time a vernacular of "tempered piety" would emerge in New England, shaping a society in which people had purposefully and self-consciously chosen to live among others whom they loved and respected.[20]

Puritans held an idealized vision of an England without temptation. They loathed certain customs and beliefs and were disenchanted with much folk and popular culture associated with English religious ways. And they shared a providentialist worldview, one that might allow a simplification of one's economic condition to achieve another end. While acquisitive, they were nevertheless repelled by the social and economic forces of change they observed in England. Puritanism was their response to unsettledness. Consequently, their migration can be seen as an "essentially defensive, conservative, even reactionary response," one "betraying a profound fear of social chaos and a deep yearning for order and control" especially in local affairs, to conform to their conception of well-ordered England. Unable to create such a world in England, they tried to create it in New England. "Moved by powerful millennial and communal impulses," they rapidly formed strong, patriarchal families, elaborate kinship networks, and visible and authoritative leaders to shape a residential community and agricultural settlement in New England, intending the settlement to "shine as a model of godly devotion and moral rectitude." Providentialists, they anticipated that God would not fail to reward their efforts with competency.[21]

The New England Experience

When puritan colonists then looked upon the strange coast of New England and believed they saw Christian paradise, their impression derived as much from expectation as from the environment. On the one hand, "New England" was an epithet—conceived, in terms of physical geography, as another England and thus of lesser value commercially than more southerly lands equating latitudinally with the Mediterranean region of Europe. This naive model of global climate, which derived from the Greek notion of *climata*, ignored atmospheric and oceanic circulation systems relative to land and water.[22] And, indeed, New England's winters would prove to be colder and its summers hotter than the English were used to. Still, the New England land offered hope of agricultural productivity. It invited settlement. The considerable seasonal variation relative to England constrained grain productivity, but not growth of luxuriant grasses in the comparatively vast coastal marshes or wide terraces of river valleys and beaver-made meadows of glacio-lacustrine plains (ancient lake beds of glacial origin) cutting through the open woods produced by burning. It was ideal for cattle raising.

As William Cronon has argued, Europeans looked at this New England landscape in their cultural terms, necessarily limiting what they saw and recorded. They failed to comprehend native American exploitation of seasonal diversity by means of mobility and subsistence cycles, and thereby failed to comprehend how humanized a landscape, how much a garden, they had encountered. Southern New England natives who had cleared land for agriculture in order to concentrate their food base had significantly reshaped the environment long before English settlement. Especially, native groups had produced through burning a vast parklike woodland habitat. Europeans justified expropriating native lands, including old fields, on moral grounds. The indigenous cultural ecology had failed in English terms to employ adequately the abundant resources at hand.[23] The consequent mapping of places and division of land in English fashion and naming of towns after English places was an assertion of Englishness on the landscape.

To this land, colonists brought their varied set of regional agricultural ways and settlement forms, many of which they wished to perpetuate. In staking out farms, as most settlers did, colonists thus created a new geography of English cultural subregions and constructed initially a complex domestic landscape that reflected different local patterns of settlement and land use developed in subregions of England.[24] But with no vested interests in a complex and finely woven cultural landscape as in England, and with little threat to community stability, the intricate weave of social structure and particularistic cultural ecologies that were themselves undergoing change in England was not repeated nor were its forms reconstituted in the same fashion. The English, detached from direct cultural sources and constraints and faced with a land of contradictory images of wilderness and garden-to-be, reached only selectively back to idealized cultural origins to constitute an England of new possibilities. The recovered England in New England, the city upon a hill, was a new creation—like any act of preservation—of a selected, imagined past.

Meanwhile, contrapuntal forces of continuity and change on the one hand and centralized and decentralized control on the other expressed themselves. Larger contexts and frameworks of action challenged persistent localism, and decentralized decision making challenged colonial authority, which in turn challenged imperial authority. As in England, individual expression and competence confronted communal striving in social, economic, political, and religious ways. Neither a reconstitution nor a reconception, New England was a puritan vision of England. But the dialectic of continuity and change played itself out in the seventeenth century, shaping a new English society internally coherent and comparatively different from both that in England and that in its first settlers' minds' eyes.

In particular, puritan leaders had hoped to plant a single residential community, so, John Cotton (1642) noted, "If we could have large elbow room enough, and meadow enough, though we had no ordinances, we can then go and live like lambs in a large place."[25] They could not. Too many people with too many competing points of view composed the Massachusetts Bay Colony to meet the exigencies of a new society in a single site. Aiming for Salem on Cape Ann, the 1630 settlers opted for Boston Bay. Initial beach-heads prospered, and puritan leaders soon found demands for land and their own ideology of converting wilderness to garden driving the occupation and settlement of more land and establishment of more communities. They acknowledged their inability to hold to the plan for a single agricultural town, and the orchestration of settlement in New England was set. As Robert East has written, "[p]uritan settlements in the early colonies divided and subdivided until it would seem that every saint would eventually have his own habitat as well as his own church."[26] Under pressure to accommodate cattle with pasture and fodder, the original towns hived again and again, and other colonists removed farther away—to Connecticut, Rhode Island, or New Hampshire—establishing the habit of planting new towns among a variety of land types beyond settled areas by the late 1630s. In broad strokes of the brush, settlers first established a range of commercial activities in a foreland of open coastal and riverine lowlands, and then, ultimately, the greater number established less commercially based agriculture in the hillier, more forested interior.

Land Types

Pastoralism was the force behind this expansion, as William Bradford noted early on in Plymouth: "No man now thought he could live except he had cattle and a great deal of ground to keep them, all striving to increase their stocks. By which means they were scattered all over the Bay quickly and the town in which they lived compactly till now was left very thin and in short time almost desolate."[27] William Wood, writing in 1634, was quite taken by the bounty of marsh and "medow": "There is so much hayground in the Countrey, as the richest voyagers that shall venture thither, neede not feare want of fodder, though his Heard increase into thousands, there being thousands of Acres that yet was never medled with." But he noted as well that "Hay-ground is not in all places in *New England*: Wherefore it shall behoue every man according to his calling, and estate, to looke for a fit situation at the first; and if he be one that intends to liue on his stock, to choose the

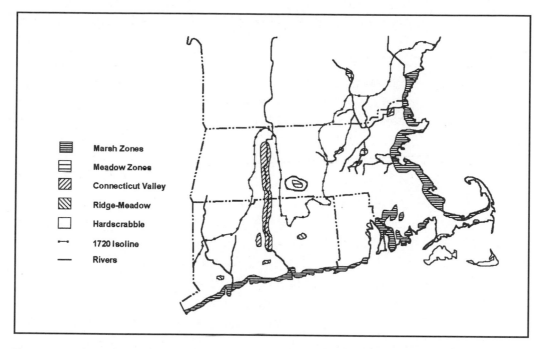

FIG. 1.2 Ecological Regions. Several kinds of grassland regions early attracted New England settlers, and settlers had taken most of these regions within the first hundred years of English settlement.

grassie Valleys before the woody mountaines."[28] And John Winthrop noted it, too, in 1635: "Those of Watertown and Roxbury had have to remove whether they pleased in this jurisdiction [of Massachusetts Bay]. The occasion of their desire to remove was for that all towns on the bay began to be much straightened by their own nearness to one another, and their cattle being so much increased."[29] Following Wood's advice, New England's settlers identified a set of distinctive ecological zones supporting grasslands—coastal marshes, freshwater meadows, and other arable islands amidst hardscrabble and forest.[30] Distribution of grasslands influenced how English settlers intent on family farming constructed their settlement geography, its orientation, its extent, and its forms (FIG. 1.2).

In *salt or tidal marsh*, frequent tidal flooding precluded growth of trees. New England's first settlers garnered as much marsh along the coast and in the adjacent tidal zone as they could to provide fodder for cattle. What they could reclaim by diking or drainage they did. Cleared, tillable land in the open, parklike woods beyond the marshes of the coastal zone also included, not uncommonly, old fields abandoned when the native population was decimated by European disease prior to permanent English settlement. Yet across the coastal foreland, in Massachusetts, Rhode Island, and Connecticut, as well as north in New Hampshire and Maine, agriculture was often secondary to trade or fishing, and it was trading opportunity by and large as much as land division that established settlement morphology: Trading places were sited for relative location and often palisaded; farms in support of trading places were then sited for access to nearby meadow (FIGS. 1.3, 1.4, 1.5, 1.6).

Freshwater meadows lay beyond the tidal zone, usually in one of New England's many glacio-lacustrine areas. Glacial meltwaters had formed large lakes across vast basins, and into these basins they had deposited fine and deep silt and sediments. Subsequent drainage patterns cut through but did not obliterate these lake basins. Meadows were the result of high water tables or frequent flooding, or both, precluding effective tree growth. Commonly beaver had reflooded portions of these areas, enhancing the effect of both siltation and production of grass. And where beaver had not already accommodated their needs, colonists themselves could shape familiar watermeadows by their own act of flooding. In the lower and middle reaches of many streams, the most attractive land was flat, black, rock-free alluvium supporting meadows. Like salt marsh, but better, natural meadows provided grasses for English cattle.

The Connecticut River, larger by far than the other rivers of the eastern lowlands of New England, flowed through ancient Lake Hitchcock, and there produced kame and alluvial terraces in great wide swaths. The valley and that of its significant tributary, the Farmington River, produced land comparable to English champion lands. Cattle could graze in large numbers, and cultivation of grains produced exceedingly large yields. Long strings of farmsteads paralleling the river formed linear settlements (FIGS. 1.7, 1.8).

An interstitial zone between the commercial foreland and the interior was pocketed with a significant, discontinuous set of sites of glacio-lacustrine origin lying in Lakes Concord, Sudbury, Nashua, and Merrimack, as well as in the Taunton Basin, an extension of Narragansett Bay. Similar basins, although less useful, are located in valleys of the Piscataqua and of streams and their tributaries eventually flowing into Long Island Sound: the Housatonic, Pomeraug, Naugatuck, Quaboag, Quinebaug, Thames, or Blackstone, for instance (FIGS. 1.9, 1.10, 1.11).

Interior New England, not far from the coastal foreland, was geomorphologically complex. One need not have removed very far from the coast before

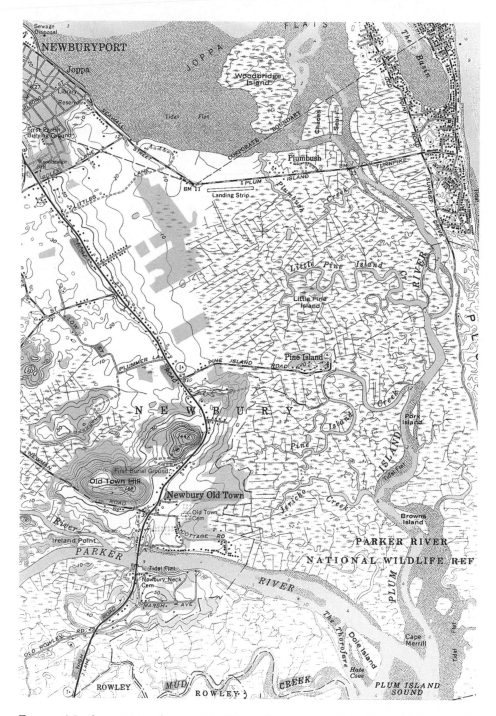

FIG. 1.3 Newbury, Massachusetts. English settlers recognized the bounty of salt marsh at Newbury, north of Massachusetts Bay in Essex County, and settled it in the 1630s. (Section of the Newburyport East, Mass. Topographic Quadrangle 42070-G7 [1966].)

FIG. 1.4 Salt Marsh in Newbury, Massachusetts. (Photo by J. S. Wood.)

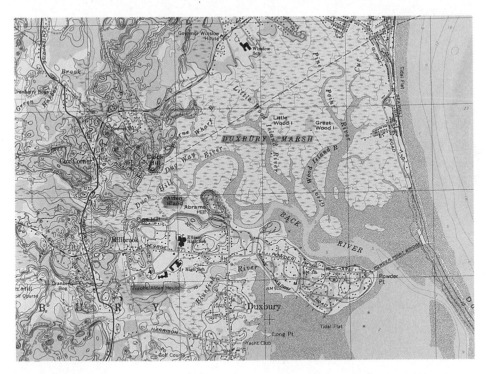

FIG. 1.5 Duxbury, Massachusetts. Plymouth Colony settlers were attracted to salt marsh and rapidly spread along the coast in search of it. John Alden found Duxbury suitable to his needs. (Section of the Duxbury, Mass. Topographic Quadrangle 42070-A6 [1974].)

encountering the less enticing sandy scrub and stony loam hardscrabble of the morainic lowlands, which the rivers interpenetrated and deep forest covered. Receding glaciers had distributed a heterogeneous, extremely stony glacial till across most of New England, upon which stood great stands of forest, the composition of which varied from south to north. Because settlers were quite conscious of differences in soil fertility, they kept to small alluvial meadows, avoiding the backbreaking English way of grubbing roots from the wretched upland soils while they could (FIG. 1.12). The "labor necessary to clear land and plant nutritionally superior grasses was simply beyond the means of most colonists until the second half of the seventeenth century" in any event.[31]

Still, scattered fortuitously amidst the hardscrabble and forest were *islands of arable land*, of relatively good workability and some agricultural productivity. A unique subclass of ridge and meadow sites, not previously noted as a set, resulted from ancient basaltic ridges scoured by glaciation and with

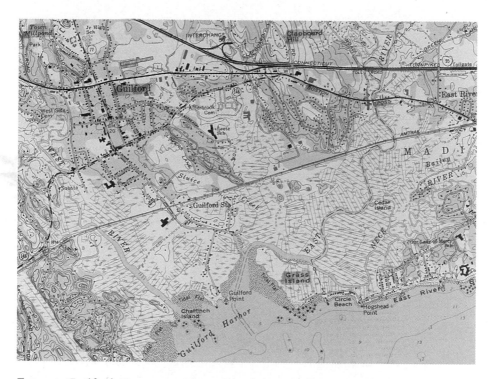

FIG. 1.6 Guilford, Connecticut. Long Island Sound offered plentiful salt marsh, and Connecticut settlers controlled the bulk of it by 1650, as here in Guilford. (Section of the Guilford, Conn. Topographic Quadrangle 41072-C6 [1984].)

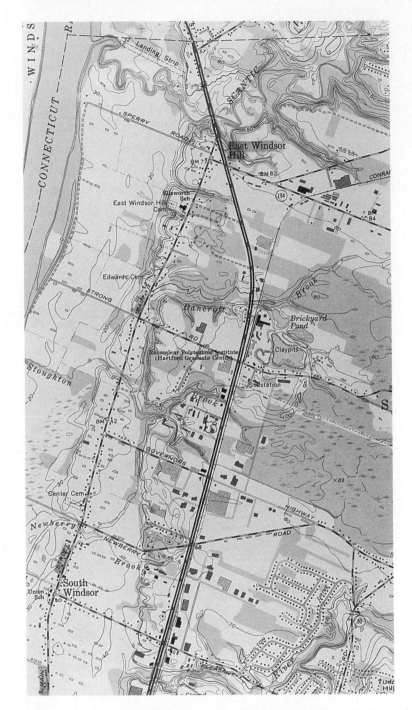

FIG. 1.7 East Windsor, Connecticut. Linearity of settlement in East Windsor reflects the bounty of Connecticut Valley alluvial terrace soils, which supported grass for cattle initially and later grew tobacco or corn. (Section of the Windsor Locks, Conn. Topographic Quadrangle 41072-N6 [1984].)

FIG. 1.8 Meadows in East Windsor, Connecticut. View is across the alluvial terrace toward the east. (Photo by J. S. Wood.)

lateral meadows of probable glacio-lacustrine origin. Three are noteworthy, forming the focus of settlement in the Connecticut towns of Newtown, Durham, and Lebanon (FIGS. 1.13, 1.14).

Glaciers had also shaped occasional well-drained drumlin hills and fertile outwash and glacio-lacustrine plains of fine clay and silt, deposited by meltwater. Sand plains and some drumlin slopes produced grass because drainage was too good to sustain tree growth. Such arable islands framed by hardscrabble and forest represented the bulk of settled soils brought into agricultural production in New England prior to the sheep-raising mania of the nineteenth century. In any one town, however, land in tillage, pasture, or meadow rarely accounted for more than 30 percent of land use and commonly made up less than 10 percent.[32]

Settling Land

The great migration of 1630 to 1642 was unusual for its short duration, great intensity, and annual variability. Pilgrim settlers at Plymouth had spread into a number of communities after 1621 to make up the Plymouth Colony of southeastern New England. After an initial few years of slow growth,

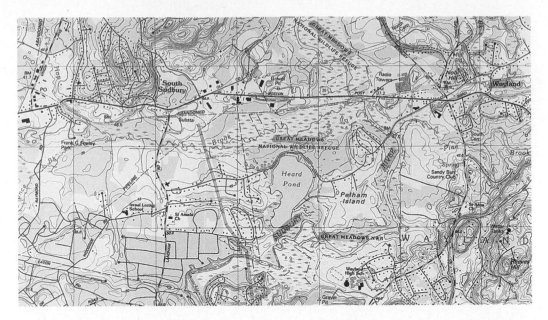

FIG. 1.9 Sudbury, Massachusetts. The English located their earliest settlements away from tidewater in glacio-lacustrine zones full of freshwater meadows, like Sudbury's Great Meadows. Wayland is the site of the original 1640 Sudbury settlement. See FIGS. 2.6, 2.7. (Section of the Framingham, Mass. Topographic Quadrangle 42071-C4 [1987].)

FIG. 1.10 Glacio-Lacustrine Zone in Eastern Massachusetts. Fresh meadows such as these that attracted early settlers now restrict suburban development. (Photo by J. S. Wood.)

g River in Woodbury, Connecticut.
od.)

Durham Mead-
here settlers
erations, if they
2-D6 [1984].)

cticut. This small intervale in an
s in the arable margins of the coastal
are salt marsh or large expanses of

FIG. 1.13 Durham, Connecticut. Unusual ridge-and-meadow sites, lik[e]
ows, offered early interior settlement opportunities in Connecticut, [w]
otherwise remained along the coast or in the Connecticut Valley for ge[n]
could. (Section of the Durham, Conn. Topographic Quadrangle 410[7]

FIG. 1.14 Durham Meadows, Connecticut. View from the ridge toward the west. (Photo by J. S. Wood.)

immigration to Massachusetts Bay then doubled in 1634, an event that generated much pressure on settlement expansion, if not so much for people as for their cattle. Given the geographical distribution of land types, it follows, I wish to argue, that siting of farms, and thus of towns and town centers, was a matter of available site conditions—grasses—as much as relative location. For all of its religious context, New England was a commercial venture. Many place-names were of English, and commonly East Anglian, market towns, not agricultural parishes or villages, and, indeed, America has always been an "urban frontier," settled outward from urban places. Entrepreneurs constructed large houses and lived in commercial places. But entrepreneurs, like other settlers who constituted the bulk of colonists, built farms, situating them so as to control New England's plentiful salt marsh and bountiful glacio-lacustrine meadows to feed their cattle.

The search took settlers along the coast both north and south from Massachusetts Bay for salt marsh and inland along the Charles, Mystic, Neponset, and Merrimack Rivers and their various tributaries for freshwater meadow.[33] Early Boston landowners relished their tidal-zone "farms" set out away from the initial settlement at places called Muddy River (Brookline) or Rumney Marsh, the latter a name that both represented English heritage and perceived environmental worth. Direct migration from England had established the New Haven Colony, made up of numerous trading and agricultural plantations set about the salt marshes of the estuaries on Long Island Sound. Remarkably, 80 percent of soils related to tidal marsh in Connecticut were settled by 1650, despite the comparatively long time it then took in Connecticut to expand much beyond the coastal foreland (FIG. 1.15).[34]

The first towns settled inland from tidewater about Massachusetts Bay, along the Merrimack River, in the Taunton Basin, and along the Connecticut River were also initially laid out in the 1630s and 1640s, and always in close proximity to glacio-lacustrine meadow. At Concord and Sudbury in the Concord-Sudbury watershed, and at Dedham between the Charles and Neponset Rivers, rivers were not used in the common fashion as town boundaries (see FIG. 1.9). Such initial towns straddled extensive areas of meadow; only later were rivers used to subdivide towns as secondary "villages" split off. Meanwhile, settlers explored for more meadow, identifying as likely next targets of settlement the lower Merrimack and the Nashua River Valleys. William Wood had observed on the Merrimack River, for instance, that "all along the river side is fresh marshes, in some places 3 miles broad."[35] The Massachusetts Bay Charter of 1629, of course, had fixed the northern boundary of the grant three miles north of the Merrimack, the present-day Massachusetts–New Hampshire boundary. Settlement at Lancaster after 1643 marked the western extension of colonization of meadows in the Concord-Nashua-Merrimack watershed. Far outlier Brookfield, settled beyond the line of continuous settlement on the rich meadows of the Quaboag River after 1660, marked the eastern reach of the Chicopee-Connecticut watershed at about the divide between Massachusetts Bay, Narragansett Bay, and Long Island Sound drainage basins.

"Want of accommodation for their cattle" in Newtown (Cambridge) by 1634, along with disputes over religion and franchise, led to the leap of settlers to the meadows of the Connecticut River Valley.[36] The portion of the lower Connecticut River Valley that ran north from Middletown in Connecticut to Northfield in Massachusetts had the most extensive meadows in New England. It was perceived as a true land of milk and honey, where not only would farming yield a marketable commodity, but money could be made trading furs with native peoples. Here settlers planted, at least initially,

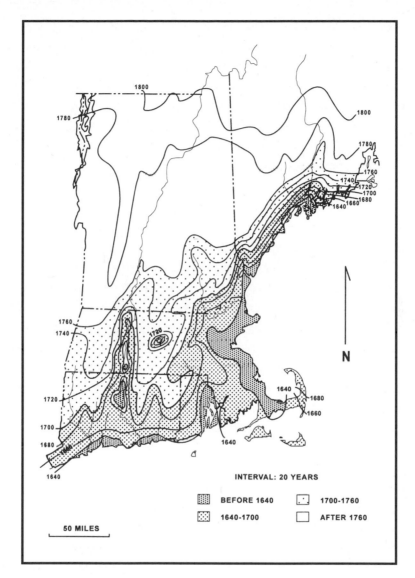

FIG. 1.15 Isochronic Map of Settlement. Isochrones, or equal time lines, of settlement show a strong geographical correlation to ecological zones.

a dozen large towns with a high incidence of the suffix "-field" in place-names before 1675. Longmeadow and Northampton (hamp or ham[m] refers to a flat, low-lying pasture near a river) further the association.[37] Frontier towns of the Massachusetts portion of the Connecticut River Valley, like Springfield, determined the northerly and westerly direction that subsequent settling would follow, but these riverine plantations were beyond the line of generally occupied territory in the seventeenth century. Grassy Deerfield, farther north still from Springfield, was successively planted and abandoned three times in a period of fifty years before the area of continuous settlement engulfed it in the early eighteenth century. And only in the eighteenth century were settlers comfortable with colonizing the rich meadows of the Penacook region in the upper Merrimack Valley in old Lake Merrimack.

Date of settlement of a town effectively correlated with size and quality of available marsh and meadow as much as with proximity to Massachusetts Bay or a secondary node generating settlement, as Dedham did for Deerfield in Massachusetts or New London did for Lebanon in Connecticut. An aerial view of today's northern reaches of Megalopolis makes clear the important presence of tidal salt marshes and freshwater meadows, now obstacles to development rather than the prized possessions of entrepreneurial land seekers of three and one-half centuries ago (see FIGS. 1.1, 1.10). Away from the coast, siting of farms, then, was as much a matter of site conditions as it was relative situation, which often appeared only after the fact of construction of highways. This is an important point. Situation—relative location—was an effect as much as it was a cause of the construction of transportation linkages, a considerable reversal of locational strategies today.[38]

By the third quarter of the seventeenth century most all of the commercial foreland and its arable margins was settled. A string of straggling fishing and trading outposts stretched almost continuously from the nominally Anglican fishing stations of the rocky shores of Maine, to the Pilgrim plantations on the marshes of Cape Cod, around to the merchant settlements about Narragansett Bay, and on to the estuaries of Long Island Sound. Another handful of trading posts with farms were clustered in the lower Connecticut River Valley from Wethersfield north, ultimately, to Northfield. A large wedge of towns with access to meadow had been planted inland from tidewater. Here, adjacent to Massachusetts Bay, north to Exeter and the Piscataqua in New Hampshire and south through the Taunton Basin in Plymouth, adjacent to the commercial foreland, and inland to Lancaster and Brookfield, was the bulk of New England's agricultural population. Here, in this wedge, inhabitants were farmers first. Here, in this wedge, English colonists shaped a new English landscape.

The implication of this New England experience is that early settlers were backwoods frontiersmen. Few really were. Colonists, especially those whose interests were commercial and who chose to locate coastal trading posts or establish staple plantations in the Connecticut River Valley, looked east to

England, not west to the interior. Farmers likewise had little interest in pioneering, except as curiosity about new lands required it, and they saw little very good land beyond their marshes and meadows and much hardscrabble to fill up. Some settlers did specialize in launching towns, moving regularly, but the great number of puritan settlers who were taking up land in the seventeenth century remained in that wedge of agriculture, in the glacio-lacustrine basins of eastern Massachusetts, even as New England's population doubled every thirty years.[39] Still, the significant population growth over the first several generations of the colonial period could not be accommodated by equally bountiful lands. From the 1630s onward, New Englanders took up land that varied in agricultural potential from lush glacio-lacustrine meadows to well-drained drumlin hills and other arable islands in hardscrabble. While puritan rhetoric made the environment appear far tougher than it probably was, those seeking farms spread only slowly from the Massachusetts Bay settlement core and secondary cores established during the first decade, as long as meadow was available. With a decline in available meadow, however, intertown mobility increased and settlers sought opportunities in islands of arable land amidst the hardscrabble. As settlers thus adopted a variety of ecological zones, they employed a mix of land uses and settlement forms, and they established a complex of cultural landscapes visible still today.

Shaping New England's Cultural Geography

What colonists brought to New England, we have noted, was an abstraction of English local ways purged of disagreeable customs and shaped by an ideal. The important similarity of New England families to English families in age structure and sex ratio allowed rapid implantation of normal familial patterns of intergenerational contact and relationships. Families drew upon familiar forms and ways of doing things, bringing with them few vestiges of religious ritual, of moral economy or class interdependence, or of medieval institutions in community, church, governance, or agricultural practice, and creating local pockets of English regional diversity. The cultural context of settlement was English, but settlers asserted themselves in ways that reflected local patterns. Some insisted on duplication of common rights in open fields for the advantages offered; others preferred their familiar freehold close. But only fragments of English culture, like rectangular land division within fields, were generally transplanted.[40] Given, therefore, multiple emigrant origins and motives, including common-field, enclosed-farm, and incorporated-borough, and given a desire for competency, no single land system and settlement form prevailed universally across physically variegated New England. Puritan settlers sought opportunities to shape a new England landscape, even if no single image of that landscape prevailed. With a wealth of what proved to be agricultural practices and settlement skills preadapted to New England's grasslands, they succeeded well enough.

The town system, itself derived in part from English ways, provided the geographical coherence and social stability necessary for expression of those English ways. Settlement by incorporated community and congregation was based on the puritan belief that society might disintegrate in a new country. Both congregational forbearance (a puritan goal) and economic enterprise (the underwriters' requirement) would fail without some guiding plan. Towns and villages brought political and religious order to the process of settlement. The town organized families within relatively independent, settled, and permanent groups of inhabitants, replacing the English institutions of local government of manor, parish, and borough, and providing clearly defined geographic bounds for the community and the congregation.

Not all towns were alike at first, nor were they perfect communities. Towns were meant to model in secular form the covenantal relationship of God and man in temporal and religious affairs.[41] But the diversity of agricultural and settlement practices that marked New England towns in the first decades was mirrored in local political custom as well. Those from market towns especially might have had experience with local government and the multiplicity of civil and ecclesiastical jurisdictions of English ways. The town, then, was a forum for different English experiences to work out farm practices, rules of land ownership and inheritance, settlement geography, and self-governance.

Towns and town governments experienced a process of simplification and standardization. Settlers in the initial towns effectively took authority over their own affairs, designing their own institutions from ancient styles of governance, such as the village assembly or town meeting, selectmen, and fundamental laws. Functional separation of town and church followed from the increased burden of secular affairs, institutionalizing the town meeting and concept of selectmen by 1635. Archaic elements of English local government were eliminated. Towns were effectively manors without lords, parishes without church officers, and boroughs without aldermen. Land proprietors and eventually freemen, who elected selectmen, prevailed. Thus towns came to provide the structure and leadership necessary to establish stability and legitimacy. They divided land, assigned rights to commons, policed community affairs, and encouraged economic intercourse, although they did not otherwise interfere with the material life of the townspeople. As diverse as they were at first in form and organization, they became increasingly alike and institutionalized both legally and symbolically throughout the colonial period.[42]

What made a town the closed society that it became was less the need to secure community in the wilderness and more the fact that towns gave away land—an action not be taken lightly or indiscriminately. By controlling the division of land, the proprietorship initially asserted political authority over community organization and saw to it that a church was established and land provided for its maintenance; that services required of the community were exacted; that community welfare was maintained; and that unwanted settlers were excluded from land ownership. The political purpose of the town, then, if not the town itself, evolved out of the economic, the system of land distribution. The town itself was not a settlement form but a vehicle for settling. Settlers, reflecting the variety of English settlement experiences that they did and having formed communities in the variety of ways that they had, employed the town as a political mechanism to provide a solution to distributing and working land satisfactory to their situation.[43] Governing councils developed the New England town to orchestrate settlement by replication, employing the related terms *village* and *district* to denote an unchartered town. The town fixed the spatial matrix of local life, serving the function of providing congregational orthodoxy and mutual security, in both military and economic terms. It proved a useful adaptation of English ways in a new England.

What in New England was different from ritualistic English experience was that towns granted land outright. To obtain and hold land in New England came to be a natural right, conferring a basic dignity, some social status, and competency. The adaptive strategy made the individual as responsible as could be for his family's economic well-being, and it produced a leveling within New England society. Commercialization of society in England at the time of the great migration was accelerated in New England, as in so many other ways, liberalizing land ownership and inheritance practices. Evolving rights to sell, transfer, and divide land, as well as partible inheritance (long the practice in the south and east of England in place of primogeniture), found full expression in New England, where the principle that every household should own land prevailed. Colonists, mostly landsmen, unlike the coastal fishermen and tradesmen whose economy predated the great migration, in turn proved to be effective agents of land accumulation. And, regardless of former occupation in England, farming was an imperative in New England; so land was to be settled, not just owned.[44] As such, land ownership became an effective adaptive strategy for converting wilderness to garden. Land accommodated independent households bound together by community covenant, and land accommodated differences among them as well. One could remove to new land in the farther reaches of a settlement's grant of land, join a newly organized town, or remove to a new colony. Land established separation as a solution to irreconcilable pluralism in English ways or religious practice. The town was not the settlement, and it required no particular settlement form. But by distributing land, the town came to be an instrument of settlement and shaper of settlement patterns.

Land distribution policy was inexact in the early decades. Settlers had to mold it, as in so many other matters, from their variety of English ways, puritan ideals, and settlement experiences. Partition of land into private holdings was not necessarily equal, being rated according to the means, rank, and inherent (i.e., puritan) virtue of each settler, as well as the amount of land it was thought each could employ. Land was thus a dividend for one's investment in the colony, including the cost of one's passage and that of one's family and servants from England. Those with some investment in cattle, for instance, received extensive tracts of valuable marsh and meadowland in the commercial foreland. But there was little New England counterpart to either a landholding elite or a large landless proletariat. Equality of holdings increased as one moved inland to the glacio-lacustrine meadows in eastern Massachusetts, reflecting a New England system of values drawn from East Anglian ways and puritan ideals.[45]

Once land was granted, individual farm families held it in fee simple, though towns placed some initial control on alienation of land to reduce speculation, and owners could forfeit land not suitably improved. A number of tracts in different quarters of the plantation and at varying distances from the town plot of house lots often composed individual estates. Such division allowed for inclusion of land of varying quality in one estate, but inexactness fostered encroachment and required compensatory allotments as well. House lots ranging from one-quarter acre to well over twenty acres formed the residential focus of a newly settled community. Size, shape, and spacing of house lots, and the degree to which they were inhabited, determined how closely gathered and geographically coherent the settlement might actually come to be. In the unfinished society of early New England, land division and transfer practices were imperfect but tolerated. Although the proprietorship often had first option on sales of land and could exclude nonresidents from purchasing land, individual enclosure and consolidation of relatively substantial estates were readily accomplished simply by trading or marketing tracts of land. Land changed hands frequently in the seventeenth century, and rapid consolidation no doubt raised the concern expressed by the General Court ruling of 1635 limiting dwellings to within a half mile of the meetinghouse in newly settled towns, those most threatened by forays by native peoples. Puritan leaders themselves were the largest speculators and least likely to inhabit house lots in the many towns in which they held property. Puritanism restrained but did not prohibit taking advantage of the commercial prospects of the proprietary system of land distribution and the accumulation of more land than a settler might need.[46]

Townspeople, in their various ways, maintained for a generation or so an essential continuity with English life as they had known it, fashioning a patchwork of different English-like landscapes. Particular cultural ecologies (regional differences in farming practice, for instance) were reconstructed in New England towns, with Yorkshire people establishing common fields and nucleated settlements, at least for a generation, as in Rowley, Massachusetts, or East Anglians proving to be well preadapted to the new physical circumstances and quickly establishing freestanding farms, as in Watertown and Ipswich.[47] Immigrants organized as groups in England could even transfer kin, neighborhood, and congregational linkages, thus perpetuating particular cultural ecologies intact in a newly constituted cultural geography. But communities were fluid and changeable; mobility within New England was great. People of a common cultural heritage, yet quite different social backgrounds and regional subcultures, each with their own customs and material forms, were intermingling. After a generation, when the bulk of the population had migrated in youth or been born in New England, few held any clear sense of the meaning of the original mission to New England. Ideals were replaced by opportunities.[48]

As New Englanders used land, new world selective pressures of settlement and resettlement especially encouraged further reduction of vestigial ways and forms, generating a process of cultural filtration marked by adaptation and innovation and leading toward more common ways of doing things and more common material culture. The logistical undertaking itself had been enormous, requiring discrimination in material culture baggage. Where open fields were established, for instance, as in Rowley and Sudbury, land divided rectangularly and owned in fee simple brought an early and often rapid enclosure as old ideas weakened in competition with the distribution of free land, as was the case in Boston. For those drawn away from their house lots for extended periods to their planting fields and farms miles distant, the East Anglian and puritan compulsion to "improve time" discouraged further such lengthy journeys when enclosure was possible in any event. Encouraged by alternate husbandry with cattle and grain in an unencumbered cultural landscape, the trend away from the common field was faster in New England than was possible in England. East Anglian settlers in towns like Watertown, Newbury, and Ipswich rapidly consolidated land from common to individual holdings, making land a saleable commodity.[49]

For those from the weak-manored wood-pasture regions of England with experience in making their own production decisions, New England's opportunities were ideal. Cattle raising allowed time to clear land beyond what old fields provided and could be enhanced by reclamation of fens. Given the wealth of grasslands, little labor was needed in this way to add significant protein to one's diet and produce a marketable commodity. Over time, settlers adapted forms of alternate husbandry to each of the land types of New England. Where grasses were greater, cattle were always more numerous. Increased numbers of cattle were brought with each successive ship, and in turn they multiplied on the luxuriant, if not wholly nutritious, native grasses. Plymouth settlers found cattle a useful commercial venture, selling stock that exceeded their domestic need to newly arriving puritans in the 1630s. By 1650 vast herds numbering several hundred grazed on grasses in the interstitial zone of tidal marsh and fresh meadow of the lower reaches of several streams flowing into Massachusetts Bay in Watertown, Lynn, Ipswich, and Roxbury, all in close proximity to Boston, and by way of Boston's harbor to markets beyond. The Connecticut Valley's rich alluvial terraces and the Narragansett Basin's marshes supported similarly large herds. After land, livestock, especially cattle, was the principal component of colonial capital, and New England was the first Anglo-American cattle kingdom.[50] Where grasses were fewer, settlers employed mixed farming and husbandry, as on arable islands amidst hardscrabble and forest, where English woodland clearance experience proved useful. And, very important, the import of English grasses, soon after the completion of the great migration, freed settlers from locational constraints natural grass sites imposed on cattle raising.[51]

Migration and diffusion—to and within New England—simplified adaptive strategies, allowing them to become more uniform than they had been in England. New England, of course, was not so removed from England finally to escape the forces of unsettledness there. Intercourse with England continued throughout the seventeenth century. The focus of settlement, after all, was a coastal enclave with a growing urban core at Boston and at other outliers of trade. A slow stream of migrants—not always a net increase—persisted. Networks of credit and kin stretched back to England. The colonists were never detached from England, and their cultural features remained English.[52] Still, a distinctive English vernacular evolved—a particularly New England configuration of English ways emphasizing nuclear family, craving for land, and dependency upon private property rights. Social homogeneity reduced differences in economic, social, and political status, thereby reinforcing communities of equals and helping settlers from diverse backgrounds succeed in creating this new society, if not the imagined puritan ideal. Only in early settled towns that had been closed to new settlers did English subregional distinctiveness long persist—even more so than in that passing train, England. Recombination and adjustment cut across the grain elsewhere, producing a new, albeit not unrecognizable, English landscape. Inheritance, ideology, and experience collectively provided the context for social development. In particular, the strong East Anglian sense of collective responsibility maintained the integrity of the nuclear family. As Jack Greene has noted, the "individual pursuit of happiness emphatically did not diminish institutions of family, community, church, and social order." It did produce competent household economies, which in turn established the utopian model for the American family farm for generations hence.[53] By the end of the seventeenth century, then, much individual town distinctiveness in forms and practices inherited from England was gone, and for good reason. A permanent provincial society had emerged. New England was a new England.

The Settlement Landscape

Settlement expansion took place, we have seen, by replication, by increasing the number of communities rather than the size of any one. Both more dispersed and more nucleated settlements emerged, the latter along portions of the Massachusetts Bay and Long Island Sound littorals; about some glacio-lacustrine meadows of eastern Massachusetts and southern New Hampshire; on terraces of the Connecticut River Valley and parallel rivers; and, much later, at ridge-and-intervale sites forming a beaded belt across central Connecticut. The long, linear clusters of affluent farms with large houses in the Connecticut River Valley especially persisted throughout the colonial period, as did nucleation in places whose primary function was always other than agriculture. In the glacio-lacustrine basins of eastern Massachusetts, however, the inhabitants of the few, famous, largely ephemeral nucleated settlements, such as Sudbury, Dedham, and Andover, dispersed at the first opportunity to build detached freehold farms (see FIGS. 1.9, 2.6, 2.7). Hundreds of other towns and villages from the first years of settlement about Massachusetts Bay framed settlements of single-family farms forming neighborhoods confined in loose clusters on islands of arable land. To be dispersed was not to be disconnected.[54]

By nucleated, I mean that dwellings and farmsteads were gathered purposefully close together, and apart from farmlands, to form a compact settlement, not simply a thickly settled region of separate farmsteads. Closely gathered settlement was a puritan ideal, as one function of the town was to inspire and perpetuate congregational orthodoxy by gathering people about a meetinghouse for maintenance of spiritual values and community concord. The ideal was clearly stated in an anonymous "Essay on the Ordering of Towns" written about 1635.[55] Settlement was to be limited to within a radius of a mile and a half, or at most two miles, of the meetinghouse. A proper ranging of different activities from the center would furnish both geographic and social order as well as a sense of symmetry and beauty to the landscape. The essay also promoted enclosure: "He that knoweth the benefit of inclosing will omit noe dilligence to bring him selfe into an inclusive condicion, well understanding that one acre inclosed, is much more beneficial than 5 falling to his share in Common." Land as private commodity rather than public common was, after all, the compelling characteristic of New England settlement.

The ideal settlement was rarely employed by New England's settlers. Governor Bradford's personal history of Plymouth records a 1621 order that adjacent house lots of one acre be allotted in Plymouth to keep inhabitants close together. But few wished to do so; Bradford noted that "many followed Christ for the loaves sake." Despite Plymouth's apparently strong religious orientation, its leaders were incapable of preventing widespread dispersal of farmsteads in the 1620s. Recall Bradford's complaint that, "no man now thought he could live except he had cattle and a great deal of ground to keep them, all striving to increase their stocks. By which means they were scattered all over the Bay quickly and the town in which they lived compactly till now was left very thin and in short time almost desolate."[56]

In Massachusetts Bay, too, leaders were no more successful at maintaining compact settlement than those in Plymouth. As early as September 1630, Massachusetts authorities were ordering settlers in the future town of Ipswich "to come away" back to the settled area.[57] The oft-cited 1635 order from the Massachusetts Bay General Court likewise required that: "hereafter, noe dwelling howse shalbe builte above halfe a myle from the meeting howse, in any newe plantacon, graunted att this Court, or hereafter to be graunted, without leave from the Court, (except myll howses & fferme howses of such as have their dwelling howses in some towne)."[58] The order came in the context of the granting of a town at Concord, the first inland town on Massachusetts Bay, and the order was designed to affect new plantations or towns only. "Fferme howses" was a reference to shelters constructed in new plantations by those who had retained residence in established towns. That any such legislation was deemed necessary is telling of the predilections of settlers to disperse about their new lands, and repeal of the legislation in 1640 casts doubt on the ability or desire of the puritan will to place requirements of God ahead of others. Land and imported English ways simply frustrated efforts to form communities into nucleated settlements.

Towns still met the need for mutual security from the uncertainty of life on a new continent, if not necessarily from native peoples or wild beasts. The logistical undertaking of settlement was considerable, and the environment enjoined settlers to work interdependently at first. We know from our assessment of cultural transfer that a majority of families had come, at least most recently, from market towns and cities, not from farms. Settling required agricultural skills, and only some immigrants had been farmers. Sharing of skills, implements, and animals continued throughout the colonial period, but it did not require compact settlement.[59] Clearing land, for instance, discouraged nucleation, while cleared land did not necessarily encourage it. More commonly, towns orchestrated rectangular division of common land, a practice distinct from communal farming in open fields, which was employed and survived in only a few New England communities where particular land resources demanded it.

As for defensive precautions, the Pequot War of 1637 was an outcome of the tensions that had led to the 1635 Massachusetts order restricting dispersal of settlement in newly planted towns inland. Inland settlement had been sanctioned for the security it was expected to provide those who remained in the initial settlements.[60] A 1637 amendment applied the order to all towns, but Watertown, a settlement of widely dispersed farmsteads located well east of the frontier, was exempted in 1639, and the ruling itself was repealed in 1640.[61] Ironically, the war provided an opportunity for observing firsthand potential inland settlement sites and acquiring natives' lands.[62]

Later skirmishes with native peoples in 1645 again led the Massachusetts General Court to stipulate safety in numbers, again for frontier towns:

> In regard to the great danger yt Concord, Sudberry, & Dedham wilbe exposed unto, being inland townes & but thinly peopled, it is ordered, that no man now inhabiting & settled in any of the said towns (whether married or single) shall remove to any other towne without that allowance of the magistrate, or other select men of that towne, untill it shall please God to settle peace againe, or some othe way of safety to the townes, whereupon this Cort, or the councell of the comon weale, shall set the inhabitants of the said townes at their former liberty.[63]

Physical security, then, was a concern in the early years of settlement and would be again from time to time, especially in the Connecticut Valley over the next century. Anticipating destruction of inland towns during King Philip's War, the Massachusetts Court regretted that "our inhabitants in the severall townes [are] in so scattering and remote a condition."[64] The point is this: General Court restrictions as early as 1630 were a response to existing conditions of dispersal. From the start of settlement, colonists held ideas about settlement that confounded both ideology and security concerns.

What best explains nucleation, where it occurred, is preadaptation to particular site conditions. Plymouth was sited for suitable anchorage and the availability of fresh water near old fields, but, as we have noted, farmers shortly thereafter dispersed to grasslands. Salem was the original company town, established in 1628 to provide order, secure supplies, and develop revenue for puritan colonists to follow, but agricultural settlement from the first was dispersed to farms in the secondary settlement of Salem Village (see FIG. 2.4). Abundant salt marsh, upon which one could depend for fodder but upon which one could not build a farmstead, encouraged settlement in 1638 in Hampton, New Hampshire, part of Massachusetts Bay until 1679. Rarely, however, did New Englanders find an adequate quantity of good land concentrated to such an extent as to encourage and support communal farming and concentrated settlement, especially when land was divided into rectangles large by English standards. The Connecticut River Valley especially offered both meadow and market access, and large tracts of land divided into rectangles stretched back from the river. Family farming of divided strips of common land, not communal farming of open fields, prevailed to form "street villages." The point is important. Because large common fields were divided into rectangles and small common fields were widely dispersed in New England towns, and included infields and outfields, the colonists' own cultural geography encouraged enclosure of fields and dispersal to family farmsteads.

Thus where favorable site conditions might be expected to have encouraged compact settlement, to allow equal access to salt marsh or meadow, purposeful nucleations of settlement did not necessarily prevail. Site conditions were important factors in locating settlements, but site conditions did not cause compact form. Of the few agricultural compact settlements composed primarily of full-time farmers working fragmented fields, only at Hampton, New Hampshire, where an abundance of salt marsh restricted settlement sites, did residents long conform to the general morphological characteristics of the compact English manor village (FIG. 1.16).

The situation in Boston is instructive. Characteristically, it was sited for a number of reasons having little to do with agriculture—a source of fresh water, a defensible position, and good harborage. The peninsula yielded little arable or pasture land, and the town soon came to control additional land, available to its inhabitants, on the north and south shores of the Bay, at Rumney Marsh and at Mount Wollaston, and up the Charles River, at Muddy River (Brookline). Some of these grants, as to John Winthrop, were quite large, but generally they served the purpose of providing agricultural land to Boston's growing population in the early 1630s, while reserving some land closer to the peninsula for closely gathered house and garden lots. The distant lands were quickly enclosed and Boston's freemen placed servants, sons, and tenants to live on these outfields and cattle stations. Notwithstanding the 1635 order regarding close proximity to the meetinghouse, many people, landowners or not, were functionally divorced from the town on the peninsula. Residents of Mount Wollaston, beyond Dorchester, formed a separate congregation of the Boston church in 1636 and by 1640 had successfully sought incorporation as the town of Braintree.[65]

In short, requirements of puritan tenets, economic and spiritual well-being, and defense easily gave way to transfer from England of well-established cultural predispositions for certain kinds of economic endeavor, land-use and

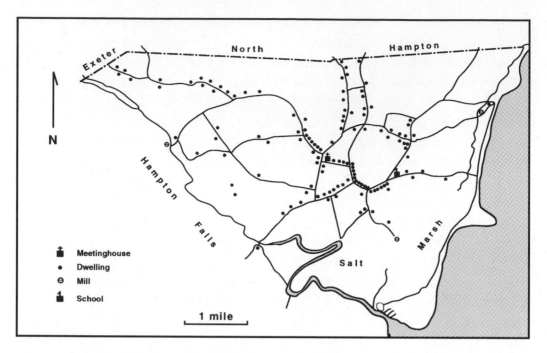

FIG. 1.16 Hampton, New Hampshire, c. 1806. Hampton is the exception that proves the rule. Abundant salt marsh supported large numbers of cattle but not sites for farmsteads. Residents retained nucleated agricultural settlement into the nineteenth century. (Redrawn from Dow 1893.)

land-division practices, and preferences for particular land types, which could not all be accommodated with a common-field system and nucleated settlement. The continued influx of settlers and discovery of favorable meadowlands in the first decade of settlement to support them of course encouraged continuous settlement expansion. The settlement ideal might suit settlers' needs as long as they distrusted the forest and its inhabitants. Perception of hazard reinforced collective impulses. But the possibilities of mobility, both social and geographic, which colonists found in New England undermined puritan aspirations for maintaining the ideal. General Court restrictions were responses to existing habits, which the court was unable to inhibit. The very importance to puritanism of transforming wilderness into garden, complemented by pressures of population growth and ecclesiastical dissension, accelerated the breakdown of the organic community envisioned in the puritan ideal, itself bankrupt by 1640, argues Peter Carroll.[66] John Martin's recent study of entrepreneurs further undermines the (Romantic) notion of communitarianism as a binding force and supports the contrapuntal notion that a community spirit, including government regulation, fostered individual expression in entrepreneurial relationships over land.[67] Experienced with a range of English ways and forms, settlers quickly sorted possible sites and established a variety of New England landscapes. But the New England encounter with the land produced rapid cultural change, much more rapid than is commonly granted. English ways and the New England land, to which English ways were well preadapted, encouraged successful settlement from the very first.

A Settlement Utopia

We can summarize this way: English settlers collectively brought cultural baggage that included in varying quantities and mixes a set of preadapted traits that encouraged successful settlement. They came as nuclear families of middling class with an expectation to own land and to build farms. They justified their adventure intellectually as one to improve one's self and to improve one's land. They brought an entrepreneurial spirit and market sensibility tempered by puritanism. They believed in collective responsibility for purposes of promoting social and economic organization and in individual responsibility to provide competency. They were not pioneers with axes intent on clearing thick woodlands, though some were experienced with woodland clearance in England. They were prepared to employ forms of alternate husbandry, such as wood-pasture farming, in the raising of cattle. They knew how to exploit marsh and meadowlands, including diking of marshes, reclaiming of fens, and constructing of watermeadows to enlarge their grasslands. They knew how to divide and work common land enclosed in individual rectangular strips. They were prepared to construct detached farmsteads in a geographically coherent relationship to one another and to their meetinghouse. Finally, they were prepared to form a syncretic cultural ecology separate from the variety of forms they had known in England.

Rich coastal and riverine ecological zones with trading places supported by commercial agriculture formed the initial settlement subregions of New England, in which settlers experimented with preadapted English ways under puritan ideology in a new environment. Here were perpetuated, for the first generation or so, a patchwork of different English-like cultural ecologies and cultural landscapes. The coastal foreland and its significant riverine extension, the Connecticut River Valley, however, were always focused outward, with inhabitants more connected and more commercial than in settlements only a few miles inland from tidewater.

In a wedge-shaped interstitial zone of fresh meadow about the Charles, Mystic, and Neponset Rivers and in the up-river glacio-lacustrine plains of the Charles, the Merrimack, and their tributaries, was a significant early (1630s–40s) experiment with dispersed settlement in proximity to lush meadow. Dispersal had occurred already on vast marshes in Watertown, Lynn, and Roxbury, for instance, but the histories of Concord, Dedham, Sudbury, and Andover all record the purposeful playing out of a tension for maintaining community in the face of individual expression in land division and land use, and thereby in government regulation of settlement. Similar tension played out later in Connecticut's similar interstitial ecological zones and cultural subregions, in towns such as Woodbury and Durham.

In the central ecological zone of hardscrabble interspersed with arable islands, English settlers fully formed the classic New England rural landscape of detached farmsteads. Despite the lack of any more marsh and meadow, forms of the mixed agriculture of the early colonial period, known in England as alternate husbandry, dominated, as they did in most ecological zones of New England until widespread commercialization of agriculture in the period of the early republic. In any one town in the interior, little land was actually in tillage, pasture, or meadow; farmsteads were clustered by the confines of bands of arable land, pasture, or meadow. Here, the classic size, shape, and organization of the New England town as a division of space to accommodate individuals on dispersed farms within a communal structure evolved.[68] An abstraction of English society had become whole, manifest in the settled towns of detached farmsteads of New England.

New England colonists from the start employed English ways of farming and husbandry, land division and settlement, governance and puritan ideology, adapting these to their newfound situation, but puritan social theory proved irrelevant in the new environment. The latent circumstances of New England's physical environment and cultural condition exerted selective pressures, providing a basis for the flowering of a new England, if not the puritan new England many sought. Paradoxically, the importance puritan thought gave to transforming wilderness into garden fused with pressures of population growth to accelerate the achievement of competence through settlement expansion to produce an economically stable society.[69]

The point here is that the expediency of settling rather quickly a new space employing familiar forms of husbandry and agriculture also required employing familiar and reliable forms of land use and land division. Fortunately for New England settlers, these forms easily suited the land they encountered. Among such forms, the common English notion of village as space for community and the practice of settlement by family farm survived this selective cultural transfer of English ways to the wilderness of New England and the subsequent reconstitution of English ways. Villages of dispersed farmsteads accommodated the centripetal requirements of venturing into the wilderness and the centrifugal forces of the American land. English settlers could find places that suited both their convictions and their needs.

"Imagining America as 'a howling desert wilderness' was a puritan conceit which became current for self-serving polemical purposes *after* the successful settlement of New England," writes David Cressy.[70] From the perspective of cultural ecology however, New England was already a garden, one in which settlers previewed the American utopian idiom—single-family, dispersed farmsteads providing competency and employing crops and animals in relation to one another—all models brought from England, preadapted to New England, and progressively adapted to varying American conditions.[71] Exceptionalism it was not.

2 · Village and Community in the Seventeenth Century

~: What was the geography of the villages and communities colonial New Englanders shaped? As noted in the previous chapter, New England settlers experimented with a number of settlement forms they had known in England. By the close of the first generation of settlement (the 1660s), a relatively standardized form of settlement had nonetheless developed: "Villages," as New Englanders called them, were pieces of territory laid out for settlement by a community of freehold farmers on dispersed farmsteads that would fashion a corporation and an ecclesiastical parish. Regional variations in settlement form did exist but reflected functional differences: coastal trading and fishing villages in which inhabitants also farmed, or interior concentrations of farmers along valuable intervale land in wide alluvial river valleys. Thus the colonial New England village was not as much a deviant form of settlement as it was an early American manifestation of English antecedents that ultimately came to characterize the form of much of the agricultural settlement expansion of the United States in the nineteenth century. The interlarding of communalistic desires and individualistic actions, expressed here as community-sanctioned individual farmsteads, continues to shape Americans' relationship with the land today. The lesson of the colonial New England village, moreover, is that the meanings we assign words are never invariant. :~

~: EARLY NEW ENGLAND COLONISTS, IT IS WIDELY BELIEVED, ESTABLISHED nucleated settlements, and these nucleated settlements enhanced community life.[1] This correlation between community function and settlement form was so important, it is further believed, that community was diminished in the eighteenth century as settlement form was loosened and many community members dispersed from nucleated villages to individual farms. But was community forbearance so dependent upon nucleated settlement? Or has the rhetoric about puritan community been so linked with the particular settlement form of the New England town as "to effect an implicit definition of community as the ideal Puritan town," and so confuse the settlement form with community?[2] This chapter suggests that a simple correlation between community function and nucleated settlement form in early colonial New England is mistaken. Highly structured communities were established; but, as in England, whence the colonists came, new communities—often called villages—developed and survived quite well without the necessity of nucleated settlement.

Community is a "social web" or, more explicitly, "a network of social relations marked by mutuality and emotional bonds."[3] Community is dependent upon common purpose, shared understanding and values, a sense of obligation and reciprocity, and collective action. As traditional community interaction was interpersonal and frequent, common space is also implied in most definitions. Space and place denote common experience; and, in the traditional view, community as experience and community as place were one.[4] The organization of the common space—the settlement form—reflects in large measure the configuration or spatial structure of the social web.[5]

The prevalent settlement form attributed to the place associated with traditional, preindustrial community is the village, or "collection of dwelling houses and other buildings, forming a centre of habitation in a country district."[6] Village and community, like place and community, are often considered one and the same and the terms are used interchangeably; but, in the primary definition of village, nucleation is strongly implied:[7] A kind of cosmological predilection to have a nucleated settlement located at the center of a community's area prevails and, in the geographical literature, is reinforced by a spatial view based on theoretical rings of decreasing intensity of land use with increasing distance from the center, on agglomeration economies, and on central places. Quite simply, nucleated forms provided the functional requirements for successful community and economy.[8]

No settlement form would have better insured community forbearance as seventeenth-century colonists ventured into the wilderness of New England. The conventional view that New England's colonial communities formed compact villages gathered around a central meetinghouse correlates nicely with an idealized social order attributed to hard-bitten, theocratic puritans; with recorded plans for villages; with literary and circumstantial historical reference to villages; with nineteenth-century maps and sketches of villages; and with present-day landscape. Yet, for all that has been said about community and settlement form in New England, it is instructive to examine once more the New England village. First, a number of scholars have shown that villages need not be nucleated settlement forms at all. Villages in Europe, including those in England, have ranged in form from quite compact, to linear, to widely dispersed neighborhoods.[9] Dispersed villages were common in southeast England, the major source area of New England colonists in the seventeenth century.[10] Second, recent studies of New England communities have dealt largely with the question of the essence of preindustrial village life in New England, the extent to which this way of life reflected its particular English origins, and the specifically American experience of these communities.[11] As a result of these studies, it has become evident to some historians that nucleation was not the constant rule for settlement form in early colonial New England.[12]

Close inspection of seventeenth-century New England villages—places specifically called villages in records of towns and governing colonial assemblies—suggests that *village* was an official designation of a community, like *town*, and that villages were subordinate to towns. Also like towns, villages were not necessarily nucleated in form. Indeed, detailed accounts of settlement form indicate that the modal form of settlement was dispersed from the 1630s onward and even many nucleated settlements were short-lived.[13] Nevertheless, New England communities existed and functioned quite well. Even when social structure or settlement form was altered, the social web that constituted community persisted. Village status encouraged such community forbearance by providing a community with land resources and placing the community and its assigned land under the auspices, guidance, and taxing power of a parent town. This status enabled the community to establish its own ecclesiastical society, or parish, or, if unsettled, to undertake settlement beyond the pale of what in time might become a town in its own right.

"In the Village Manner"

New England colonists' yearning for land was great, and available land was a critical factor in establishment of New England villages. Civil and religious liberty was important for settlers who came to New England, of course, but owning land and all that ownership implied were the most impelling reasons for both initial colonization and inland settlement.[14] The goal of puritan settlement in New England was noble: There was to be a covenanted community established in a new England, a congregation of individuals bound by special compact. But abundant land had an unsettling effect. New Englanders expanded settlement by replication, by increasing the number of communities rather than enlarging any one. Not satisfied with crowding along the shoreline, in Salem or about Boston Bay, settlers spread inland when and wherever they could. Much of New England is hardscrabble; once salt marshes, Indian old fields, and riverine meadows (intervales) were taken, settlers were forced to settle land more marginal than what first settlers had found. As New Englanders spread across the land, they established a settled landscape of places, many called villages and all designed to foster community well-being.

The New England town system was designed to bring order to these communities. The town was a community of settlers incorporated as an administrative unit to encourage settlement and establish political and religious institutions within clearly defined geographic boundaries and, thus, perpetuate community. But a town was not a settlement. Only through land proprietors, in whom was vested local authority and who were responsible for distributing land, did towns come to be instruments of settlement (FIG. 2.1). Colonial magistrates made extensive grants of land to town proprietors and to individuals in their favor, so, according to Governor Winthrop, "that (when the towns should be increased by their children and servants growing up, etc.) they might have place to erect villages, where they might be planted, and so the land improved to the more common benefit."[15] These "villages or plantations" were to be developed into new, freestanding communities with certain conditions required to assure success of the community.[16] The Town of Lynn, Massachusetts, one of the original towns about Massachusetts Bay, was especially in need of the grant for Lynn Village. The fifty families that came to Lynn in 1630 had laid out farms from ten acres to two hundred acres in size and had settled these farms in all parts of the original town grant.[17] But by 1639 more land was required, and the General Court was generous:

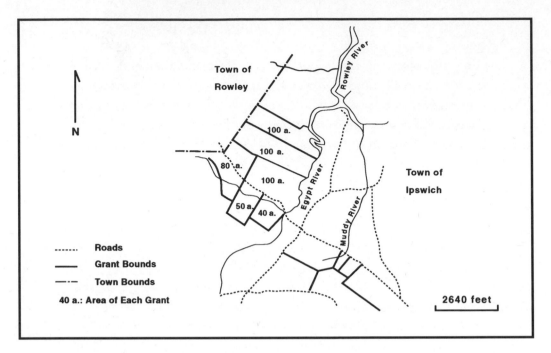

FIG. 2.1 Ipswich Village Grants, c. 1640. Ipswich Village, or the Egypt River Grants of the Town of Ipswich, comprised a number of large tracts of land parcelled out from the town's common-land holdings to its proprietors soon after settlement. (Redrawn from Jewett and Jewett 1946, p. 297.)

> The petition of the inhabitants of Linn for an inland plantation at the head of their bounds is granted them 4 miles square, as the place will affoard, upon condition that the petitioners shall within 2 years make some good proceeding in planting, so as it may bee a village fit to conteine a convenient number of inhabitants, which may in dewe time have a churche there, & so as such as shall remove to inhabit there shall not with all keepe their accomodations in Linn above 2 years after their removall to the said village, upon paine to forfeit their interest in one of them, at their owne election, except this Court shall see just cause to dispense further with them; & this village is to bee 4 mile square at least by just content.[18]

New England towns were thus settled, according to Timothy Dwight, widely traveled president of Yale College, in "*the village manner*: the inhabitants having originally planted themselves in small towns."[19] Dwight continued:

A town in the language of New England, denotes a collection of houses in the first parish, if the township contains more than one, constituting the principal, and ordinarily the original, settlement in the Parish.... A Street is the way, on which such a collection of houses is built; but does not at all include the fact, that the way is paved.... *Nor is it intended that the houses are contiguous, or even very near to each other.*[20]

While Dwight's statement is characteristic of the eighteenth-century landscape with which he was familiar, his description is appropriate for the seventeenth century as well. A century and a half before Dwight wrote, Captain Edward Johnson described Watertown, like Lynn one of the original towns about Massachusetts Bay, as: "a fruitful plat, and of large extent, watered with many pleasant Springs, and small Rivulets, running like veines throughout her Body, which hath caused *her inhabitants to scatter in such manner,* that their Sabbath-Assemblies prove very thin if the season favour not."[21] Similar descriptions, individual town records and maps, and even

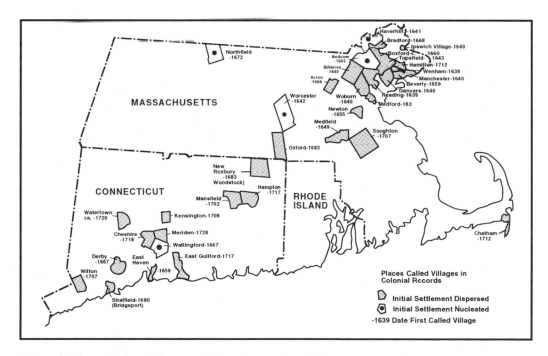

FIG. 2.2 Places Called Village in Colonial Records and Their Corresponding Settlement Forms.

57

idiosyncratic town histories confirm that seventeenth-century settlements, like Lynn or Watertown, were more often than not settled in a dispersed fashion.

Dispersal was especially characteristic of places explicitly called villages in colonial records (FIG. 2.2). Some of these places, like Billerica, first mentioned as a village in the colonial records of Massachusetts Bay in 1642, received new grants of land:

> All the land lying upon Saweshine Ryver & between that & Concord Ryver, & between that & Merrimack Ryver, not formerly granted by this Court, are granted to Cambridge, so as they may erect a village there within 5 yeares, & so as it shall not extend to prejudice Charlstowne village [Woburn], or the village of

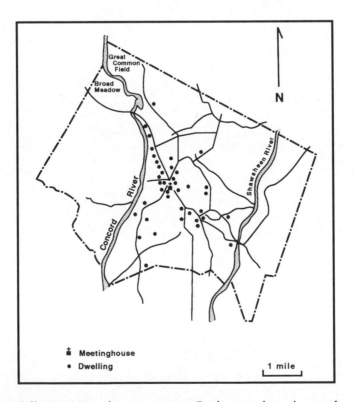

FIG. 2.3 Billerica, Massachusetts, c. 1660. Settlement along the meadows of the Concord River in the village that became Billerica was dispersed. (Redrawn from Hazen 1883.)

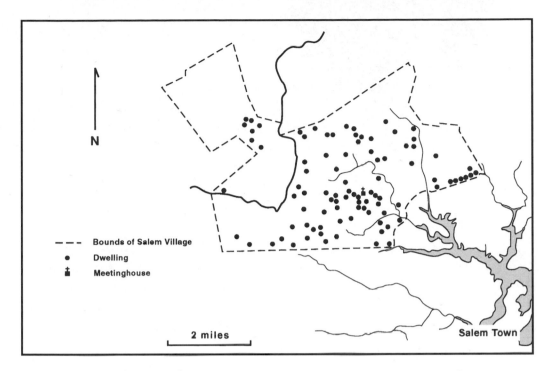

FIG. 2.4 Salem Village, Massachusetts, 1692. Salem Village was an outlying area of dispersed settlers in the Town of Salem that eventually became the Town of Danvers. (Redrawn from Upham 1867.)

> Cochitawit [Andover], nor the farmes formerly granted to the now Governor of 1260 acres.[22]

By 1660 more than forty families had established farms in Billerica, forming a settlement that partially paralleled the Concord River but otherwise was dispersed (FIG. 2.3).[23]

Other villages, like Manchester, Beverly, and Salem Village, now the Town of Danvers, were outlying neighborhoods of the original Town of Salem. The dispersed inhabitants of Salem Village, called the "farmers of Salem," broke off from "Salem Town," where Salem's merchants resided. Salem Town was not becoming too crowded for farmers, but farmers had long before moved out into an interstitial area beyond the reach of comfortable weekly commuting to the meetinghouse (FIG. 2.4).[24] As in many other towns in Massachusetts and Connecticut, Salem's settlers were simply too widely dispersed from homesteading on great lots, distant divisions of land, not to split into more manageable social, religious, and (eventually) political units—villages.

The Meaning of *Village*

A number of issues follow from the manner in which the term *village* was used in early colonial New England. First, not all settlements were called villages and not all villages were dispersed settlements. Villages seem generally to have been secondary settlements, for a time part of or subordinate to another town (FIG. 2.5). None of the very first settled towns in either Massachusetts Bay or Connecticut, and few primary or first-order towns, granted independently of any other town, were called villages.[25] There were three exceptions. Andover and Haverhill were first-order towns reserved by the Massachusetts Court as villages and granted to companies of men from a number of the original towns about Massachusetts Bay. The nucleated settlements of both towns were short-lived. As at Sudbury and Dedham, nucleated forms proved useful in establishing initial settlements in the deep woods but not for general farming; farmers dispersed within a generation, leaving no nucleated settlement in Andover and only a small commercial settlement in Haverhill (FIGS. 2.6, 2.7; see also FIG. 1.9).[26] The vicinity of Worcester in Massachusetts Bay was first mentioned for a village in 1642 because of the presence of lead mines, but the venture did not succeed. In 1667 a committee was established to view the vicinity of Quinsigamond Pond for a village. Worcester was settled and abandoned twice, however, before permanent settlement occurred in 1713. The relatively compact but linear form of settlement that came to prevail in Worcester was important for defense, and later for central-place activities, but not for open-field farming.[27] The second-order settlements of Northfield, Massachusetts, and Wallingford, Connecticut, were also more clustered than dispersed. Riverine topography favored linear settlement in both places, and both were threatened by native people. Wallingford had to be abandoned in 1675. Northfield was not permanently settled until after 1713.[28] In all other settlements expressly called villages in colonial records, dispersed settlement seems to have prevailed.

Though such villages were established throughout the first century of settlement in Massachusetts Bay and Connecticut, the meaning of the term *village* seems to have changed over time. In Massachusetts Bay, where the term was generally used only in the seventeenth century and thus earlier than in Connecticut, a village charter was an instrument of land distribution and town formation. Population was greater in Massachusetts Bay than in Connecticut, and inland settlement proceeded more quickly. Hence, Massachusetts Bay towns were subdivided or required new land grants earlier, often

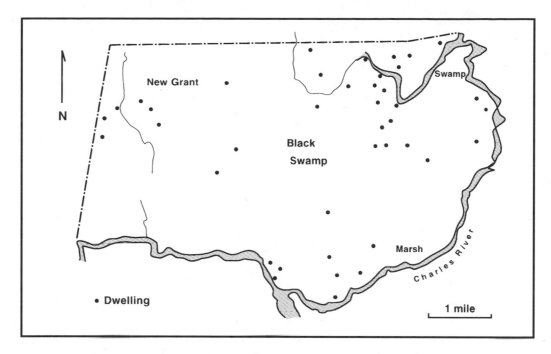

FIG. 2.5 Medway, Massachusetts, 1713. Medway formed from meadowland originally part of Dedham and, after 1649, the Village of Medfield. With settlement in 1660s, Medway became a village of Medfield. It was incorporated in 1713. (Redrawn from Jameson 1886, p. 46.)

within a decade or generation of initial settlement. The area allocated for a town in Massachusetts Bay could hold only so many people before the community split into new communities or overflowed. In Connecticut, on the other hand, dispersed settlements were divided from older towns as well, but only long after the same process had generally occurred in Massachusetts Bay. In contrast to Massachusetts Bay, English agricultural practice, including common-field agriculture, persisted longer in Connecticut, larger reserves of land were held for future generations, and stricter control was placed on land division. Moreover, with a smaller initial population, population pressure took longer to build up. Hence, there were fewer requests for new communities, and until the end of the seventeenth century the Connecticut Court and Assembly were reluctant about liberally granting new villages.[29]

By then, *village* had come to mean something different in Connecticut than in Massachusetts. As early as 1659 some dispersed inhabitants of New Haven, Connecticut, were asking to be a separate village of East Haven.

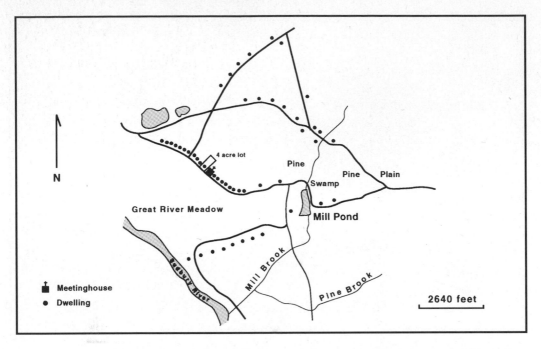

FIG. 2.6 Sudbury, Massachusetts, c. 1640. As was common among several first-order towns granted in the 1630s inland from tidewater in the glacio-lacustrine lands of eastern Massachusetts, Sudbury's original settlement was laid out in small lots, many actually set some distance from the meetinghouse. See also FIG. 1.9. (Redrawn from Hudson 1889, p. 76.)

They agreed to meet conditions of their "Village grant" by laying out a five-acre meetinghouse lot, constructing a meetinghouse, and settling a minister.[30] Village status was finally granted in 1707, and records of the subsequent dialogue between inhabitants of East Haven and the Connecticut Assembly reveal the changing meaning of *village*:

> This Assembly considering the petition of the East Village of New Haven, do see cause to order that they shall be a village distinct from the township of Newhaven, and invested and privileged with all immunities and privileges that are proper and necessary for a village for the upholding of the publick worship of God, as also their own civil concerns; and in order thereunto, do grant them libertie of all such offices as are proper and necessary for a town, and to be chosen by themselves in order and form as allowed by law for each and any town.... As also the said village have libertie to have a school amongst themselves with the privilege of the fortie schillings

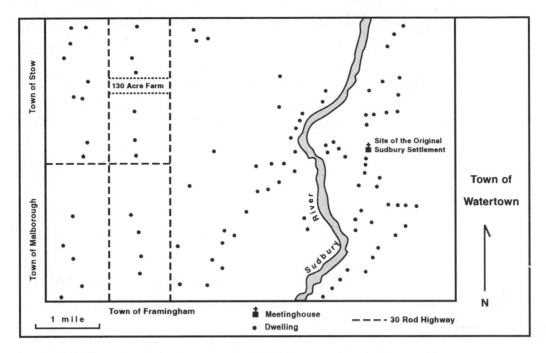

FIG. 2.7 Sudbury, Massachusetts, c. 1708. Sudbury's original settlement quickly dispersed westward across the Sudbury River. In 1723 that portion east of the river became East Sudbury and today is the Town of Wayland. (Redrawn from J. Brigham in Hudson 1889, p. 124.)

upon the thousand pound estate as every town hath by law; and also shall free their own village charge, and maintain their own poor, as all towns are obliged by law to do; and be fully freed from paying any taxes to the town of Newhaven.[31]

East Haven residents read more into their charter than the Assembly had meant to concede them, and in 1710 the order had to be qualified to read that "there is nothing in the said act that concerns property of lands, or that excludes the village from being within the township of New Haven."[32] Even this failed to settle the matter. In 1716 East Haven was "to have no other powers than those that are common to other parishes."[33] In short, land distribution was no longer the purpose or prerogative of a village, but a village still formed a community for social and religious functions. Consequently, when the inhabitants of Wilton petitioned for separation from Norwalk in 1726, the Assembly was quite specific about what *village* had come to mean in Connecticut: "Upon the petition . . . praying to be a village by themselves enjoying parish privileges, and that they may be called by the name of Wilton Parish: This Assembly do hereby grant the said inhabitants be one village."[34]

Occasional references not specifying any particular place suggest that *village* was used by some to mean any settlement, especially any recent or prospective settlement.[35] But in most cases, a village was self-consciously and legally ordained as a community. In the seventeenth century, a village had sufficient independent status and authority to establish and foster spiritual as well as economic, social, and political well-being for its inhabitants while still being part of a parent town. By the eighteenth century, a village was at least an ecclesiastical parish.

The Cultural Context

Several points spelled out in the previous chapter bear repeating. The traditional view that colonial New England villages were necessarily nucleated settlements housing rural communities practicing open-field agriculture is based on the premise that New Englanders were so predisposed. That is what Englishmen were supposed to do. Moreover, nucleated settlements met the requirements of both mutual protection in the wilderness and puritan tenets about how communities should be organized spatially to maximize political and religious order.[36] But though English colonists shared a common heritage, England was hardly homogeneous in social structure. Englishmen came from a variety of social backgrounds and regional subcultures. Most had some familiarity with agriculture, but rural England in the seventeenth century was not composed exclusively, even largely, of corn-and-stock peasants farming open fields and living in nucleated settlements. Areas devoted more to livestock and less to grain tended toward dispersed settlement.[37] Thus, no singular folk tradition or set of rules and material forms existed. No single model of how an agricultural community was to operate or how a settlement was to be formed prevailed.[38] The English village that many colonists left behind was not necessarily a nucleated cluster of dwellings and outbuildings adjacent to a church and manor and encircled by common fields. How an English village functioned to provide a sense of community was more important than the form it took. The village was an interdependent, rural society carrying on family-oriented agriculture. The village functioned to provide economic security for its inhabitants, and its inhabitants shared a common social purpose.[39]

Not only did England embody a heterogeneous landscape of settlement forms, but the society colonists were leaving behind in England was in the throes of significant institutional changes, including changes in land division and tenure. England was experiencing a crumbling of old customs of farming in the face of subtly increasing commercialization of agriculture and voluntary enclosure. The bulk of New England colonists, though not necessarily the dispossessed, came from portions of the east and south of England especially undergoing change. They brought with them to New England a strong notion that land ownership would provide both prestige and economic security.[40] Their desire for land was compounded by a spirit of individualism in politics, society, and ideas that had grown and developed in sixteenth- and seventeenth-century England. Hence, New England settlement must be viewed in the context of a tension between a longing for individual private control of land in a garden—and individual economic security—and a communal forbearance in a wilderness—social security. In all of their endeavors, large numbers of English colonists were driven to seek both individual expression and covenanted communities.[41]

Driven as they were, and with no vested interests in replicating a singular English way of life. Englishmen in New England could mold a new cultural landscape. Thus, while colonists drew upon familiar forms and ways of doing things, they probably brought with them little excess cultural baggage, few vestiges of medieval institutions in community, church, governance, or agricultural practice. As a result, English local institutions were reshaped within each New England community to meet the particular needs and backgrounds of the inhabitants.[42] But because people of a common cultural heritage yet with quite different social backgrounds and regional subcultures, each with their own customs and material forms, were intermingling, further reduction of vestigial ways and forms and adaptation and innovation eventually took place. Such intermingling led toward more common ways of doing things and more common material culture.[43] By the end of the seventeenth century, much distinctiveness inherited from England was gone.[44]

Both the common English notion of community and dispersed settlement survived the cultural transfer of English ways to the wilderness of New England. Such community not only could accommodate the centripetal requirements of venturing into the wilderness, but in its English variety of settlement forms it could also accommodate the variety of individual needs and experiences of New England's colonists. Requirements of defense and economic and spiritual well-being easily gave way to direct transfer from England of well-established cultural predispositions for certain kinds of economic endeavor, land-division practices, and preferences for particular environmental conditions that could not all be accommodated in a nucleated settlement form. As livestock raising was especially significant in early colonial New England, settlers were prompted to secure as much intervale or salt marsh as they could while still remaining loyal to the evolving concept of the New England town.[45] One could choose either nucleated or dispersed settlement; but the modal form of community settlement that characteristically emerged in an early colonial New England, torn between individual expression and community covenant, was the dispersed village; and English custom encouraged it.

Village and Community

What is important from the foregoing discussion of settlement form is not only that villages were often not nucleated settlements in early colonial New England, but that villages functioned as communities regardless of settlement form. No one doubts that community was achieved in early colonial New England villages. The process of community building was not necessarily easy; but, aided by the common English heritage of the colonists, by the fact that many communities were purposefully gathered from parent communities in England or were formed in New England of old neighbors or acquaintances, and by the provision for land distribution, community building was accomplished. As in England, *village* meant *community*. As in England, villages were well-knit rural societies carrying on family-oriented agriculture, constituting distinct social and religious groups, and providing collective security for inhabitants. Indeed, community cohesion may have grown stronger in New England, and New Englanders continued to nourish such localism as a value to be cherished.[46] Congregational control of the church and local political control, including collective regulation of land distribution, encouragement of local enterprise, and coordination of communal activities, provided for a distinctive sense of community identity. Shared ideology insured societal uniformity and cohesion. Even economic exchange was fundamentally local. Trading relationships were familiar and intimate. Moreover, available land had released colonists from an age-old cultural tradition of communal frugality in land utilization. Finally, available land meant political responsibility based on freeholding could actually be more widely held within the community.[47]

Dispersed settlement did not necessarily imply remoteness and isolation, a denial of community, even in a society driven to individual expression. Interaction caused by daily, weekly, seasonal, and annual congregational and political responsibilities took place within an established social structure, and the interaction itself was more important than the degree to which settlement was nucleated. The real colonial New England village was a network of social and economic linkages, a social web, not a cluster of dwellings. Within the social web, a basic conflict between human striving for individual expression and a similar strong need for collective experience and a place to belong was played out. People were villagers, under an umbrella of social control and economic security, while living dispersed upon their own farms.

The New England community's network of interaction had a physical manifestation. Common cultural features of colonial maps of New England villages and towns are a node, paths, and edges—or the meetinghouse, roads, and town boundaries. Other buildings or dwellings and property boundaries are less often shown, especially on the earliest extant maps. The meetinghouse, the focus of community activity, was often exaggerated beyond proportion to indicate its location. Indeed, the meetinghouse—well situated often at an elevation, standing alone or accompanied by a parsonage, in time a tavern, perhaps a blacksmith, and by chance a farmhouse or two—was the dominant feature of the village landscape throughout the colonial period. No particular sacredness was attached to the meetinghouse itself, but the meetinghouse was the embodiment of the community, a tangible manifestation of the intangible political and religious life of the community—even if it stood alone, as Captain Edward Johnson described the meetinghouse in Roxbury, Massachusetts, in the 1630s. "Their streets are large, and some fayre Houses, yet they have built the House for Church-assembly, destitute and unbeautified with other buildings."[48] One hundred and fifty years later, community centers looked little different, as Meriden, Connecticut, first called a village in 1728, illustrated (FIG. 2.8).[49] The town road network, extended to interconnect dispersed farmsteads, enhanced the situation of the meetinghouse, providing access for all in the community. The physical circumscription of bounds added to the sense of place, and the annual perambulation and intertown contentiousness over bounds recorded by provincial assemblies attest to the significance of town boundaries.[50]

Bounds, of course, could not be too extensive, or intratown contentiousness (also recorded by town meetings and provincial assemblies) might arise
and a new community might have to be established. Equitable organization
of space within reasonable bounds for dispersed settlements was the overriding consideration in the formation of new communities. As seventeenth-
century settlement reached into extensions of land granted for villages and
plantations, and settlers were required to travel considerable distances to
meeting and so often petitioned for establishment of a separate community,
a village with its own meetinghouse could be sanctioned and social order
maintained. As residents withdrew still farther from the affairs of the original community, the town, they might petition for their own separate town
incorporation. Because parent towns were often reluctant to release such
communities within their bounds and thus reduce their tax base, as residents
of East Haven, Connecticut, had learned, such division was slow. Nevertheless, division of dispersed communities into new villages and towns was an
important process in the evolution of the New England settlement landscape.[51] As long as social and economic linkages remained unbroken, community prevailed. When linkages were stretched too far, the effect was hardly
a rejection of the idea of community. As in 1630, when too many settlers had
gathered on the shores of Massachusetts Bay to form a single community, division created new communities.[52] By the end of the colonial period, early
settled towns had been subdivided and more recently settled towns granted
in such a fashion that the landscape of New England came to resemble a
great mosaic of equal-sized communities.

Also by the end of the colonial period, the notion of community as it had
been known in early colonial New England was being challenged. Economic
and social linkages that maintained community were strained. Yet the infor-
mal and intimate relationship of self-conscious, colonial communities bridged
differences, including the new abstract theological differences of the Great
Awakening that had given rise to dissenting congregations within communities and that had assumed great rhetorical importance in provincial politics.
A multiplicity of operating cultures—a pragmatic, family-based community
culture concerned with local economic and social affairs, superficially over-
lain by a more abstract culture concerned with religious and political issues,
all interpenetrated by emerging external associations—helps explain the apparent persistence of "peaceable kingdoms" well into the eighteenth century.
Community was not necessarily diminished; it simply accommodated change.

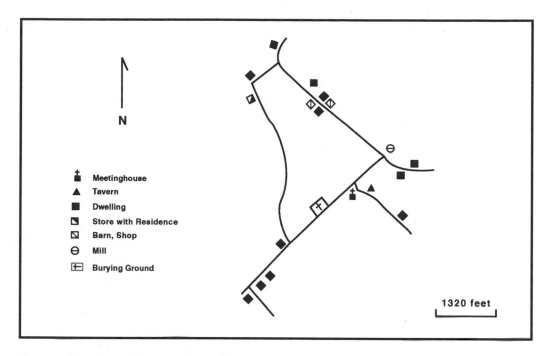

FIG. 2.8 The Central Portion of Meriden, Connecticut, c. 1780. Meetinghouses at town centers, like Meriden, were the symbolic and geographical centers of New England's communities. (Redrawn from Gillespie 1906, p. 342.)

Settlement form, long dispersed, had little to do with it.[53] Methods of land distribution within towns, increasingly individualistic and competitive rather than community-based as the colonial period passed, may have had much to do with transforming what was recognized as community in the seventeenth century to a form of community more appropriate to the eighteenth century.[54] That, however, is another study.

Conclusion

David Lowenthal reminds us that the preservation of relict artifacts may overemphasize the role an artifact played in a past landscape.[55] The village encountered in New England today, white-painted, black-shuttered, classical-revival dwellings, churches, and stores abutting a tree-shaded green, reflects not continuity with New England's colonial past but a most dramatic change. The change took place in the Federal period, in the last generation of the eighteenth century and the first generation of the nineteenth century.

Economic affairs became increasingly less localized and more regional, and New Englanders broke out of traditional culture molds to create a landscape of commercial places where meetinghouses had long stood alone.[56]

Only then, as the form of settlement changed to become nucleated, did the term *village* take on its present-day connotation. To early colonial New Englanders, who were not necessarily predisposed toward nucleated settlement, *village* only meant *community*. The New England town was the source of land for most individuals and thus initially the instrument for providing economic security and encouraging settlement. A well-bounded corporate space, inhabited by people who sensed they constituted a community distinct from any other, was sufficient to provide the order and cohesion long attributed to nucleated settlement. Indeed, closely interdependent, collaborative communities of colonial New England themselves allowed nucleated settlement, where it had been implanted, to wither. Social order did not require nucleation. In the colonial meaning, the village was a social web in which puritan tenets worked well enough.

3 · The Architectural Landscape

~: Not only has our reading of past settlement landscapes erred so that we have projected nineteenth-century villages back to the seventeenth century, but we have misread the architectural forms in the landscape as well. We have taken those buildings that remain visible today as representative of the architectural landscape of the colonial period. Using the Direct Tax Census of 1798, Michael Steinitz shows that most houses in central Massachusetts in particular and the state as a whole were actually smaller, had fewer stories and less ornamentation, and were more dispersed than we have commonly believed. Indeed, one-story houses outnumbered double-pile, two-story houses, the classic New England farmhouse of an imagined landscape, by a ratio of seven to one in the study area. At the same time, regional variation occurred in houses, indicating regional differences in wealth related to good lands, a point made in Chapter 1. Also, clearly from the architectural record, a great house rebuilding was under way by the 1790s, presaging change in villages as well. Subsequent chapters translate this rebuilding into the new village landscape. This focus on the largely disappeared architectural landscape and its misrepresentation reiterates points made for the broader settlement landscape of the period. :~

~: THE CLAIMS OF THE ACADEMIC DISCIPLINE OF AMERICAN GEOGRAPHY for an interest in the realm of vernacular architecture go back over sixty years. In 1925 geographer Carl Sauer established the methodological basis for the Berkeley School of cultural geography with his essay "The Morphology of Landscape," an attempt to introduce the notions of cultural process into a discipline that was essentially ahistorical and antitheoretical in its orientation.[1] Sauer borrowed freely from the European traditions of human geography to promote in this country the concept of the cultural landscape as an appropriate object of geographical study. In "The Morphology of Landscape," and in his later writings, Sauer repeatedly drew attention to the importance of what he called common house plans and structures as significant records in the landscape, as expressions of family organization, as outgrowths of local economies, and as embodiments of traditions carried on through time and space.[2]

Sauer's empirical research unfortunately did not include systematic studies of North American vernacular architecture. However, in 1936, one of his students, Fred Kniffen, published "Louisiana House Types," a pioneering work that identified and mapped that state's most common architectural characteristics, including selected plan configurations, roof types, and porch constructions.[3] Kniffen's article made the "shotgun house" a part of every cultural geographer's vocabulary, and it was here that he introduced the monolithic concept of the "I-house" into the study of American vernacular architecture. Kniffen's early demonstration of methodological possibilities inspired relatively few followers, although other Berkeley-trained geographers subsequently generated a number of regional architectural studies.[4] Throughout the 1940s and 1950s the investigation of regional architecture remained a very minor component of American cultural geography,[5] despite its advocacy in the 1950s by maverick geographer J. B. Jackson, who as founder and editor of *Landscape* magazine aimed to make the common house the focus of a new, indigenous, humanistic American geography.[6]

In the 1960s, however, two widely influential pieces of writing appeared in the geographical literature: Fred Kniffen's "Folk Housing: Key to Diffusion" and Henry Glassie's *Pattern in the Material Folk Culture of the Eastern United States*.[7] Together these statements reshaped our vision of the cultural landscape of the eastern seaboard during the colonial and early national eras. They focused specifically on the common dwelling house as a key diagnostic indicator of the distinctive patterns of folk culture generated in the new social and physical environments of North America. Kniffen and Glassie used the classic methods of the cultural geographer: They went into the field and recorded what they saw. They also relied on predecessors who had looked at the landscape and systematically documented it, particularly the surveyors and photographers of the Historic American Buildings Survey, who had amassed a large archive of information in the 1930s. What emerged in the late 1960s, however, was a dynamic model that defined several distinctive cultural source regions along the coast, from which people, ideas, and artifacts diffused into the continental interior of the humid east. What followed the establishment of the model was a lively debate on the processes of cultural transfer, the significance of environment, and the extent to which changes in house form reflected fundamental shifts in social and cultural attitudes.[8]

Implicit in the work of the 1960s and much of what followed were claims of access through the surviving elements of material culture to the perceptions and aspirations of people who were otherwise unrepresented or underrepresented in the historical record. The rediscovery of the common house gave access to the world of the common people, or so it seemed. But while the Kniffen and Glassie model suggested the interregional diversity of common dwellings in use during the colonial and early national periods, it did not address the issue of how representative its diagnostic sample of surviving houses was. More recent historical research clearly points to serious methodological problems with the cultural geographer's traditional reliance on field reconnaissance of a small number of surviving buildings to reconstruct historic patterns.

Rethinking the Architectural Landscape

Work over the past decade by archaeologists, architectural historians, and social historians in the Middle Atlantic and Chesapeake regions, for example, suggests that the images of the vernacular landscape that Kniffen and Glassie initially generated for these areas were in fact not representative of the types of houses inhabited by most people. In the Chesapeake, it is now clear that the predominant house through the end of the eighteenth century was not a two-story I-house. For all but the wealthiest residents of the tidewater region, home typically meant a small, short-lived, flimsy, one- or two-room structure. Thus, the eighteenth-century "folk" landscape of this region was characterized by small, impermanent dwellings, of which few aboveground

traces remain.[9] One of the present and future tasks of all students of vernacular architecture is to help push forward a reevaluation of the regional models
of Kniffen and Glassie in light of the past decade's research, and to develop a
more detailed and representative picture of the housing of the great culture
hearths of the eastern seaboard. Using research developed on housing in
eighteenth-century central Massachusetts, this chapter identifies some directions that these revisions might take.

The Kniffen and Glassie image of northern New England suggested an
egalitarian landscape dominated by comfortably large, two-story houses.
Three eighteenth-century house types were identified by Kniffen, and two
additional types were recognized by Glassie. These types included two-story,
central-chimney hall-and-parlor houses; two-story, central-chimney salt-box
houses; and one-story central-chimney Cape Cod cottages. The most common survival in the region is the large, two-story, double-pile, central-chimney house, sometimes called "the New England Large," which is often cited in
the literature as the most representative house type in interior New England
during this period. A number of two-story, central-hall houses also survive.[10]
Field observations, then, suggest an eighteenth-century landscape dominated
by large, two-story houses that make up four of the five regional types. This
is the image that has continued to be set forth in such works as Pillsbury and
Kardos's *Field Guide to the Folk Architecture of the Northeastern United States*,
Virginia and Lee McAlester's *Field Guide to American Houses*, and most recently Allen Noble's *Wood, Brick and Stone: The North American Settlement
Landscape*.[11]

Worcester County, Massachusetts

Field reconnaissance for the Massachusetts Historical Commission's State
Survey Program confirms these characteristics of the surviving eighteenth-
century landscape. Worcester County, in the central part of the state, had
over sixty-one thousand inhabitants occupying more than nine thousand
dwellings in 1800. Two-thirds of the standing eighteenth-century houses are
substantial two-story buildings, and all five of the New England dwelling
types are indeed present. Yet this surviving "folk" architectural fabric represents at best 10 percent of the houses standing in 1800, a sample skewed very
strongly toward the upper end of the socioeconomic scale. It primarily includes the largest and best-built houses, as well as those constructed in the

1780s and especially the prosperous 1790s.[12] As in the Chesapeake and Middle Atlantic regions, the fragments of the eighteenth-century vernacular landscape that survive in this part of New England overrepresent an "elite" folk landscape: the domestic environments of the families of the most successful farmers, land speculators, merchants, artisans, clergymen, and professionals. Somewhere below this lies a much less visible middle landscape for which the terms *typical* or *representative* would be more meaningful. This differential survival rate, part of what R. W. Brunskill calls the "vernacular threshold," appears to be characteristic of most historic, rural landscapes. The best-built houses of a historic period are often overrepresented among extant examples, whereas substandard and even middling houses survive in very low numbers, if at all.[13]

In Massachusetts, both the recovery of these lost elements of the landscape and the establishment of the characteristics of the most common dwellings are possible through the use of the Federal Direct Tax Census of 1798.[14] This census was a detailed inventory of property that recorded a number of measurable dwelling features, including exterior dimensions, building material, story height, number of windows, amount of glass, and number and type

Fig. 3.1 Gershom-Brigham House, c. 1750. In the central uplands of Massachusetts, small, one-story buildings such as this in Westborough were the most typical dwelling form at the end of eighteenth century. (*Some Old Houses of Westborough* 1906.)

of outbuildings. The enumerators then assigned each house a dollar value.[15] This systematic documentary evidence strongly indicates the extent to which inferences from surviving buildings have been misleading. A picture emerges of a far different cultural landscape, one that varied remarkably from town to town, and one that also clearly reflected significant economic stratification within towns. It was a landscape characterized by much smaller and meaner dwellings than has been assumed up to this point (FIG. 3.1).

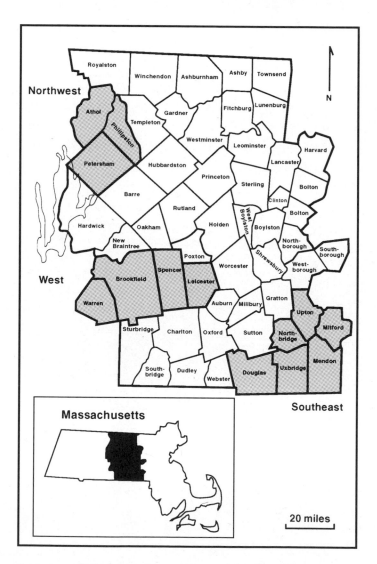

FIG. 3.2 Location of Worcester County Towns. The figure depicts those towns for which 1798 Direct Tax Census information survives, indicating subregional clusters of towns. Inset indicates location of Worcester County within the state.

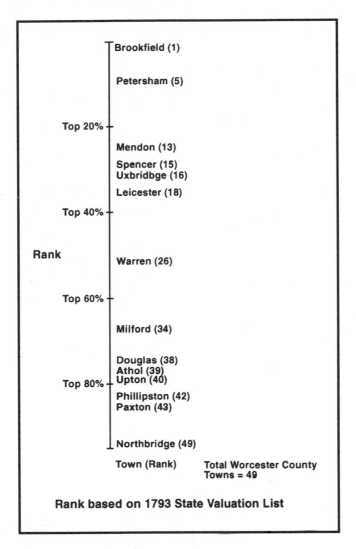

Brookfield (1)

Petersham (5)

Top 20%

Mendon (13)
Spencer (15)
Uxbridbge (16)
Leicester (18)

Top 40%

Rank

Warren (26)

Top 60%

Milford (34)

Douglas (38)
Athol (39)
Upton (40)
Top 80%
Phillipston (42)
Paxton (43)

Northbridge (49)

Town (Rank)   Total Worcester County
                     Towns = 49

Rank based on 1793 State Valuation List

FIG. 3.3 Sample Towns Ranked by Aggregate Wealth in 1793.

In the balance of this chapter I use the data from the Direct Tax Census to establish patterns in the eighteenth-century architectural landscape of fourteen Worcester County towns for which detailed information survives concerning the nearly twenty-three hundred dwellings that made up the complete housing stock.[16] The fourteen towns are located in three clusters in the southeast, west, and northwest parts of the county (FIG. 3.2), areas that differed in the timing and sequence of settlement and growth in the eighteenth century. In 1798 the average length of permanent settlement of the towns in the southeast was ninety-two years. In the west it was eighty-one years. In the northwest it was only fifty-eight years. Based on the 1793 state valuation lists, the towns also represented all levels of aggregate local wealth (FIG. 3.3). They included Brookfield, the richest town in Worcester County, a large, old, and affluent agricultural town in the west. They also included Northbridge, a small, recently created town in the southeast, which in 1793 was the poorest community in the county.

The detailed housing data for these towns are quite revealing. In 1798 the floor-plan sizes of dwellings (as measured on the exterior of buildings) varied considerably. At the bottom was the 140-square-foot house (measuring 10 feet by 14 feet), valued at $25, owned by Grindal Thayer of Uxbridge. At the top was the 3,002-square-foot, two-story residence of Luke Baldwin of Brookfield, with its forty-five windows and adjoining stable, wood house, and outhouse. For the entire sample, the average house-plan size was 831 square feet, much smaller than the typical surviving house. When the house-plan sizes are scaled at 50-foot intervals, their distribution reveals two peaks— one around 600 square feet, and another near 1,000 square feet (FIG. 3.4). In addition, the data indicate that the houses of up to 1,000 square feet were mostly one story in height. Only beyond 1,100 square feet, well above the mean of 831 square feet, did two-story houses dominate. On a finer scale, at 10-foot intervals, the plan sizes for all houses follow a relatively continuous increase from about 320 square feet to 1,200 square feet, with what appear to be regular, periodic peaks of occurrence of particular house-plan sizes (FIG. 3.5). While much more work needs to be done in relating these figures to actual house plans, one possibility is that the smaller intervals may reflect incremental increases in room size, while the larger may reflect additional rooms.

The distribution also strongly demonstrates the persistence of small dwellings at the end of the eighteenth century. While small houses are known to have remained in use in other New England regions such as Cape Cod, their continued presence in the interior beyond the initial settlement phase has been less widely recognized.[17] Yet in 1798, inland Massachusetts still had its one-room houses, such as the $10 dwelling of William Jewel of Boxborough in Middlesex County, which was enumerated as "one poor little miserable low house, no window, no glass." In Worcester County, 24 percent of the dwellings enumerated were less than 600 square feet in area, and 14 percent were less than 500 square feet. (A dwelling of 600 square feet might still have had a plan with two moderate rooms of 15 feet by 16 feet each and a lobby or hall.) Houses of this size or smaller are now known to have been

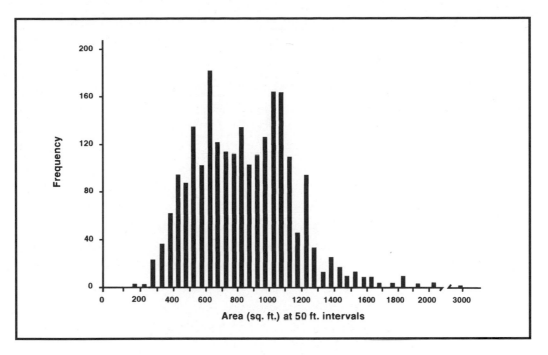

FIG. 3.4 Frequency Distribution of House-Plan Sizes in 1798 at Fifty-Foot Intervals.

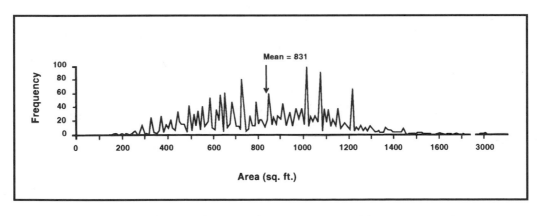

FIG. 3.5 Frequency Distribution of House-Plan Sizes in 1798 at Ten-Foot Intervals.

typical of other regions of the eastern seaboard during this period.[18] The tax census data show not only that they were much more numerous in New England than indicated by the survivals, but also that, at least in Worcester County, they were the most common class of building.

In contrast to these smaller buildings, the effective areas of many of the region's large houses were further extended through the addition to the main block of the house of specialized domestic spaces, such as kitchens, wood houses, and wash houses, as well as stables and chaise or carriage houses. In 1798 these domestic outbuildings were largely limited to the highest valued houses in a community; their appearance in the middle range of houses was rare.

House values in 1798 ranged from George Halstatt's $4 "log-house" (the only one enumerated in Worcester County), measuring 28 feet by 18 feet and located in Petersham, to the Luke Baldwin mansion in Brookfield, the largest house in the sample, assessed at $3,000 (FIG. 3.6). The bulk of the region's houses were assessed at less than $350, with the peak in the interval between $100 and $150. Real differences in median house value were apparent among towns and among the three clusters of towns. As a group, the western towns had higher median values than the two other clusters. In both the west and the southeast, the younger towns of Leicester and Uxbridge had significantly higher house values than their neighbors. At the same time, other towns in these subregions, such as Spencer and Douglas, lagged notably behind, as did the younger towns in the northwest.

The tax census also reveals that, at the end of the eighteenth century, one-story dwellings in Worcester County outnumbered two-story buildings by a ratio of two to one. This is exactly the reverse of the proportion indicated by survivals in the field. While local variations in proportions of one- to two-story houses existed, according to the tax census one-story houses dominated thirteen of the fourteen towns. In six towns, one-story dwellings made up 75 percent or more of the total; in three of these they made up 80 percent or more. Both the southeast and northwest subregions show a trend toward an increase in the proportion of two-story buildings with length of settlement. Yet the younger towns of the northwest did not have significantly higher proportions of one-story houses than many older towns in the southeast. The towns of the west, however, had a greater proportion of two-story buildings than either of the other subregions, and Leicester had an exceptionally high proportion (66%) of two-story buildings.

The distribution of one- and two-story houses among economic groups within each community also varied considerably (FIG. 3.7). Five economic classes were identified in the county, adjusted to natural breaks in the data. The curves show the changing proportions of two-story buildings for the top four value classes in each town. Not surprisingly, two-story structures constitute a very high proportion of the houses in the upper value groups. However, in nine of the fourteen towns, there is a sharp drop in two-story build-

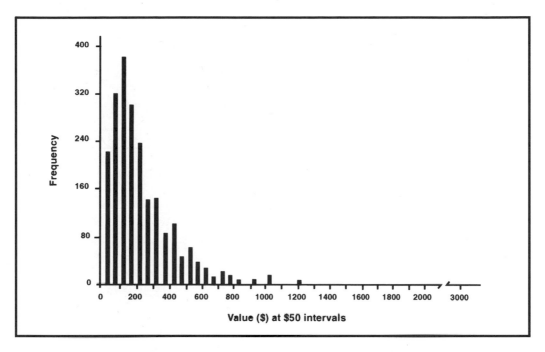

FIG. 3.6 Frequency Distribution of House Values in 1798.

ings in the upper-middle value group. In the five remaining towns there is a sharp drop between the middle and lower-middle value groups. Two-story structures, then, were not only a minority in the region; they were also concentrated in the highest valued group of houses in each community, only occasionally extending in significant proportions into the upper-middle value group. In only one town (again, Leicester) did two-story houses make up more than half of the middle value group. In contrast, in most towns one-story houses made up 80 percent to 90 percent of the middle value range and a majority of the upper-middle range. Clearly, the most common dwelling in this interior area at the end of the eighteenth century was not a two-story, five-bay, double-pile structure, but a more modest one-story building. In fact, while the ratio of one-story to all two-story buildings was two to one, one-story houses outnumbered double-pile, two-story houses by a ratio closer to seven to one.

In 1798 the cultural landscape of Worcester County was hardly egalitarian. The differences in material standards of living between the upper and lower fifths of the population were marked. Variations in house size, height, and value were evident both locally and regionally. The data suggest the emergence of a hierarchical pattern in the cultural landscape, but one that

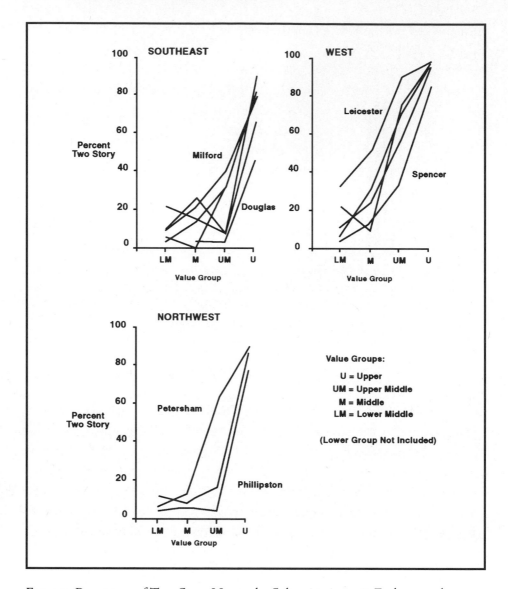

FIG. 3.7 Percentage of Two-Story Houses by Subregion in 1798. Each curve shows the changing distribution of two-story houses among value groups in an individual town. Not all town curves are labeled.

did not directly reflect length of settlement or aggregate local wealth. These variations in the landscape must have been readily observable as signs of individual affluence or poverty. John Brooke, in his study of the region, has suggested that Shays' Rebellion pitted one-story regulators against two-story gentry-merchants.[19] Certainly the social significance of the height, symmetry, mass, and ornamentation of the region's architectural landmarks must be measured in relation to the smaller, one-story dwellings that sheltered the majority of the population.[20] Soil survey maps strongly suggest that in agrarian Worcester County at least part of the local variance in housing stock can be understood in terms of significant differences in the soil resource base and the workability of the land.[21] In the older southeastern part of the county, towns like Douglas, Northbridge, and Upton had (and still have) such a high proportion of rocky, poorly drained soil that the use of the land for anything beyond pasture must have been extremely difficult. In contrast, western towns like Leicester, Paxton, and Brookfield were situated in a belt of prime soils. In these towns, a high proportion of the land is fertile, relatively stone-free upland till, which readily sustained the mixed agricultural practices brought to the region by its settlers. Possession of fertile, productive soils and access to the rudimentary road network gave clear economic advantages to a minority of families. But in a region in which only a third of the soils are highly productive, it is not surprising that the means of most yeoman families were sufficient only to construct relatively modest dwellings.

Across Massachusetts

How representative is the Worcester County region of the New England culture hearth as a whole? In order to answer this question, analysis of the federal tax census has been extended to thirty-three additional towns located in other regions of Massachusetts, towns that are distributed among its other major cultural and physical subregions: the coastal lowlands of the east, the Connecticut Valley, and the western highlands. At this point only one variable for these towns has been examined: story height. Nevertheless, on the basis of the evidence for forty-seven Massachusetts towns for which relevant schedules survive for eighty-six hundred houses, it appears that only in the northeast in Essex County, one of the oldest, wealthiest, and most densely populated agricultural regions of the entire east coast, can a general case be made for the widespread existence of larger, more substantial houses at the end of the eighteenth century (FIG. 3.8). Here, in towns near the coast like Danvers, Topsfield, and Middleton, more than 80 percent of the houses were two stories in height. Further inland in Essex County, along the Merrimack River, nearly three-quarters of the houses in Andover were also two-story buildings (FIG. 3.9).

Yet early settlement and location near the coast were no guarantee of widespread construction of larger dwelling houses. South of Boston in Plym-

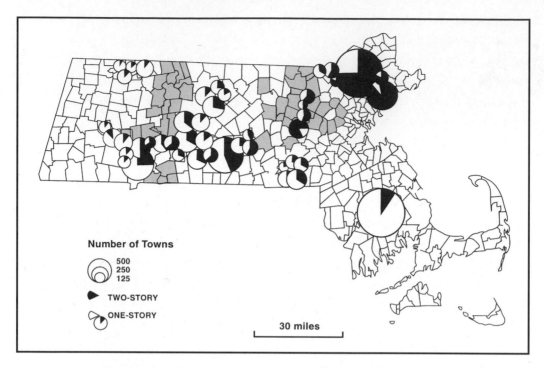

Number of Towns

500
250
125

TWO-STORY

ONE-STORY

30 miles

FIG. 3.8 Percentage of One- and Two-Story Houses in 1798. The figure depicts forty-seven Massachusetts towns for which 1798 information survives. The shaded regions indicate towns with known substantial, late-eighteenth-century grain surplus information (from Pruitt 1984).

outh County, the large, old town of Middleborough was located only a dozen miles inland from Plymouth Bay. Of Middleborough's six hundred dwellings, more than 90 percent were still one story in height at the end of the eighteenth century. Away from the coast, a one-story landscape prevailed. In the recently settled hill towns of the Berkshires west of the Connecticut Valley, the proportion of one-story houses was consistently near 90 percent. However, in a few areas in the Connecticut Valley itself and in Middlesex County in the east there are a number of towns in which two-story houses made up half of the local housing stock.[22] While not as old and wealthy as the Essex County region, these areas were experiencing a significant intensification of market-oriented agriculture in the last quarter of the eighteenth century. Based on research on the agricultural economy of Massachusetts in this period by Bettye Pruitt, it appears that the Middlesex and Connecticut Valley towns fall within the two distinct Massachusetts regions that were producing substantial grain surpluses by the 1770s.[23] In the Middlesex area in particular, these surpluses resulted from investment in land improvements that led to much higher yields per acre. It seems quite possible that the cycle of prosperity and reinvestment set into motion in these towns included a transformation of the landscape through the construction of new, larger, two-story houses. Researchers in the Chesapeake region of Maryland and Virginia have found a strong correlation between regional shifts to a grain-farming economy and the construction of more substantial houses.[24] This very cursory look at Massachusetts evidence indicates a similar relationship between late-eighteenth-century high farming and the appearance at the end of the eighteenth century of a two-story landscape in the most prosperous towns of interior New England.

Conclusion

In his recent *Shaping of America: A Geographical Perspective*, geographer Donald Meinig portrays the "New England Farmstead" of 1800 with a paint-

FIG. 3.9 Stanley-Lake House. In older, prosperous regions such as Essex County, Massachusetts, phased additions to small, original structures resulted in a 1798 landscape of large, two-story dwellings, like this in Topsfield. In this case, a late-seventeenth-century core was enlarged by early- and mid-eighteenth-century lateral extensions. (Photo by M. Steinitz.)

4 · Villages in the Federal Period

~: Social and economic relationships of New Englanders with one another and with people elsewhere changed dramatically in the late eighteenth and early nineteenth centuries. Although economic historians debate when and to what degree this change occurred, the previous chapter identified its effect on the architectural landscape. The settlement landscape also clearly recorded change, with the rise of center villages (inland country market towns, in effect) across New England. Along with increased interaction as measured by growth in trade, transportation, and communication, for instance, town centers evolved into commercial places. Town centers had long been places of social and economic interaction in New England towns. Meetinghouses were located there, as were occasional taverns. Town roads were laid out to that location, focusing interaction there. Central-place theory helps explain the rise of these villages. This theory offers some insight into the manner in which increasingly extralocal interaction focused on particularly advantageous sites, such as town centers, and facilitated growth and development of the system of villages, now no longer dispersed communities. The concept of elaboration further helps in understanding the effect of advantageous situation of some places over others in the context of urbanization. Moreover, some places that were successful at one time were not so later. Literally and figuratively these villages, bypassed as urbanization proceeded, slid downhill. :~

~: THE VILLAGE ONE ENCOUNTERS TODAY IN THE LANDSCAPE OF NEW England was formed in the Federal period, in the final decades of the eighteenth century and the first decades of the nineteenth century. The villages were new places of commerce, not the simple agricultural-community centers thought to have dotted the colonial landscape. The new village was a central place, what geographers commonly call an active marketplace that dominates and is central to a market area (FIG. 4.1). Yet New England villages were not immaculately conceived. The rise of these commercial villages reflected not the creation of something new out of whole cloth, but an elaboration of an existing settlement system, a legacy of the colonial period and a manifestation of long-standing cultural habit.

Elaboration here means the detailed working out or development (or decline) of the system of the New England villages in their historical and geographical context. Human geographic patterns reflect cultural habits of interaction and organization. Such geographic patterns, however, tend to persist long after the cultural habits that produced them have faded away. Because they persist, geographical patterns condition subsequent human activity. In New England, the town has always been the culturally significant unit of settlement. The colonial town center provided dispersed farmers with comfortable access to a centrally located meetinghouse by means of an elaborate town road network. When a meetinghouse proved too eccentric in its location for a portion of the congregation, division took place so that every family had its own town center nearby. Although local exchange was more than sufficient to support the presence of central-place activities—by part-time practitioners—the rural economy simply did not support many central places, and inland commercial villages were few and far between.

The Federal period, in contrast, witnessed a more commercial rural economy, or at least an economy able to support central places. Farmers left agriculture to take up full-time commerce, processing, and professions, and by relocating they gathered together to make central places out of what had been colonial town centers. A marked geographic separation of production and ultimate sale of goods had occurred, and town centers, already centrally and uniformly spaced and interconnected by town road networks, provided dispersed farmers comfortable access to centrally located clusters of stores and shops. Even the directions in which goods flowed persisted. The flow of goods between commercial villages followed lines of credit and exchange developed by traders during the colonial period and, though turnpikes later

FIG. 4.1 A View of Ware Village, Massachusetts, c. 1837. This view from Prospect Hill near the Northampton Road suggests the character of a thriving early-nineteenth-century village, in this case a factory-place/central-place hybrid. (T. Moore Lithographics, in A. Chase 1911. Courtesy, American Antiquarian Society.)

captured flows of goods, such roads did not redirect flows. Hence, New England villages emerged within and came to represent an increasingly elaborate regional system of central places, reflecting the level and intensity of activity that characterized the Federal period but founded on a precommercial colonial settlement system. In short, the town center provided an appropriate site for a central place where New Englanders were predisposed to congregate. The settlement system persisted.

Theory of Central Places

Central-place theory seeks to explain logically the localization of economic exchange at centrally located places and the resultant geographical distribution of such places. The number and type of commercial functions performed in any market center are related to the size and relative location of the center and to the center's position in a hierarchy of market centers or central places. A central place, as distinct from any settlement, is a mediator of local commerce with the outside world. This "surplus importance" or "central importance" of the place, as it has been called, produces "centrality," or the ability of a place to provide goods and services in excess of the needs of its residents. A crossroads, even with a church and tavern or store, is not necessarily a central place without a degree of centrality. Centrality of a place, therefore, refers less to its location than to its function as a provider of central goods and services, including noneconomic or cultural offerings that nevertheless seem to respond to laws of economic behavior.[1]

Theoretically, the service areas of central places will be arranged in such a way as to take on a hexagonal shape because this is the most efficient subdivision of space. New England towns, or settlement patterns anywhere, are rarely hexagonal, but the spacing of settlements is remarkably regular in reality. Because of this regularity, central-place theory is often invoked to explain the evolution and arrangement of settlement patterns.[2]

Most historical geographers invoking central-place theory have related the development of an expansive and hierarchical diffusion of a central-place system across the landscape, either in the Christallerian mode or, for instance, as Vance has predicated in his mercantile model.[3] What the New England experience of the Federal period appears to illustrate, however, is something different. The development (and later decline) of the central-place system is not so much the emergence of new locations or places offering central goods as it is a shift in scale—the development of centrality at already established places or the elaboration of the existing settlement system.

In a historical view, the relative importance of central places can change markedly over time. For instance, the appearance of functions and the proliferation of establishments should parallel population growth, though population growth alone is hardly an adequate measure of the centrality of a place.[4] Moreover, as McManis has noted, a central-place system was inherent in the New England town system, but exception should be taken to his inference that a particular site within each town was necessarily and consciously designated to be a future central place.[5] Nevertheless, as Christaller argued, "the rational scheme of the system is not itself changed; only the decisive factors are changed." Put another way: "The rule is that the older system previously determined always determines the more recent system developed under other economic laws and conditions with other types of central goods and other ranges of these central goods."[6]

In this regard, the development of a central-place system should not necessarily be viewed as a diffusion of locations or places, but may also be seen as a diffusion of the creation of centrality or the increased demand for central goods, giving rise to central places at existing settlement sites within a persistent settlement system. Change in centrality, because of a shift in the scale of a rural economy, can produce a shift in the scale of a central-place system and the proliferation or decline of central places.

Understanding of the notion of elaboration hinges on the distinction between a central place and what Christaller called auxiliary central places and dispersed places. The presence of institutions of exchange does not measure the central importance of a place. Only extralocal exchange is regarded as a basis for centrality and, notwithstanding clear evidence of exchange, few central places actually existed in colonial rural New England. Dispersed goods and services were provided at dispersed places, at the homes or farms of producers, the locations of which were hardly determined by any economic advantage with respect to other places. In this regard, colonial New England towns, comprising many dispersed places where localized exchange had taken place, have been misconstrued as central places.[7]

Many noneconomic activities, however, still required a measure of centrality. As a matter of cultural practice, the town center's meetinghouse provided a gathering place for social, political, and religious activities. The colonial New England tavern, too, had a role that went well beyond serving cider and rum to locals or providing meals and lodging to occasional passersby. It was also a place where people gathered to exchange news and opinions or to engage in personal business. Meetinghouses were sited and re-sited to insure a central location for the town's cultural activities. Many entrepreneurial New Englanders, fully conscious of the importance of a central location, thus located their tavern next door to the meetinghouse or urged that the meetinghouse be constructed nearby. The colonial town center was an auxiliary central place, dependent for its existence on the comings and goings of townspeople but hardly a place of much extralocal exchange.[8]

What follows is an abbreviated attempt to illustrate the notion of elaboration in a settlement system. In an analysis of the emergence of central places in early-nineteenth-century New England, no abstract systems are identified and no test of central-place theory is intended. But it is clear from the New England experience that well-developed cultural habits of interaction and organization, not simply the emergence of a commercial society, set the regular pattern of settlement that the commercial society adopted. Culture underlies settlement patterns—something of which Christaller was well aware.[9]

New England Towns

We have learned in previous chapters that most settlements in the colonial period, regardless of when settled, were composed of loosely gathered neighborhoods of farmers. The modal form of settlement was dispersed. Agricultural settlements, what Christaller might have identified as dispersed places or at best auxiliary central places, ranged in form from very compact, such as at Hampton, New Hampshire, to the isolated farmsteads of squatters, such as at Framingham, Massachusetts.[10] Commercial places, ranging in size from small landings to such urban places as Boston, were nevertheless important components of the settlement landscape, even if their number was relatively limited in the colonial period and they were concentrated along tidewater or within easy reach of tidewater.[11]

Towns were the basis for settlement, and within towns the meetinghouse was the symbolic focus of the settlement, regardless of how compact or dispersed settlement was in the town or of how much dispersed or centralized exchange occurred. The location of the meetinghouse might have been planned from the start, or it might have been the result of considerable controversy and negotiation. Meetinghouse sites located by legislative fiat or before settlement took place were removed to a preferable site if they proved to be "uncentrical."[12] Once the site for a meetinghouse had been set, however, roads were laid out to it, which is to say that a maze of trails was established within the town by common usage, so that all farmsteads might have access to the meetinghouse. The location of the meetinghouse with respect to the distribution of population within a town was therefore always more important than geometric centrality.

Division of Towns

Not everyone could be satisfied with the location of the meetinghouse. Many early settled towns, especially in Connecticut, were quite large and, as the population of a town increased and spread farther and farther from the meetinghouse, controversy over the location of the meetinghouse inevitably arose. Controversy was usually resolved by the establishment of a new community, whether as an ecclesiastical parish (*village* in the terms of the colonial period) or immediately as a town. The price of town growth in Massachusetts in the seventeenth century was internal strife and contentiousness, as residents of Watertown, Sudbury, Andover, and scores of other towns had all learned. Only divine intervention could have kept "broyles" from developing within a town over the distance that inhabitants of one neighborhood or another might have to travel to the meetinghouse. Ultimately, separation from the parent town was the only means by which a new meetinghouse—as a symbol of a new local community and unanimity—could be obtained. In Connecticut, parish status seems to have been more significant than in Massachusetts, and many neither petitioned for, nor were granted, town status until after the 1760s.[13]

Town division was not an unforeseen event. Many early Massachusetts Bay grants stipulated that lands could extend six or ten miles or more from the meetinghouse to accommodate anticipated population increases and the development of new communities within a town. Windham, Connecticut, was laid out as three parishes initially. But two conditions were usually necessary before a community was divided. A new community needed a population of sufficient density and geographic continuity. Moreover, there needed to be some hardship on the part of this population in getting to the meetinghouse, too great a distance or an intervening obstacle, such as a river. There also appear to have been critical thresholds for population size and distance. The experience of a large number of towns in Massachusetts suggests that division, usually to form a town, resulted when a new community had grown to about thirty or forty families. Boxfield in eastern Massachusetts was denied separate incorporation from Rowley until 1685, when about forty families had been settled. In 1673 the incorporation of Brookfield, beyond the frontier, required that the "Township" could not be divided until forty or fifty families had been settled. In Connecticut in the eighteenth century, on the other hand, successful petitions for parish status received by the General Assembly were usually granted when signed by twenty or thirty families. Indeed, Haller suggested that a critical "zone of population" for splitting was about two hundred households. As household size generally ran about five or six, he may have meant about two hundred people. or some thirty-five head of household. As important as a critical size was the distance that separated the petitioning families from the meetinghouse. Almost invariably the stated distance on Connecticut petitions, including hazardous river crossings, exceeded three miles and averaged about five or six miles.[14]

Town division continued throughout the eighteenth century as long as population spread out in large towns. Although population might continue to increase, however, the distance between meetinghouses soon stabilized in settled areas, and town division—or at least subdivision of towns into parishes—ran its course. Consequently, in granting petitions for separation, colonial assemblies seem to have taken it for granted, consciously or not, that a comfortable spacing between meetinghouses was about five to six miles and that this spacing provided a proper area for a New England town.[15] By the end of the colonial period this geographic modus operandi had created new congregations and a familiar mosaic of towns across New England, and it had also created a network of town centers almost uniformly spaced from Boston to Lake Champlain (see FIG. I.2).

When division generally ceased across inhabited New England in the last quarter of the eighteenth century, towns and the remaining parishes averaged about thirty-five square miles in area, and meetinghouses were thus spaced about six miles apart, the square root of the area.[16] The earliest settled towns and their parishes, especially about Massachusetts Bay and southeastern New Hampshire, were smaller than the average, having been considerably divided into areas of about twenty to twenty-five square miles and with meeting-houses spaced four and a half to five miles apart. Mainland towns of Rhode Island, Providence Plantation, where a meetinghouse could be built any-where by anyone, were always larger; no permission was needed to form a parish or town in order to build a church. Towns and remaining parishes most closely matching the mean area were established in large numbers in the eighteenth century, especially throughout central New England. With the experience that town division had provided, the thirty- to forty-square-mile size was confirmed when, in the 1730s and later, relatively standard-sized, approximately square towns with a reserved, central meetinghouse lot were laid out in the Massachusetts military grants and in the colony grants in Connecticut. The practice flourished in northern New England. Between 1760 and 1764 Governor Benning Wentworth of New Hampshire granted 129 standard-sized towns in great tiers west of the Connecticut River.[17] As these towns were settled, plans for the location of the town center and set-tling lots were usually ignored, but town boundaries and a sense of commu-nity from a common locale and a shared meetinghouse remained largely unchanged.

Town Centers

The distinguishing feature of the colonial settlement landscape in the rela-tive absence of compact settlement was the town center, symbolizing in tan-gible form the intangible web of human relationships that constituted the town. The meetinghouse was the material manifestation of the political and religious community. No particular sacredness was attached to the meeting-house itself and not everyone was a church member, but relative proximity to the meetinghouse was a significant factor in rural life. The importance of roads was determined by their directness to the town center. Having a nearby meetinghouse was an overriding consideration in the expansion of settle-ment and, thus, the cause of town division.

The tavernkeeper-trader was the only townsman to do enough business to require a central location—aside the meetinghouse lot. The tavern, often a farmhouse parlor, was the second most important public place in town, and few town centers were without one or more.[18] Whereas the meetinghouse was an important place for private business, socializing, and politics, it was not uncommon for public business to repair from the meetinghouse to the more comfortable quarters of the tavern. An influential citizen, or one who hoped to be influential, might have appropriated a lot for the meetinghouse and often the materials needed to construct it. The meetinghouse at Lexing-ton, Massachusetts, was donated to the town by the local tavernkeeper. The Effingham, New Hampshire meetinghouse was located on "Lord's Hill"— almost in front of Lord's tavern. And in Westmoreland, New Hampshire, an entrepreneur offered a barrel of rum to the teamsters moving the disassembled meetinghouse, if they would unload the meetinghouse next to his tavern. They did, and there it stood.[19]

In central-place terms, therefore, the town center was an auxiliary central place. The community or congregation provided the threshold, or minimum population, for the meetinghouse and other activities that might locate at the town center for local intercourse and exchange. The range, or the maximum distance over which exchange would occur, defined the effective boundary line between communities. Radial movement of traffic to the nearest central place (theoretically) causes centers with similar order activities—like New England town centers and later center villages—to be spaced at approxi-mately equal distance from one another over a uniformly populated and pro-ductive area. Thus, in colonial New England, when the range of a meeting-house was large and there was sufficient population to meet a threshold for a new community, division created a new town with its own town center. Across much of glacier-scrubbed, boulder-strewn, and later-settled New En-gland, however, towns of standard size with town centers of standard spacing were laid down upon a map, and then upon the landscape, without regard to population density.

Economic and Social Context

The dispersed settlement that dominated in colonial New England reflected the rural economy. Yet the rural economy was not fixed. Throughout much of the colonial period, and especially in the eighteenth century, transformation from predominantly subsistence to increasingly (though never dominantly) advanced commercial agriculture occurred. It is conventional wisdom that the transformation gained momentum in the second half of the eighteenth century and culminated in a burst of commercial activity in the Federal period.[20] Although it is not clear when this transformation began or how rapidly it took place, the corresponding rise of central places, the focus of concern here, clearly indicates change had occurred and a threshold of economic activity had been reached during the last half of the eighteenth century.

The Colonial Rural Economy

Colonial New England yeomen made their living close to the land. Land ownership was an important ingredient of the rural economy, and inland almost everyone was a farmer first. Farmers lived comfortably by their standard and actually accumulated some wealth, but New England's hardscrabble seems hardly to have allowed much marketable surplus for one's endeavor: "Their farms yield food—much of cloathing—most of the articles of building—with a surplus sufficient to buy such foreign luxuries as are necessary to make life pass comfortably; there is very little elegance among them, but more of necessaries."[21] By producing as many kinds of food and materials as his effort and time allowed, a farmer could maintain this standard of living with irregular participation in an exchange economy beyond the bounds of the town. Thus, extralocal trade would have been too sporadic and the rural economy alone not sufficient to support commerce at central places inland.[22]

The low agricultural productivity in New England appears to have resulted not just because land was poor, nor from poor market opportunities or inadequate transport, but mostly because of the cultural context. Colonial New Englanders were enmeshed in a web of social relationships and cultural expectations that may have inhibited the free play of market forces.[23] The land was no different during the heyday of New England agriculture in the Federal period; colonial farmers were aware of market opportunities, and those near coastal commercial villages could always find markets. But a deficiency in pasturage and fodder, the inefficiency of technology based on hand sickles, and a scarcity of labor combined to limit productivity and income. The inadequacy of transportation, moreover, was a consequence and not a cause of agricultural productivity. Given the marginal quality of most land, colonial New Englanders were largely general farmers supporting most of their own agricultural needs and marketing what surplus vegetable, grain, or animal products they could.[24]

This is not to argue that New England farmers were self-sufficient, and they did not care to be. But as a result of relatively low agricultural productivity, most did not participate greatly in regional markets. Long-distance trade, of only a few score miles, was in luxuries and when opportunities presented themselves, but not generally in any great quantity of bulk goods. The economy was fundamentally local, and trade was dominated by local society, not the reverse. As a result, farmers developed special skills to supplement agricultural surpluses, and most occupations were represented locally. In the aggregate, local exchange was important to an extent hardly suggested by the meagerness and pettiness of individual transactions. But local exchange could not very well support full-time nonfarmers, if it did not require central places of any magnitude or close geographical proximity. Production and exchange remained largely dispersed within each town's geographic realm, and with the tangle of credit relationships that developed within a community the community itself became "a dispersed general store."[25]

Economic Change

The transformation from an economy based on local exchange at dispersed places to an economy focused on central places had clearly begun in New England by the last quarter of the eighteenth century. There is good reason to believe, as well, that change may have resulted in part from the economic imperative of a local land crisis — overpopulation in short — which resulted in new economic endeavors and increased social stratification in New England.[26] Change was underscored by the considerable development in the early 1770s of new port villages such as Norwich, Connecticut, and Wickford, Rhode Island (FIG. 4.2). The Revolutionary War, moreover, accelerated the change already under way in the colonial rural economy and ushered in a quickening of the commercial element in the rural economy throughout the region in the subsequent generation.[27]

Because most rural New Englanders had not generally participated to any great degree in extralocal trade, they suffered little harm when trade was cut

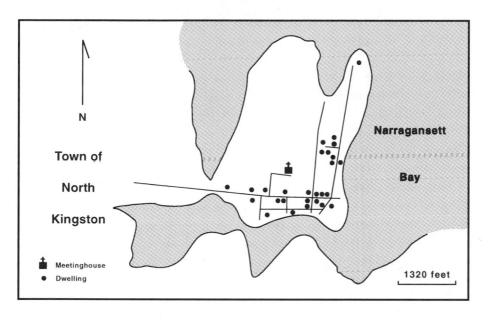

FIG. 4.2 Wickford, Rhode Island, c. 1780. The port village of Wickford began as a real estate venture in 1711 and flourished in the 1770s. Today, Wickford, left relatively untouched since the early nineteenth century, has more eighteenth-century houses than any other New England village of comparable size and age. (Redrawn from C. White 1947.)

off by economic encumbrances and retaliatory measures of nonconsumption and nonimportation before the Revolution and by the war itself. On the contrary, the war encouraged domestic industry and commercial agriculture and incited rising expectations inland.[28] The immediate effect of peace in 1783, however, was economic depression. Farmers were plagued by financial confusion, low agricultural prices, and heavy taxation. As before the Revolution, many farmers found the market frustrating. The results showed. In 1790 real per capita income in the United States remained below the level it had achieved by 1770. But by 1790 the tempo of transactions appears to have increased and the regional economy to have become more productive and more complex. Per capita income was growing, accelerated by the increasing availability of currency and by commercial opportunities generated by European wars during the 1790s and early 1800s. Merchant capitalists, engaging in any trade that might prove profitable, came to dominate fast-growing places everywhere, and from 1781 to the Embargo Act in 1807 New England achieved considerable prosperity that led many New Englanders to seek new occupations off the farm and new means of increasing investments.[29] It was thus evident to an observer in the 1790s that "Their imports have not been swelled in proportion to the increase of their population and wealth. The reason is clear, viz. the constant introduction of new branches of manufacture amongst themselves, and a great extension of the old branches."[30]

In agriculture as well as in household production no clear break occurred between the locally oriented rural economy of the colonial period and the increasingly outwardly oriented rural economy, but the balance had shifted. In relative terms, productivity remained low, communication and transportation poor, processing unsophisticated, and subsistence a persistent dimension of everyday life. Agriculture itself never became a flourishing enterprise for many New Englanders, but trade was far less localized than it had been in the colonial period. An increasing distance intervened between the locations of production and consumption as farmers became more dependent on outside markets, and thus central places, for the sale and purchase of goods. With regular exchange, favorable and stable prices, and cash, farmers slowly but consciously increased productivity.[31]

The change in agriculture was complemented by unprecedented organization and concentration of business enterprise. Corporations, franchised to carry out banking and insurance, internal improvements in transportation and communication, and pioneering in manufacturing, increased from 7 in 1780 to well over 300 in 1800. Another 1,700 corporations were chartered in New England in the next 30 years, most reflecting the removal of manufacturing activities from independent household producers into the hands of entrepreneurs.[32] The widespread diffusion of banking was an especially important indicator of the percolation of enterprise and investment capital into the backcountry in the Federal period. The 14 banks in New England in 1800 could only be found in the larger urban places. Within 20 years, however, there were more than 100 banks widely spread across New England in over 60 central places, many of which had not existed before 1780.[33]

The turnpike epitomized the internal improvement effort of the period and visibly manifested the invisible economic network that was spreading across New England. The first turnpike in New England was chartered in 1792, and charters reached their zenith with over thirty new charters a year when the economy peaked in the mid-1800s. A turnpike charter was a franchise to connect a number of towns with a passable road in exchange for collecting a toll. A corporation either took over responsibility for maintaining a string of local roads or laid out and maintained a new road between town centers. Successful turnpike corporations were those that properly judged

the traffic they could absorb and generate, but turnpikes were never very lu-
crative investments in themselves. Investors counted more upon collateral returns than upon direct returns in the matter of tolls.[34]

Turnpikes were laid down on existing road networks as often as possible
to strengthen existing traffic patterns. In long-settled areas of southern and
eastern New England, traffic had always flowed to nearby commercial villages that acted as intervening collection and distribution points for Boston
or New York. Especially in Connecticut, where no particular market center
was dominant, turnpikes were used as means of improving existing roads,
not of extending the road network. Most Connecticut turnpikes were thus
short links between nearby towns. Litchfield, an important place in the colonial road network, was intersected by a half dozen turnpikes, and, "in due
time, it became almost impossible to get into or out of our town without
encountering a toll gate." In northern New England trading patterns were
not as well established as in longer-settled areas. Long turnpikes were laid
out like the spokes of a wheel to connect the new settlements to Portland, to
Portsmouth, and to Boston, where trade had always gravitated and the
source of much of the credit extended in New England.[35]

With more produce to be hauled than before, there was also a development in carriage. Until the Federal period, the poor quality of what passed as
roads meant that travel was generally by foot, horse, sled, or two-wheeled ox
cart. Carriages were limited to the wealthy, and wagons were more common
in the middle colonies. By the end of the eighteenth century, however, chaises
and four-wheeled, horse-drawn wagons known as Pennsylvania rigs were frequent sights on New England town roads and turnpikes, and numerous town
histories recorded with some emphasis the appearance of the first wagon or
chaise in town. In 1789 there was a wagon in Meriden, Connecticut, and in
the early 1800s in Brunswick, Maine, and, by 1790, a two-horse chaise in
Framingham, Massachusetts. Wagons were considered unusual in Bedford
and Billerica, Massachusetts, only until the turn of the century.[36]

Four-wheeled, horse-drawn stages were especially common means of carriage in the Federal period. The first stage between Boston and New York began operation in 1772, and three six-day trips were scheduled a week in 1787.
But with increasing demands for travel and improved roads, stage lines proliferated, and more and more towns were linked to one another. The first
stage through Nashua, New Hampshire, in 1795 "was an occasion of great
public interest." The covered vehicle pulled by two horses ran once a week
from Amherst, New Hampshire, to Boston, with an overnight stop in Bil-

lerica, Massachusetts. A weekly stage between Boston and Charleston, New Hampshire, was operating by 1801, and there were three a week from Hanover, New Hampshire, to Boston in 1807.[37]

Merchants were not only moving increasing quantities of goods, but they were advertising their stocks or their particular demands for backcountry surpluses and doing so widely in the newspapers. After 1790 few merchants did without advertising, and few major towns were without their own "advertiser." Though New Englanders were highly literate, fewer than twenty newspapers were published in New England in 1780. By the close of the century, however, nearly eighty were being published and, although by 1820 there were still fewer than one hundred newspapers, publication and readership were widespread even in the most recently settled areas of western and northern New England. The postal service helped. The number of postal routes and offices expanded at an enormous rate after 1790 to meet the demand for increased communication. New Englanders were now inextricably linked to the world outside the geographical limits of the town.[38]

The Rise of Center Villages

Questions remain as to how dramatic the transformation in rural economy was and how rapidly it occurred. Certainly over the period of several decades in the last half of the eighteenth century the rural economy became more complex and outreaching. At some point, moreover, a threshold was reached that let loose the rise of villages across New England in the Federal period. Regular trade connections and increasing occupational specialization were now sufficient to support permanently gathered villagers. Many village entrepreneurs—like blacksmiths or local doctors and lawyers, for example—did not participate in the trade of agricultural and handicraft products that now extended beyond the bounds of the town. All, however, depended on and took advantage of the wealth that the new trade generated. Across New England, stores and shops and offices, courthouses and academies, and residences of nonfarmers—all material manifestations of the maturing of the rural economy—were gathered about hundreds of meetinghouse lots. Storekeepers, blacksmiths, lawyers, cordwainers, doctors, tanners, hatters, saddlemakers, harnessmakers, coopers, tinsmiths, and printers, all came to locate at these existing colonial town centers. At these central locations, now inextricably linked to the world beyond the colonial town, travelers by horseback, wagon, and stage, emigrants, and large numbers of independent teamsters

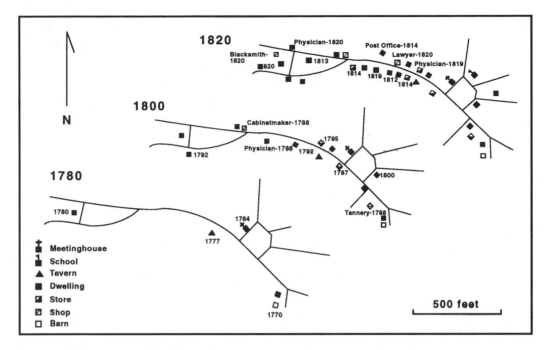

FIG. 4.3 Francestown, New Hampshire, 1780–1820. A store opened on the common in Francestown the year the federal Constitution was drafted. Other activities followed, many locating along the turnpike running past the meetinghouse lot. (Redrawn from Cochran and G. Wood 1895, p. 415.)

driving along new turnpikes, all were stopping and transacting business.

The first store in Francestown, New Hampshire, was opened on the meetinghouse lot the year the Constitution was written. The following year a cabinetmaker opened a shop and a doctor set up practice nearby. Within a generation a "lively and enterprising" commercial village had emerged (FIG. 4.3). In the 1760s several entrepreneurs planned a village in Pittsfield, Massachusetts, where their four settling lots came together. They built large frame houses but could attract neither the meetinghouse nor other activity. Twenty years later, however, an agglomeration of stores and taverns, a lawyer, a doctor, and a number of artisans and millers had gathered about the meetinghouse lot. By 1800 the town center was a substantial village (FIG. 4.4). The village at Framingham, Massachusetts, started in much the same way. Between 1790 and 1805 the town center acquired a new tavern and a store, two blacksmiths, a hatter, a cordwainer, a tanner, a lawyer, a carpenter, a doctor, a saddlemaker, a mason, and an academy.[39]

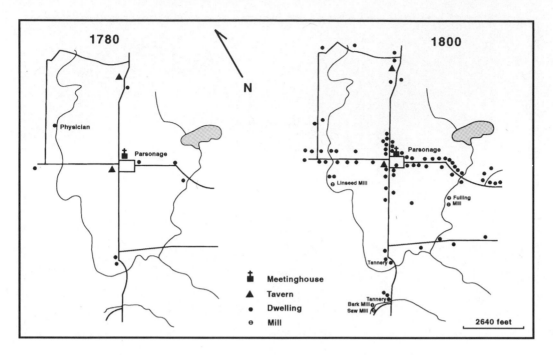

FIG. 4.4 Pittsfield, Massachusetts, 1780–1800. Despite a conscious attempt to start a village in 1760, not until the end of the century did Pittsfield's village become a substantial place. (Redrawn from J. E. A. Smith 1876, p. 4.)

Other places grew larger or remained smaller, but the same process of accretion was repeated in towns across New England. Regardless of how long a town had been settled, what form colonial settlement had taken, or what the nature of the rural economy had been and now was, full-time storekeepers, artisans, and professionals, by locating at town centers, were creating commercial villages (FIGS. 4.5, 4.6, 4.7, 4.8, 4.9). By 1800 in Gorham, Maine, there were two stores, two coopers, two shoemakers, a blacksmith, and a joiner. In addition to having the first store in the county in 1790, the future shire town of Middlebury, Vermont, was quickly accumulating a blacksmith, a cabinetmaker, a hatter, a physician, a saddlemaker, a harnessmaker, and even a college. Within twenty years it had become "one of the principal villages in Vermont." Burlington, Vermont, also hardly twenty years old, had a "commercial village" of some esteem by the first decade of the nineteenth century. And in Walpole, New Hampshire, a business center was developing around the meetinghouse lot toward the end of the 1790s (FIG. 4.10).[40]

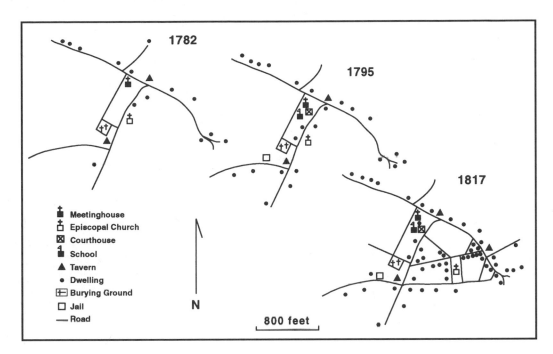

FIG. 4.5 Dedham, Massachusetts, 1782–1817. Settlers first planted a compact village at Dedham in the 1630s but dispersed within a generation. In the Federal period, a new center village developed at the same town-center site and soon flourished. (Redrawn from Rice and Brown 1972, 2:158; "Dedham Village in 1795" 1903; and "Dedham Village in 1817" 1903.)

FIG. 4.6 Dedham Village in 1795. (Painting by Jonathan Fisher in "Dedham Village in 1795" 1903, opp. p. 39. Courtesy, American Antiquarian Society.)

FIG. 4.7 Dedham Village in 1817. (Painting by D. Bingham in "Dedham Village in 1817" 1903, opp. p. 71. Courtesy, American Antiquarian Society.)

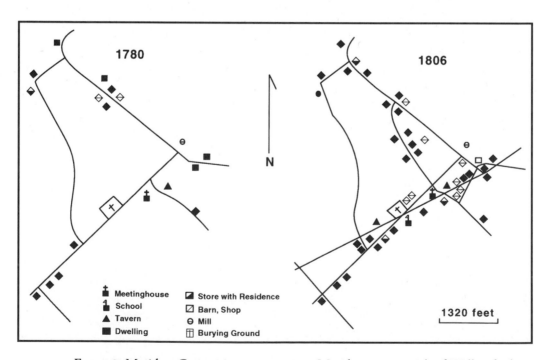

FIG. 4.8 Meriden, Connecticut, 1780–1806. Meriden was a parish of Wallingford until separated in 1806. (Redrawn from Gillespie 1906, p. 342.)

FIG. 4.9 Southern View of the Churches of Meriden, Connecticut, c. 1835. Meriden eventually developed into far more than a center village. (Barber 1838, p. 229. Courtesy, American Antiquarian Society.)

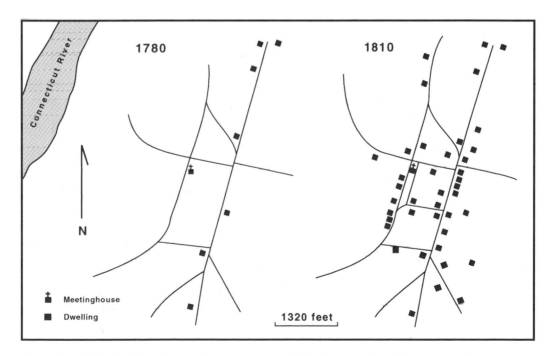

FIG. 4.10 Walpole, New Hampshire, 1780–1810. Walpole was originally composed of farms stretching along the Connecticut River. (Redrawn from Frizzell 1963.)

Stores, the connecting link for extralocal exchange and often outliers of mercantile firms, especially marked change. The first store in Hampton, Connecticut, opened in the late 1780s and on the Hill in Thompson, Connecticut, in 1794. Western Massachusetts towns competed in offering inducements to traders to settle in their communities in the 1780s. Ashfield, Massachusetts, had its first store about 1789, and one was built about 1795 near the meetinghouse in Bernardston, Massachusetts. A mercantile business began out of trading in miscellaneous articles at the tavern in Middlefield, Massachusetts; there was a separate store in 1804. Stores were first opened in 1790 in Rindge, New Hampshire, and Springfield, Vermont; in Gilmanton, New Hampshire, in 1791; in Jaffrey, New Hampshire, in 1792; and before 1800 in Salem, New Hampshire. A village began to form in the 1790s around several traders and professionals in Buckfield, Maine; there was a store in Belfast, Maine, by 1796; and one in Turner, Maine, before 1800.[41]

Relative Location

Because of some geographical variation in the division of towns during the colonial period, some geographical variation existed in the spacing of the new central places. The distance between villages was sometimes short in long-settled areas, such as eastern Massachusetts; in areas where productive soils could support a denser population, as in the Connecticut River Valley; in locations where mill villages had sprung up; and along major turnpikes. The distance was greater in late-settled areas of northern New England, in part because the population there remained more thinly scattered than in southern New England, but also because town centers were always more distant from one another.[42]

The underlying pattern of settlement set in the colonial period persisted in the upper reaches of the New England central-place hierarchy as well.[43] In the Federal period most commercial villages of the colonial period grew into cities and were still the ultimate sources of credit and supplies and destinations for agricultural produce. The largest of these places—Boston, Providence, Portsmouth, and many Connecticut ports—were still tied to the sea. By and large they retained their relative ranking locally, if not regionally, as development proceeded. Many inland commercial villages of the colonial period—Litchfield, Northampton, Worcester, and Concord—were still larger, more important places than their neighbors in the Federal period. Other villages like Wickford, Rhode Island, Ipswich, Massachusetts, and Windham,

Connecticut, failing to achieve the necessary threshold, remained small. In northern and western New England some town-center villages, such as Pittsfield, Massachusetts, Burlington and Windsor, Vermont, and Concord, New Hampshire, took on additional activities and grew large. Their growth represented a geographical extension and sorting of higher-order central places into later-settled northern New England.

Central-Place Sorting

No central-place system is static, and settlement patterns experience a constant sorting process. Notwithstanding the established settlement pattern of the colonial period, geography was ultimately cruel to many new central places. What often made — or broke — a village was its highways. Horace Bushnell found that "it is possible to tell whether there is any motion in a society by observing whether there is activity in its roads."[44] And to Josiah Temple, roads were nothing less than the material foundation of moral virtue:

> The record of its highways is the history of the material growth, the public spirit, and the relative importance of a town. When its roads radiate from a common centre to the circumference, and that centre is the meeting-house, you will commonly find an intelligent, moral, and religious, as well as thriving community. The people have faith in God and faith in each other; are social and helpful; are mindful of individual prosperity, and the prosperity and position of the town. Where the roads mainly lead through or out of town, they give sufficient warning to strangers to continue their journey.[45]

Traffic, and thus the road network, determined in large measure where central places would be located and which ones would ultimately flourish.[46] From the time a town was first settled, a centripetal network of town roads had been laid out from the meetinghouse or the meetinghouse had gravitated to an important intersection in the road network. Because road networks focused on, or radiated from, the town center and because through routes were strings of local roads, an entrepreneur could expect townspeople and passersby alike to be found going past the town center. The bustle of the Federal period brought increased traffic directed by the existing road network past the town center.

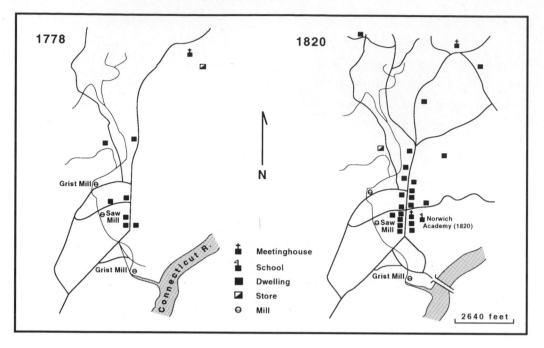

FIG. 4.11 Norwich, Vermont, 1778–1820. Norwich's original town center gravitated to a location closer to mill seats to form a factory-place/central-place hybrid. (Redrawn from P. White and Johnson 1973.)

Turnpikes, whether wholly new roads or not, generated additional trade and focused it. In the 1790s a tavern, a blacksmith, and a couple of houses were all that would be found at the town center at Thompson Hill, Connecticut. But the traffic along the Providence and Springfield stage line that intersected a new turnpike from eastern Connecticut to Boston on the Hill generated real estate speculation in the early 1800s. Other hilltop centers typically did not develop or soon failed if access roads were too arduous or too steep. The courthouse of Windham County, Vermont, on Newfane Hill, was removed in 1827 to nearby Fayetteville because the latter was more accessible. The village that had emerged on the Hill in the 1790s consisted of a courthouse, a jail, a meetinghouse, an academy, three stores, two hotels (or taverns), a variety of shops, and some twenty residences. But the hilltop location was too inaccessible, and by 1860 not one building remained to mark the original site.[47]

New industrial places, such as Lowell, Lawrence, Manchester, and many smaller factory villages, began to bloom about mill sites as localization of manufacturing took place in the Federal period.[48] These places were laid

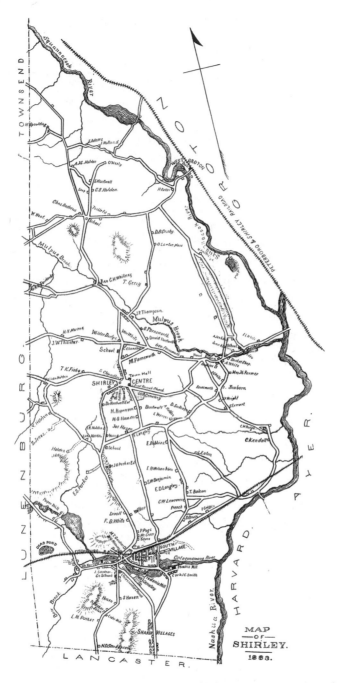

FIG. 4.12 Map of Shirley, Massachusetts, 1883. Shirley Center remains today an unusually wonderful example of a center village, but the action by the second half of the nineteenth century was in the South Village of Shirley. (Chandler 1883, opp. p. 17. Courtesy, American Antiquarian Society.)

down on top of and largely independent of the long-standing settlement pattern, sited as they were by water power. The system of factory places eventually was merged with the system of central places. By the process of sorting, factory-place/central-place hybrids emerged more durable than many places dependent only on trade or on manufacturing, as in Ware, Massachusetts, or Norwich, Vermont (FIG. 4.11; also see FIGS. 4.1, 6.7). The meetinghouse in Waitsfield, Vermont, had become dilapidated by 1840, and the center of business had entirely shifted away from the common to a nearby mill seat. Yet several dwellings, two blacksmiths, a store, a potash works, and a physician had all been located about the common in the first decade of the century. In Cummington, Massachusetts, the shift of commerce from the hilltop center to Main Street along a mill seat on the Westfield River began in the 1790s and was completed in the 1840s. The store and tavern on the hill closed in 1841, two years after the church was removed, though growth at the new center peaked in that decade as well. Today Cummington Hill is marked by a solitary plaque.[49] The geographical character of the central-place system was distorted accordingly from the system of colonial town centers that had originally underlain it (FIG. 4.12).

In central-place terms, during the general increase in economic activity in the Federal period, the thresholds of local commercial activities were exceeded and central places sprouted across New England. The region was soon saturated with little central-place villages, and for many town centers in the later settled, less populated upland areas, thresholds proved too high or ranges too low. There were simply too many towns and town centers for the limited population. A sorting process was soon under way: Marginal sellers and marginal villages at each level of the hierarchy were eliminated from the central-place system. Many hilltop centers failed to develop or, like Cummington Hill and Newfane Hill, were abandoned in a "downhill slide" to better connected, more accessible places only a short distance away.

Conclusion

New England's center villages were neither spontaneously conceived nor generated simply by the rise of central-place activities and then distributed across the economic landscape. The parameters of economic change in late colonial New England remain unclear, but the location and morphology of new central-place villages reflected the colonial New Englander's long-standing geographical ideas of how and where communities should be established in the wilderness. The pattern of settlement was long embedded in the landscape before there were central places to speak of. The rise of central places resulted, it appears then, from a shift in the scale of economic activity—the development of centrality at existing places. Centrality and central location both gave advantage to villagers who kept shop by the meetinghouse lot, but the arrangement of town centers had long provided most New England farmers with central places before there was ever need for such places. The rise of center villages in the nineteenth century was both the material manifestation of contemporary economic experience and an elaboration of an existing settlement system.

5 · The Village as a Vernacular Form

~: The previous chapter took a theoretical view of the rise of center villages as parts of a settlement system. This chapter treats center village form in descriptive terms. As successful traders and artisans established themselves in town centers about meetinghouse lots—town land that remained open in the center—so center villages grew by accretion. The center village was a new, proto-urban form with few antecedents. Only a handful of inland trading towns and shire towns of eighteenth-century New England looked and acted anything like these new urban places. Architectural fashion dictated what was constructed to house village dwellers and their enterprises; hence one does not find villages made up of colonial farmhouses and barns, but of the fine contemporary houses and outbuildings that "city" dwellers might have constructed, especially the two-story dwellings characteristic of the rebuilding described in Chapter 3. The rise of villages required continued construction, but after a period of some economic stability had set in by the 1820s and 1830s, residents undertook village improvement projects, such as forming and seeding greens or commons, building walls about burying grounds, and generally discarding the rubble of the building of the previous period. By this time as well, the village we see today had taken on an appearance that we would clearly recognize. :~

～: THE COMMON NEW ENGLAND CENTER VILLAGE IS A VERNACULAR FORM developed in nineteenth-century America. What seventeenth-century New Englanders had called a village was an outlying community of farmers living on dispersed farmsteads. From the beginning of settlement in the late 1620s, New Englanders avoided nucleation whenever they could. The settlement landscape inherited from the colonial period greatly affected the relative location and the morphology of the nineteenth-century village, but the form was distinct from seventeenth-century agricultural settlements in England and New England. At most, the new village resembled the handful of inland commercial places established during the eighteenth century. Hence, villages, now as in the nineteenth century, are composed largely of nonfarm buildings and associated dwellings, not farmhouses (FIG. 5.1).

Colonial Towns and Villages

Regardless of colonial New Englanders' penchant for dispersal, the fashion in which they organized the colonial settlement landscape is important for understanding how the contemporary village took shape. Notwithstanding religious motives for emigration, New England's colonists yearned to own land, and the control over its distribution was a crucial factor in directing the course of settlement. Expansion took place by replication of communities, by establishing new communities in a common mold, and the New England town system was designed to bring order to these new communities as they established settlements. The town was an incorporation of settlers, an administrative unit to encourage orderly settlement within clearly defined geographical boundaries. Thus, preference for dispersed settlement does not deny that New Englanders shared a strong sense of community, nor does it imply remoteness or isolation. Regardless of settlement form, communities functioned quite well. Townspeople formed congregations, regulated land distribution, encouraged local enterprise, and coordinated communal activities. Ecclesiastical and political responsibilities were performed within an established social structure. Such community identity was important despite dispersed settlement.

The colonial New England community's network of linkages and interaction had a physical manifestation. The meetinghouse was the dominant feature of the settlement landscape, the focus of community activity. Here about the meetinghouse lot, settlers located their meetinghouse, burying ground,

FIG. 5.1 View of Newbury, Vermont, from Mount Pulaski, c. 1850. This clear view—clear because the landscape was much more open in the middle of the nineteenth century than it is today—illustrates the characteristic vernacular and proto-urban form of the nineteenth-century New England center village. (Lithograph by B. F. Nutting. Courtesy, American Antiquarian Society.)

nooning sheds, and Sabbath Day houses, which in time a tavern, a blacksmith, and a farmhouse or two might encircle to form a town center (FIG. 5.2). A tavern sometimes served as the sole public building on the site, the place for town governance until eighteenth-century town houses formalized this function. Social and political activity thus focused on the town or village center, the place that symbolized the community. Importantly, this land, the meetinghouse lot, which would become in the nineteenth century the village common, was not part of the colonial common land for cultivation or pasturage. Boston Common is the exception that proves the rule. Truly a common pasture, Boston Common was located in a peripheral site on Boston's peninsula, not at the center of the original settlement where the meetinghouse and statehouse stood. Meanwhile, the town road network interconnected dispersed farmsteads with the meetinghouse, thereby enhancing its situation.

As long as the town was not too large in area, physical circumscription of town boundaries added to the sense of community.

Equitable organization of space within a reasonable distance for dispersed settlement was the overriding consideration in the formation of new communities. As seventeenth-century settlement reached farther from the established town center and more settlers were required to travel a considerable

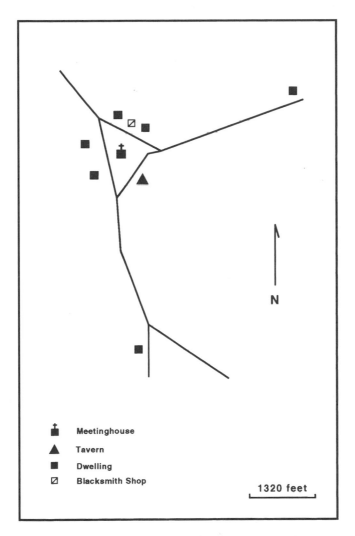

Fig. 5.2 Lexington, Massachusetts, 1775. The town center in Lexington, first settled in 1642, illustrates the limited encirclement of the meetinghouse lot by the late eighteenth century in most New England towns—even those as important in American history and located as close to Boston as Lexington. (Redrawn from Hudson 1868, p. 173.)

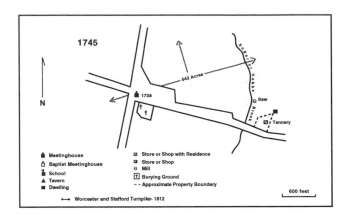

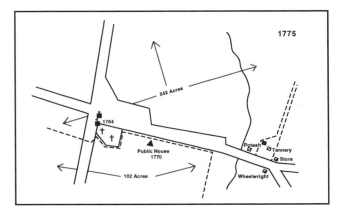

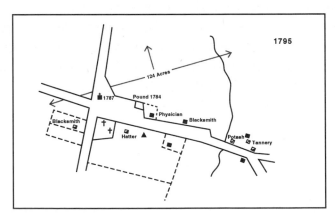

Fig. 5.4 Sturbridge Center, Massachusetts, 1745–1835. Like other former town centers, Sturbridge experienced great growth in the early nineteenth century. This unusual sequence of maps well documents the encirclement of the common and consequent formation of the center village. By 1835 the village began to look much as it does today. (Redrawn from Levine 1971.)

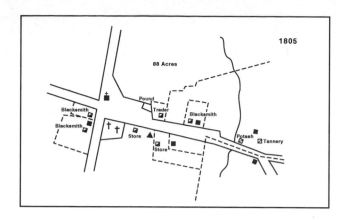

1805

88 Acres

Pound
Trader
Blacksmith
Blacksmith
Blacksmith
Store
Store
Potash
Tannery

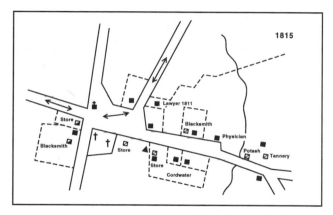

1815

Lawyer 1811
Store
Blacksmith
Blacksmith
Physician
Store
Store
Cordwater
Potash
Tannery

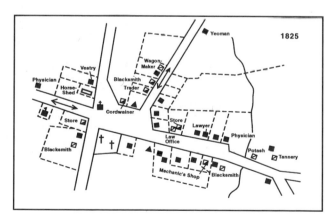

1825

Yeoman
Wagon-Maker
Vestry
Physician
Blacksmith
Horse-Shed
Trader
Cordwainer
Store
Store
Lawyer
Blacksmith
Law Office
Physician
Mechanic's Shop
Blacksmith
Potash
Tannery

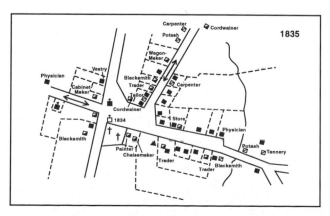

1835

Carpenter
Cordwainer
Potash
Wagon-Maker
Physician
Vestry
Blacksmith
Cabinet-Maker
Trader
Carpenter
Tailor
Cordwainer
1834
Store
Blacksmith
Physician
Painter
Chaisemaker
Trader
Potash
Tannery
Blacksmith
Trader

taken, full-time storekeepers, artisans, and professionals who located at town centers were creating center villages that resembled Litchfield, Windham, Worcester, and Concord.

There was an opportunistic quality about these new center villages. Few were planned, and speculation was rife as encirclement of meetinghouse lots took place. Center village lots, like turnpike shares and mills of various sorts, proved to be sound investments. Researchers at Old Sturbridge Village have documented lot subdivision and tenancy for Sturbridge, Massachusetts (FIG. 5.4).[6] The land around the town center, initially a single lot, was partially subdivided by 1775. Development began in the 1790s, marked by considerable turnover of land, stores, and shops. Between 1795 and 1805, four new, substantial dwellings were built, doubling the number of residences at the town center and bringing some stability to the developing village. By 1815 the town center had become a considerable place, and by the end of the next decade the form of the village was set.

Researchers at Old Sturbridge Village have further found that by the 1830s, nonindustrial center villages in inland country towns in Massachusetts—what they call "white villages," for their predominantly white-painted houses and buildings—ranged in size from six or seven up to seventy or more houses. The average size was a village of twenty-nine houses, while the median size was twenty houses. Numbers were smaller in Middlesex and Worcester Counties in the central uplands. Houses were structured loosely and gathered informally in small lots in some proximity to one another. House lots included outbuildings such as stables, barns, woodsheds, and privies, and most lots had gardens.[7] In time, stylish homes dressed main thoroughfares leading to and from center villages and thereby framed village commons, neatly captured in woodcuts by John Warner Barber in the 1830s (FIG. 5.5).

Not every town center was a commercial success. When the meetinghouse was poorly located with respect to activity in a town, the village might be situated near a mill or a landing. Competing villages might also emerge. Turnpike villages, often stretching out along one or more axes of movement, were especially likely to flourish.[8] By contrast, many hilltop centers did not develop and often failed, especially if access roads were too arduous. In the most extreme cases, this downhill slide left only the old burying ground and a small, open remnant of the old meetinghouse lot at an intersection of roads, as in Cummington, Massachusetts. Particularly in northern New England, where settlement was later than in the south, there was little vested interest

FIG. 5.5 Sturbridge, Massachusetts, c. 1835. John Warner Barber captured Sturbridge superbly. The view is from the southeast as the travelers approach Hobbs Brook. (Barber 1839, p. 608.)

in meetinghouse sites. Nevertheless, the dispersed enterprises of the colonial period gave way to those that were purposefully relocated to the "right" central places in the early-nineteenth-century Federal period. It was a cruel but efficient geography.[9]

Architecture of Center Villages

Development of center villages was concurrent with New England's cultural flowering, as reflected in architectural style. Villagers crowned their success—or at least their pretensions—with palatial town houses. The center village of the Federal period was built to entice and impress, to enhance the prestige and influence of the villagers, to show enterprise and good taste. As early as 1785, Sheffield, Massachusetts, was "a most beautiful village. There are several persons of easy circumstance and several buildings here." In Connecticut by the early 1800s "the south Killingly settlement though but a mere hamlet, three or four houses and a shop clustering around the meetinghouse, had a very imposing aspect in the eyes of that generation, and by common consent was dignified as 'The City'—a name that clung to it for many years."[10]

Fig. 5.6 Thompson, Connecticut, c. 1835. This view of Thompson Hill, as this center village in northeastern Connecticut was called, illustrates the village ensemble with large Federal and Greek Revival structures about a formative town common. The three-story Federal Revival house to the right of the church stands majestically still today. (Barber 1838, p. 422.)

Elias Boudinot, remarking on the changing countryside of southwestern Connecticut in 1809, found "the houses, along the road and in the Villages, are greatly increasing—well built—neatly painted (generally white) and beautifully situated." White had become popular for exterior walls in the Federal phase of the classical revival. Pomfret, Connecticut, had "fine houses" built on the street in the 1790s, and in Thompson, Connecticut, "many large and commodious houses were built along the line of the turnpike." In Pittsfield, Massachusetts, at the turn of the century, "very shabby and uncomfortable abodes were, on the main streets, extremely rare." [11]

At the end of the eighteenth century, houses on the "Main Street" in Concord, New Hampshire, "were built two stories, with what is called a hip-roof, with two front rooms, a door in the middle, and entry and hall running through, and an L, one story, on the back side, for a kitchen." [12] Houses of this Georgian style had been built in Boston for over a generation, but they were not common in rural New England, as noted in Chapter 3. Because of this lag in the diffusion of architectural style, Georgian houses built about the town center in Royalston, Massachusetts, and Norwich, Vermont, were in the height of local fashion when Greek Revival was appearing in coastal cities. A Federal house of three stories with a symmetrical facade and a balustraded hipped roof was built in Thompson, Connecticut, in 1798, but few houses constructed in the new villages were as pretentious (FIG. 5.6). Most were plain, two-story Georgian structures, perhaps with a flattish roof and a balustrade. The first such house in Royalston was built in 1806. Eight more similar houses were built before 1830, somewhat after the Federal style had declined in favor elsewhere.[13] By then, the Greek Revival was becoming common in the new villages, although few houses exhibited an exacting classicism. The style was marked by the liberal use of pediments and columns for embellishment and by the turning of houses so that the gable end faced the street (FIGS. 5.7, 5.8). Hence, the Reverend N. H. Chamberlain of Canton, Massachusetts, remarked, "Strictly speaking, the houses of our New-England villages have no style whatsoever; though, by numberless repetitions in building ... most of our houses have to be considered as built in the New-England style"[14] (FIG. 5.9).

FIG. 5.7 Goshen, Connecticut, c. 1835. Goshen, like Upton, Massachusetts (see FIG. 5.8), illustrates the "grecian" or "New England" style so pervasive in new, nineteenth-century center villages. (Barber 1838, p. 468.)

Fig. 5.8 Upton, Massachusetts, c. 1835. Upton's center village reflected attempts to express classical taste. (Barber 1839, p. 623.)

Fig. 5.9. Main Street Looking East, Peterborough, New Hampshire, c. 1860. This early photograph suggests the continued repetition of the "New England" style, including both gable-front and gable-end houses, which Chamberlain criticized in 1858. (Courtesy, Peterborough Historical Society.)

126

FIG. 5.10 Brooklyn, Connecticut, c. 1835. The architecture of churches followed contemporary fashion as they replaced colonial meetinghouses. Congregants might turn the old meetinghouse or merely redesign it. New churches exhibited the same classicism as houses did. (Barber 1838, p. 415.)

Meetinghouses

Rebuilding the meetinghouse was an important part of the development of villages. The 1780s and 1790s witnessed the culmination of the town division process, and by the 1800s many colonial meetinghouses were dilapidated and poorly situated. Congregations removed colonial-style, boxlike meetinghouses or replaced them with classically proportioned churches. Especially if a town center had not attracted or generated its share of commercial activities, it was necessary to re-site the meetinghouse to accommodate the settled population of the mature town or parish. Hence, new churches were constructed near the places where townspeople shopped.

Style was used to distinguish the town-center meetinghouse from the new village church. Colonial meetinghouses had been box- or barnlike structures with entrances on the long side, opposite the pulpit. Instead of a spire, there might be a bell tower at one end. In the new, classically proportioned church, the entrance and pulpit were shifted to opposite gable ends. This design was also distinguished by a marked increase in ornamentation and addition of a

FIG. 5.11 Durham, Connecticut, c. 1835. Durham, one of Connecticut's ridge-and-intervale sites, experienced renewed development as it became a center village. (Barber 1838, p. 523.)

spire. An older meetinghouse might be renovated to conform to gable-front style by turning the structure ninety degrees—or by moving the road to the new front—and by adding a pediment and a steeple.[15] Wealthy congregations could afford to hire a reputable architect, but most church designs, like those of houses, reflected a builder's translation of Georgian, Federal, or Greek Revival notions into a vernacular that has remained popular in American church design to this day (FIGS. 5.10, 5.11).

Village Commons and Greens

Commons as we know them today generally emerged only in the nineteenth century with the rise of center villages and with disestablishment of town from church. Center villages formed, we have noted, in the early years of the new American Republic as proto-urban places focusing increased agricultural trade and commerce. The New England village or town common had evolved out of the colonial meetinghouse lot, the land reserved or designated for the ecclesiastical society at the literal or figurative center of each town or village grant. Disestablishment of church and town produced secular town commons from public portions of residual meetinghouse lots (FIG. 5.12). In contrast, Taunton Green was set off in the 1640s as a training green for the militia from part of a much larger common land. It differs, therefore, from the typical common derived from the meetinghouse lot. In the absence of a meetinghouse lot or training green in late settled areas of northern New England, these essential features of the New England village were often added. Thus, by emulation if not by initial design, town centers across New England came to look much the same. Clearing the lot allowed for militia drill. Fencing off the burying ground or a portion of the common allowed its occasional use for pasturage. Later, as part of a beautification impulse, center village residents removed what remained of previllage nooning sheds and Sabbath Day houses and other relicts of the colonial town center. They seeded commons (literally turning them into greens), built walls about burying grounds, and generally discarded the rubble of recent building, but true center village improvement and purposeful creation of village greens awaited the second half of the century (FIGS. 5.13, 5.14).[16]

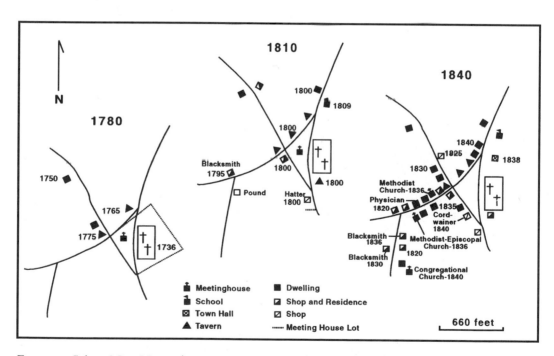

FIG. 5.12 Salem, New Hampshire, 1780–1840. Development of the center village at Salem illustrates the transformation of the meetinghouse lot into town common with disestablishment of church and town. By 1840, moreover, the meetinghouse had been removed from what had become the common to an eccentric location south of the village, and villagers and townspeople had built two other churches as well. (Redrawn from Gilbert 1907, p. 364.)

FIG. 5.13 New Canaan, Connecticut, c. 1835. In an unusual Barber illustration, New Canaan's common, set off by a stone wall from the burying ground, contained stumps and trash. (Barber 1838, p. 386.)

The centennial following the Civil War initiated the new phase of village improvement for those villages surviving the downhill slide. Commemorative "centennial" trees and monuments memorialized New England's contribution to the Revolution and the Civil War and enhanced the symbolic quality of village commons as in many villages they became wonderfully pleasing village greens. Elms were especially popular because of their distinctive branching pattern and rapid growth (FIG. 5.15). Fruits of village improvement, Victorian gazebos, bandstands, fountains, and sculptured flower beds, along with fences that kept traffic off plantings, enabled townspeople and villagers to use greens for endless community activities, such as carnivals, auctions, fairs, games, and patriotic celebrations (FIG. 5.16).

The term *green* is more commonly used today in southeastern Massachusetts, Connecticut, and Rhode Island, as well as in later settled northern New England than it is in early settled Massachusetts Bay, but the form and both terms—commons and greens—have diffused westward.[17] Wherever congregations of New Englanders established settlements in the nineteenth century—in upstate New York, Ohio's Western Reserve and Firelands, or farther west along the "yankee runway"—they configured open public space in

130

FIG. 5.14 Taunton Green, Massachusetts, c. 1830. This watercolor painting illustrates the level of stage traffic in Taunton, while at the same time suggesting attempts to keep that traffic off the open green and protect trees, a very early effort at village improvement. (Anonymous. Old Sturbridge Village Photo by Henry E. Peach. Courtesy, Old Colony Historical Society.)

FIG. 5.15 The Unitarian Church, Town House and School House, Lancaster, Massachusetts, n.d. Purposeful village improvement is clearly visible in this illustration. Lancaster residents took pleasure in their village common and worked to enhance and protect plantings, which appear to include elms. (Courtesy, American Antiquarian Society.)

FIG. 5.16 Petersham Common, Massachusetts. This late-nineteenth-century painting celebrates not only the national pastime of baseball, but the wonderfully improved and maintained village common on which villagers played. (Painting by C. F. Bosworth. Old Sturbridge Village Photo by Henry E. Peach. Courtesy, Petersham Historical Society.)

FIG. 5.17 Courthouse and Other Buildings in Norwich, New York, c. 1840. Down the yankee runway, wherever New Englanders moved westward, they configured public spaces similar to those in New England center villages. (Barber 1841, p. 102. Courtesy, American Antiquarian Society.)

central places. And, as in New England, today's village inhabitants enjoy this remarkable product of thoughtful New England use of land (FIG. 5.17).

Conclusion

The social and economic revolution that gave rise to the New England village was short-lived. The village was not only the material manifestation of worldly enterprise, but its victim as well. By the second half of the nineteenth century, encirclement of the village green was complete, and the commercial and classical revivals had run their course. Little subsequent alteration of the villagescape took place. Scores of poorly situated trade centers declined in prosperity when economic conditions changed. Most villages survived, but few remained the bustling places they had been in the first several decades of the nineteenth century.

At that time, New England villages were still relatively new places, as an 1858 observer noted:

> The first marked trait in our houses in the rural district, and in large measure also in our cities, is a fragility,—a want of permanence exceedingly suggestive of the instability of our American life. A village, with its scattered white houses, often reminds one of an encampment, with its white tents, that to-morrow morning, at the sound of the bugle, will be struck, and disappear.... Most men, receiving no transmitted home of ancestry as their house of residence, build as though there was no posterity. Thus our village houses seem often to have had no past, and but slight promise of a future.[18]

Clarifying the origin of New England villages provides context for understanding this perspective. The New England village did not derive in any direct fashion from English antecedents. It was not a peasant agricultural village transplanted to colonial New England, nor was it modeled after the region's eighteenth-century waterside market towns. In form, the New England village of the nineteenth century most closely resembled the eighteenth-century inland shire towns and marketplaces that resulted from a building up of commercial structures and associated dwellings about a meetinghouse lot. The rapid encircling of other meetinghouse lots in the nineteenth century, the consequence of serious speculation in real estate and investment in commercial enterprise, produced the early nineteenth-century New England center village, a true vernacular town form so superbly captured visually in woodcut, lithograph, view, and painting (FIG. 5.18).

FIG. 5.18 Lancaster, Massachusetts, c. 1853. The New England village is a significant vernacular—and Romantic—element in the American cultural landscape. (Courtesy, American Antiquarian Society.)

It is unfortunate that the marketplace villages that proliferated in nineteenth-century New England have come to symbolize far more than yankee enterprise.[19] Concord's fame as a historical and literary site has, implicitly, at least, linked all New England villages with a stereotyped puritan colonial past. These communities now carry this Romantic burden that obscures the real origins of this significant element of the American vernacular landscape—which the next chapter addresses.

6 · *The Settlement Ideal*

~: Proper reassessment of the nature of the village and its role in New England life requires an inquiry into the origin of its symbolic meaning, the persistence of this symbol in American culture history, and the implications of that symbolism for today. Why and how did the New England village become an important American cultural icon? In this chapter, I assess the role of nineteenth-century elites—writers, travelers, lithographers, landscape architects, social reformers, and historians—in inventing a geographical past that never existed. I discuss the intertwining of the invention of the village tradition with the creation of an appealing settlement ideal within the context of Romanticism and economic change. The settlement ideal emerged from a relationship between Jeffersonian agrarianism in counterpoise with industrial urbanism in the context of an urban conception of country. It was tied as well to the domestic revival movement, intended to improve family life by shaping appealing places. Creating places to match fictional places—or even real places—as a means to attempt recreation of relations of people in that place has for some time been an important commercial enterprise as well, and is reflected in contemporary American suburban developments. :~

~: THE NEW ENGLAND VILLAGE REPRESENTS A PAST WE HAVE GAINED. The village is the material symbol of a strongly held American tradition of New England covenanted community, cultural enlightenment, and democratic self-government. Few historical or geographical descriptions of the United States fail to refer to the formative communities served by the village of tree-shaded green surrounded by a tall-steepled church and white-clapboarded shops and dwellings. Few fail to illustrate this tradition with a proper woodcut or photograph (FIG. 6.1).

The village tradition is invented. Puritan communities were commonly dispersed settlements, as we have noted in previous chapters. While constructing compact center villages in the nineteenth century, Romantic New Englanders also invented a tradition of puritan antecedence, in which villages served as geographical metaphor for inherited pastoral ideals. Ralph Waldo Emerson, preeminent voice of his age, articulated a settlement ideal incorporating the benefits of city and country alike. "Build, therefore, your own world," he wrote in *Nature* in 1836.[1] Contemporary elites tried just that, justifying the past and legitimating the present. Writers codified a regional sense of place and diffused widely a Romantic vision of village life in New England, attaching it to new nineteenth-century center villages and thereby confusing sentiment with settlement. Landscape architects and social reformers, meanwhile, employed center villages as experiential models and contrived places to reform habits of human interaction, affirming the settlement ideal and suggesting a suburban vision. The settlement ideal is perpetuated today in gentrified center villages like Litchfield, Connecticut. The suburban vision endures as well, lived in fashionable center villages like Concord, Massachusetts, expressed across America's landscape as residential subdivision "villages," and recently recovered in "neotraditional" town planning.

This study of the *idea* of the New England village as elitist construction, Romantic tradition, settlement ideal, and suburban vision is an interpretation of a range of village landscapes juxtaposed with literary and scholarly texts. I distinguish between traditions of town and of village. The New England town was designed as an organizational instrument of land division and community formation. It has served gallantly with the grid as a Neoclassical, functional model for trans-Appalachian settlement. Villages, on the other hand, were secondary settlements of New England towns, bearing the connotation of nucleated form only after the Revolution. While New England's nineteenth-century villages largely constitute an ordinary landscape,

Drawn by J. W. Barber—Engraved by S. E. Brown, Boston.

LENOX, MASS.

The above is a southern view of the public buildings. The first building seen on the right is the Town-House; the next building, three stories in height, is Wilson's Hotel; the next building north is the Court-House, near which is another public house, to which the jail is attached. The Congregational Church is seen on an elevation in the distance. The spires of the Episcopal Church are seen between the Town-House and Wilson's Hotel.

FIG. 6.1 Lenox, Massachusetts, c. 1835. This nineteenth-century view evokes the village tradition of covenanted community, cultural enlightenment, and democratic self-government. The center village of Lenox, formed in the nineteenth century, epitomized New England virtue for literary elites who flocked to the Berkshires later in the century. (Barber 1839. Courtesy, American Antiquarian Society.)

our collective view of that landscape has been shaped by elites. Hence I focus on the village as an elite construction, one derived from a Romantic tradition that flowered in the antebellum period. Villages housing a culturally enlightened populace became symbolic models for a place-seated pastoral community during this New England Renaissance. I employ two villages in particular — Litchfield, Connecticut, and Concord, Massachusetts — as epitomes of the settlement ideal. As elite places in the eighteenth and nineteenth centuries, as today, they truly were models for, and Romantic reconfigurations of, the village tradition, which I relate to place-making. This study exemplifies that we create our own geographies, consciously or not, and that geographies in our minds are crude approximations or inelegant models of those on the ground, and vice versa. In creating our own geographies, we justify those of the past and legitimate those of the present.[2] Literally and figuratively, we build our own worlds.

The Village in American Culture

Scholars recognize a number of important American settlement experiences, and several settlement forms stand as important regional icons. Certainly the Medieval bastide and the Neoclassical grid have had seminal morphological influence on the American settlement landscape.[3] Among these settlement experiences and influences, the New England village, ritualized in Thanksgiving holidays, Christmas cards, and innumerable Romantic novels and movies, has a special standing in American cultural history and geography.

In the collective American mind, the historical New England village represents a new Eden or second Zion. It is, says historian Page Smith, the archetype of American small towns, standing for community forbearance in a period of strict political, religious, and societal discipline and economic stability. Frugal and thrifty, industrious and hard-bitten, puritans employed villages to convert wilderness and establish a Jeffersonian middle landscape of rugged-individual yeomen formed into self-governing communities. The most intense community experience of modern time, the village remains a reminder of lost innocence.[4] The village expressed the Protestant ethic and the Enlightenment ideal of the noble yeoman. The village was setting for embattled farmers striking first blows for American independence, making it as well an expression of the geographical iconography of American nationalism. Analogous to the Greek *polis*, the village housed independent ecclesiastical societies, academies, and lyceums, giving it an aura of cultivation and discernment: "The village school-house and the village church are the monuments of our republicanism; to read, to write, and to discuss grave affairs, in their primary assemblies, are the licentious practices of our democracy," wrote Edward Everett.[5]

The village, some would argue then, was the high point in human social and political evolution. Ranked with the western farm and the state university, this utopian community has been viewed, ironically, as a most effective answer to the anti-American propaganda of communism.[6] One of a troika of symbolic landscapes—along with main street and suburbia—the village carries "connotations of continuity," as the cultural ideal of a place-seated, pastoral community.[7] "The cult of the New England village" is the "most distinctively New Englandish contribution to the American social ideal."[8]

The line between real and symbolic is fuzzy at best. Historians and geographers have conventionally defined the village as a nucleated settlement in which inhabitants were linked by a set of complex interpersonal relationships. This perspective, in which settlement form and social organization were intimately interconnected, is important to be certain, but as conventionally expressed it is ahistorical and ageographical. It confuses sentiment and settlement, failing to appreciate the material nature of the place as both shaped by and shaper of those interpersonal relationships—or, to quote Donald Meinig, "at once a mold and mirror of the society that create[d] [it]."[9] Like most traditions, the village tradition is a deeply held idea standing in stark contrast to the actual landscape.[10]

Constructing the Village Landscape

Whatever the village means in American cultural history and geography, it was not, in the colonial period, the exceptionalist nucleated settlement form portrayed in the tradition. Edward Channing noted over a century ago that New Englanders chartered villages as second-order ecclesiastical parishes, either by subdividing a chartered town's territory or by granting a town new territory on the settlement frontier. A handful of eighteenth-century villages inland from tidewater and away from the Connecticut Valley—Concord and Worcester in Massachusetts and Windham and Litchfield in Connecticut (all shire towns, or county seats)—were nucleated (FIG. 6.2). Not until the nineteenth century, however, did *village* clearly designate nucleated settlement.[11] Then New Englanders first formed present-day center villages at colonial town centers as early manifestations of urbanization under mercantile capitalism. Indeed, most center villagers of the early nineteenth century were neither wealthy traders nor proletarian workers. They were members of an emerging, enlightened middle class that filled ever-widening mercantile and artisanal niches in the period of the early republic (FIG. 6.3).[12]

The New England landscape underwent continued reconfiguration in the nineteenth century, suggesting economic decline. Marginal agricultural areas experienced farm abandonment, but agricultural productivity elsewhere in New England even increased.[13] Industrialization also marked the landscape, reconfiguring the emerging urban system of New England. Hence, many center villages achieved the heights of their commercial success even as they underwent village beautification. Well situated for agricultural marketing in the period of the early republic, many were misplaced and miscast by mid-century in an America increasingly dominated by industrial capitalism, as Ralph Waldo Emerson noted: "Of late years, the growth of Concord has been slow[;] without navigable waters, without mineral riches, without any con-

FIG. 6.2 A View of Concord [Massachusetts] taken in 1776. Concord was one of the few urban places inland during the colonial period, hence its military importance in 1775. (View by S. Hill. Courtesy, American Antiquarian Society.)

FIG. 6.3 Petersham, Massachusetts, c. 1835. Center villages were formed in the first decades of the nineteenth century about meetinghouse lots. (Barber 1839.)

siderable mill privileges, the natural increase of her population is drained by the constant emigration of her youth." Yet others sought places like Concord, increasingly choosing them as home while doing business elsewhere.[14]

Inventing the Village Tradition

The early nineteenth century witnessed both the building of center villages in New England and a transition from Neoclassicism to Romanticism as cultural idea in the English world, economic change stimulating both. Romanticism encouraged the orchestration of the organic, evoking an impression of picturesque complexity and employing a preternatural landscape as source of historicist metaphor. Fusing categories of history and fiction, it echoed an interest in the literary uses of the past and fostered as well a nostalgic empathy for New Englanders' authoritarian ancestors and their self-governing communities. It was not out of place for Rufus Choate to deliver an oration at Salem in 1833 entitled "The Importance of Illustrating New England History by a Series of Romances Like the Waverly Novels" (of Sir Walter Scott), which summarized the popular opinion of the day. What Choate proposed was no less than the appropriation of place and invention of tradition to justify the past and legitimate the present.[15]

Romanticism's New England manifestation presaged the literary invention of the region and exploitation of local life and landscape to literary ends through traditions of landscape poetry, regional prose, and commemorative discourse. Literate New Englanders of the "village enlightenment" were encouraged and empowered to build new and larger worlds.[16] Heeding Emerson, they did. Even as they built center villages—and as agricultural retreat and industrial expansion altered the landscape—the village became a metaphor for inherited ideals of stable puritan community and democratic society. No conspiracy ensued, but all could see local manifestations of the changes Emerson had noted in Concord. Romanticists who lived in, observed, wrote about, and portrayed villages ingenuously fused New England-as-tradition with nineteenth-century village-as-setting to invent New England village-as-tradition. Romanticism glorified New England village ways, creating as orthodoxy the village tradition that served as reflection of both a glorious past and a brimming future.

Literary elites—Catherine Maria Sedgwick, Nathaniel Hawthorne, Henry Ward Beecher, Harriet Beecher Stowe, and Sarah Orne Jewett, for instance—created the necessary illusion of steadfast village life. Travelers and social observers like Timothy Dwight and Anne Royal verbally described an attractive scene, which illustrators, especially John Warner Barber, captured superbly. Emerson and Henry David Thoreau encouraged a complementary, harmonious, pastoral ideology. Social reformers like Catharine Beecher and Charles Loring Brace invoked the village as model for domesticity and community. Landscape architects like Andrew Jackson Downing, Calvert Vaux, and Frederick Law Olmsted fabricated an appealing suburban aesthetic. Political scientists and historians in pursuit of the origins of the New England town meeting—Joel Parker, Herbert Baxter Adams, and Edward Channing, for instance—articulated a scholarly tradition as well. Collectively, Americans transposed the nineteenth-century center village with a colonial instrument of land division and orderly settlement, inventing a geographical past that had never existed. Interwoven, complementary strands of literary, artistic, and scholarly interest projected the center village as both physical setting and source of communal bonds back to apocryphal seventeenth-century origins, whence came legitimization of the nineteenth-century worlds New England elites were building.

Village as Geographical Metaphor

Roots of the New England village tradition as second Eden or new Zion go deep. One can discern the idea in William Bradford's "Of Plymouth Plantation" (1647), but it flowered in the Romantic period. The nostalgic pastoral "Greenfield Hill" by Neoclassical establishmentarian minister and scholar Timothy Dwight anticipated Romantic poetry. Describing the dispersed rural settlement space of late colonial New England, the poem enthusiastically celebrated the New England way of life. Dwight's 1790s *Travels*, a sober, Neoclassical landscape inventory marked with Romantic indulgences, further depicted New England towns as the highest form of civilization yet achieved. Dwight spawned, intellectually and spiritually, several subsequent generations of Romantic boosters of the New England tradition, who celebrated New England village life and landscape.[17]

Catherine Maria Sedgwick's novella, *A New England Tale*, was the first noteworthy fictional depiction of New England village life. Only by the 1820s, with changes in publishing and the literary market, could professional writers reach a national audience and support themselves commercially by their art. *A New England Tale* is, then, for multiple reasons, a landmark in American regional literature, reflecting the parallel developments of professionalism, commercialism, and literary expression of regional self-consciousness. It helped further to make Sedgwick's hometown of Lenox, Massachusetts (see FIG. 6.1) the literary seat of the Berkshires for the remainder of the nineteenth century. In this work, she articulated the basis for a cult of domesticity and social reform by conveying the notion that New England village life was "a most favorable milieu for nurturing of human happiness and virtue." [18] Paradoxically, not all glossed over degeneracy in the rural countryside—the slovenliness, idleness, poverty, habitual drunkenness, and violence of some of its inhabitants.[19] Hawthorne's novels especially drew attention to smothering puritan intolerance. Yet reality could not dissuade readers of the Romantic virtues of New England village life.

Center villages caught travelers' eyes. Scotsman John Duncan noted the "singular neatness" of New England villages, and Benjamin Silliman, passing through Sedgwick's Lenox in 1819, observed that "probably no small town in England is so beautiful as Lenox, nor have the Europeans, in general, any adequate idea of the beauty of the New-England villages." To Anne Royal "the villages, the lofty white steeples of the churches, peeping up through the trees, perhaps three, four, or five miles distant, may give some idea of the scenery [of the Connecticut Valley]." [20] Likewise, Nathaniel Hawthorne recorded in his *American Note-Books* blissful walks through the Essex County, Massachusetts countryside of the 1830s, a countryside punctuated by villages. In his 1831 "Sights from a Steeple" in Salem, Massachusetts, Hawthorne observed that "in three parts of the visible circle whose centre is this spire, I discern cultivated fields, villages, white country seats, the waving line of rivulets, little placid lakes, and here and there rising ground, that would fain be termed a hill." [21]

One might obtain such a picturesque view, we learn from illustrators, because the landscape was open and cleared much more so in the nineteenth century than today (see FIGS. 6.2, 6.5, 6.6, 6.7). Emerson noted that "The health of the eye seems to demand a horizon. We are never tired, so long as we can see far enough." Early-nineteenth-century New Englanders could indeed see far enough in the open landscape.[22] But illustrators of the 1830s and after, concerned with capturing the essence of New England's towns, also sought filled space to record in their views and prints. Center villages with tall-steepled churches accommodated this need and became lithographic as well as literary icons of New England life in the popular imagination of the nineteenth century.

A Usable Past

Concord, Massachusetts, and Litchfield, Connecticut, served the need for a usable past in Romantic literature. Among the very elite places of the late eighteenth and early nineteenth centuries, they provided models for the village tradition and came to epitomize the settlement ideal. East coast, liberal, Unitarian, and transcendental Concord and Connecticut Valley-inspired, conservative, Calvinist Litchfield reflected early-nineteenth-century sectarian differences.[23] As sectarian division blurred in an increasingly cosmopolitan New England, both became central elements in the literary landscape of nineteenth-century New England—Concord as archetype in the first half of the century and Litchfield as inspiration in the second half.

Concord and Litchfield were neither unique literary havens, nor were they removed from the ferment of change in nineteenth-century New England. Like center villages across New England, they underwent wrenching economic and social adjustments—commercialization of agriculture, elaboration of division of labor, rise of a middle class, and disestablishment of town and church. But these villages were different from other center villages as well. They were shire towns, like Sedgwick's Lenox, especially important, higher-order places housing elites in the countryside of early-nineteenth-century New England. Moreover, they were among the half dozen or so places that had been inland urban villages in the late colonial period; they indeed had a colonial past. And Concord lay in close proximity to Boston, coming eventually to serve as an urban residence beyond the city. Litchfield's residents literally reconfigured the place as a Romantic embodiment of the settlement ideal.

It was in transcendental Concord, argues literary historian Alfred Kazin, that nature became an American art and religion. Emerson, like Hawthorne, Thoreau, Bronson Alcott, and William Ellery Channing, came to Concord, Van Wyck Brooks has suggested, "by a natural attraction that seemed to reside in the tranquil atmosphere."[24] Concord was the first settled town inland from tidewater in Massachusetts Bay, and by the nineteenth century, the most famous small town in America. It proved a proper Romantic setting; its gentle, two-hundred-year-old cultural landscape stimulated and mirrored the writing of its famous residents, who conceptualized the scene in sophisticated terms. Emerson's Concord view, reported in *Nature*, suggests, for instance, both the quality of the scene and something of the transcendental origin of geographers' notion of landscape:

Drawn by J. W. Barber—Engraved by J. Downes, Worcester.

CENTRAL PART OF CONCORD, MASS.

The above is a northern view in the central part of Concord village. Part of the Court-House is seen on the left. Burying-ground Hill (a post of observation to the British officers in the invasion of 1775) is seen a short distance beyond. The Unitarian Church and Middlesex Hotel are seen on the right.

FIG. 6.4 Central Part of Concord, Massachusetts, c. 1835. Cosmopolitan Concord, to which Emerson had moved in 1834, was an archetype for the village tradition. (Barber 1839, opp. p. 455. Courtesy, American Antiquarian Society.)

When we speak of nature in this manner, we have a distinct but most poetical sense in mind. We mean the integrity of impressions made by manifold natural objects. It is this which distinguishes the stick of timber of the wood-cutter, from the tree of the poet. The charming [Concord] landscape which I saw this morning, is indubitably made up of some twenty or thirty farms. Miller owns this field, Locke that, and Manning the woodland beyond. But none of them owns the landscape. There is a property in the horizon which no man has but he whose eye can integrate all the parts, that is, the poet. This is the best part of these men's farms, yet to this their land-deeds give them no title.[25]

Thoreau, too, found Concord an ideal world in which to live—his cottage at Walden Pond was located in an extensive wood only a mile and a half south of Concord's commercial core but was, in Thoreau's words, "as far off as many a region viewed nightly by astronomers."[26] *Walden* portrayed a village-centered landscape of a settled core surrounded by successive rings of field

FIG. 6.5 Southeast View of Litchfield, Connecticut, from Chesnut Hill, c. 1835. Bustling Litchfield served as literary and social model of domestic virtue and village tranquility. See also FIG. 7.3. (Barber 1838, opp. p. 456. Courtesy, American Antiquarian Society.)

and forest. This fried-egg image of center yolk in the midst of encircling white is classic village-as-tradition.

Yet, too, "Virgilian Concord" had long been more cosmopolitan than other center villages.[27] Concord had been the leading inland urban place in eastern Massachusetts in the colonial period. Rebels had stored arms in Concord, destination of the infamous British assault of April 1775. Throughout the British occupation of Boston, it served as the site of Harvard College. The Town of Concord had all the virtues of the rural countryside about it, while the center village of Concord had many of the amenities of Salem or Boston. Emerson and Thoreau built worlds, the idyllic image of which, like most Romantic images, was fuzzy. Concord, by the 1840s, could encompass both Walden Pond and an urban place connected to the world beyond by the Fitchburg Railroad (FIG. 6.4).

Litchfield in the early nineteenth century was a bustling, urbane place as well (FIG. 6.5). The early settlement and shire town for northwestern Connecticut, it had a law school and was an important publishing center before the Revolution. During the war, American military operations between the Hudson and Connecticut Rivers were directed from Litchfield. To Timothy Dwight, writing in the 1790s, Litchfield ranked not far behind older Connecticut Valley towns as repositories of New England civic and religious virtues in the purest and most concentrated form.[28] Litchfield provided an ideal incubator for a literary tradition that blossomed in the mid-nineteenth century.

The Litchfield reminiscences of its minister Lyman Beecher, Dwight's student at Yale, provided grist for the fictional writing of his children. They consciously aspired to the ideological retrieval of preindustrial village life they had known there. Harriet Beecher Stowe's nostalgic *Oldtown Folks* (1869) idealized a close-knit, Calvinist village of the post-Revolutionary period, when most such places were just forming about colonial meetinghouse lots, and alluded to John Winthrop's colonial ideal of a "city upon a hill." Her *Poganuc People* (1878) even more self-consciously focuses on New England village ways, with emphasis on the intellectual life of a cultivated people. Stowe presented the Litchfield-like town and its people with optimistic zest, echoing Dwight's enthusiasm for New England and the New England town.[29]

Norwood; or Village Life in New England, Henry Ward Beecher's Civil War era novel, emphasized the continued importance of picturesque place for human values. Despite nineteenth-century change in life and landscape, "The remote neighborhoods and hilltowns yet retain the manners, morals, institutions, customs and religion of the fathers. The interior villages of New England are her brood-combs."[30] The novel, for which Beecher was advanced the then unheard of sum of $30,000, was so influential in New England that the south precinct (or second parish) of Dedham, Massachusetts, took the name of Norwood when chartered as a separate, suburban Boston town in 1872.[31] Litchfield, meanwhile, was past its commercial prime. Unlike Concord or Norwood, the hilltop village was inaccessible to direct rail linkages. It was left up to "summer people" to restore it as a Romantic embodiment of New England tradition in a "colonial" village.[32]

Romantic Reflection

Thoreau wrote in his *Journal* in 1856 that "I have never got over my surprise that I should have been born into the most estimable place in all of the world, and in the very nick of time, too."[33] The rise of center villages in the early nineteenth century was a response to an urbanizing world. The generation of New Englanders who formed center villages in the nineteenth century saw traditional ways of life rapidly retreat from the onslaught of individual enterprise, industrial opportunism, and mechanical prowess. In the larger context, sentimental pastoralism, Leo Marx has written, "enabled the nation to continue defining its purpose as the pursuit of rural happiness while devoting itself to productivity, wealth, and power." Similarly, Thomas Bender has convincingly argued, New England elites, seeking "symbolic harmonization" of city and country, were simultaneously creating a positive urban vision.[34] Villagers themselves propelled the machine onward, steaming down iron rails past Walden Pond, along the path Thoreau walked to Concord's center village. Although New Englanders lamented the passing of their rural landscape, it was New England's center villagers who were not supporting marginal farmers and who were building mills and railroads. They found the source of their cultural enlightenment and their commercial enterprise in their puritan heritage. Colonial fathers in Boston and Salem and New Haven, after all, had hardly spurned worldliness. They had, in their fashion, quite successfully laid a foundation for the economic and cultural development of the nineteenth century.

The Romantic reinventing of puritanism, with all of its "Jekyll and Hyde aspects," and the creation of the myth of puritan antecedence were important parallels to the formation of the village tradition. Puritans had established social order, economic security, and local self-government, employing villages to convert wilderness from the realm of evil to a world of the sublime. Center villages across New England were first forming when Dwight wrote "Greenfield Hill" in 1794 and in economic decline by midcentury when Thoreau was at Walden Pond. Therefore, pictorially adept representations of the past did not violate the sensibilities and historical understanding of Romantic readers.[35] True, villages were only caricatures of puritan virtue in the world of literary imagination, but New Englanders took Romanticism seriously. It justified the past, the characteristic economy of which was in decline, and legitimated the present. Out of this Romantic vision, the idea of *the* New England village was constituted and rooted deeply in a newfound tradition of moral rectitude.

The linkage between construction of center villages and invention of village tradition is so proximate in time that one might even ask if the idea of the village were a self-fulfilling prophecy that New Englanders wrote and copied. Discourses like Horace Bushnell's "The Age of Homespun"—which Bushnell's mentor Dwight would have found familiar—aroused interest in "improvement" of village landscapes after midcentury. Romantics reconstructed and transformed center villages, like Lenox, as both setting for and reflection of nineteenth-century Romanticism.[36] Center villagers, as well as "summer people" arriving by rail from Boston, New York, and Philadelphia,

FIG. 6.6 Princeton, Massachusetts, c. 1886. Romantic, bucolic, pastoral, and picturesque, Princeton was already past its prime when this photograph was taken. (Courtesy, American Antiquarian Society.)

observed "a pastoral landscape of smooth expanses of short grass, bordered by translucent groves of trees." They continued a "cult of the past" and historicized the landscape to evoke an ahistorical colonial tradition, of which Litchfield was a most important example.[37] That tradition was embellished in the Colonial Revival architectural style in the 1880s, epitomizing an agrarian society and inherited landscape characterized by "domesticity, dedication, difficult yet satisfying labor, and a nourishing connection with nature."[38] Romanticism's aesthetic was perpetuated into the latter half of the century by a delight in the picturesque, continuing to mold both the geographical imagination of Americans and their landscape (FIG. 6.6).[39]

Many late-nineteenth-century observers took a less than approving view of the New England setting, suggesting that as the rural economy had faded so had some of the moral rectitude. New England had become "the most conceivably left-over place that rapidly self-transforming America could provide," the village now a metaphor for sentimentalized pastoralism (FIG. 6.7).[40] By then, however, connection between center village and colonial community—between village-as-setting and New England-as-tradition—was confounded. The literary elaboration of the tradition had become reality. Villages, literary

sought to reform the city by bringing city and country, and the respective values for which they stood, into a "contrapuntal relationship." This vision of cityscape in counterpoise with the natural landscape was articulated by Emerson and Thoreau and was manifested, Bender suggests, in the planning of Lowell, Massachusetts, in the social reform of Charles Loring Brace, and in the landscape architecture of Frederick Law Olmsted. Olmsted sought, in a new urban landscape, to overcome divergent rural and urban values by bringing aspects of the countryside to the city.[46] Robert Gross has developed this argument further, noting correctly that urbanization involves not only growth of cities but development of linkages between country and city.[47] If, in the encounter of country and city, the nineteenth-century urban vision of which Bender writes was never realized, a settlement ideal was. The encounter of country and city served to establish a dialogue whence evolved a reconception of place and community that allowed the advantages of the city without living there.

Emerson desired the best of both country and city: "I wish to have rural strength and religion for my children, and I wish city facility and polish. I find with chagrin that I cannot have both." He accepted the "dichotomy of city and nature not as a conclusion but as a point of departure."[48] The city for Emerson served as metaphor for larger and deeper concerns: "The test of civilization is the power of drawing the most benefit out of cities," he wrote.[49] Emerson strove to harmonize urbanism and nature, to articulate the ideal of a place embodying the best of city and nature alike. Concord, recall, was no rude village. Emerson's world became a middle ground having the attributes of agrarian community in an increasingly nonagrarian society, in which the presence of center villages marked change. Emerson continued to fulfill his "vocation" within the context of Boston, only eighteen miles away. He treated Concord as a suburb of Boston, to which he commuted by rail at least once a week.[50] Thoreau, in his manner, complemented Emerson, seeking a gentle landscape balanced between natural and artificial and believing one could live permanently in neither city nor wilderness. Thoreau distinguished country from wilderness and from meaner rural agricultural regions remote from "the ferment of novel ideas." This position reflected no sentimental pastoralism, with its theme of withdrawal from society into an idealized landscape. Thoreau's was a thoughtful and complex ideal, a metaphor for a middle ground between and in transcendental relation to opposing forms of civilization and nature. Emerson's and Thoreau's conception of country was an urban conception, one developed from the perspective of the city.[51]

Elaboration of the Settlement Ideal

Emerson's and Thoreau's conception of country was elaborated by social reformers and landscape architects in the decades that followed. Catharine Beecher's 1841 *Treatise on Domestic Economy* was the definitive statement on American domestic ideology, albeit a patriarchal one in which women were removed from places of business and industry. The work and its successor editions and imitations articulated the ideal of domestic harmony in an urbanizing world associated with the detached, single-family, picturesque cottage in a bucolic setting.[52] Beecher was familiar with that setting, having grown up with sister Harriet and brother Henry in Litchfield in the early decades of the century, when Litchfield was quite cosmopolitan for the time. Charles Loring Brace, born in Litchfield, tutored by Dwight's student Horace Bushnell, friend of Olmsted, and influenced by Emerson, used New England community life as a standard for organic, spontaneous community. He structured the asylum, ironically, as an orderly eighteenth-century village, of which Litchfield was a rare example, to stand in contrast to the industrial city he observed at midcentury. The settlement ideal had come pragmatically to reflect "a moral position perfectly represented by the image of a rural order, neither wild nor urban, as setting of man's best hope."[53]

The middle ground that Emerson and Thoreau found in Concord was a slice of John Stilgoe's "borderland"—a literal frontier between rural and urban, whence Stilgoe finds the origins of the American suburb. Proponents of the early rural-cemetery movement sought access to the borderland, where they contrived spaces for the living and the dead. Mount Auburn Cemetery, constructed outside of Boston in 1831, for instance, presaged a new, open urban landscape and inspired the emergence of the city park movement in the middle of the nineteenth century.[54]

Andrew Jackson Downing, Calvert Vaux, and Frederick Law Olmsted sought to landscape this middle ground. They insisted on an artifact that evoked the natural and organic character of the perfect village life and bore the associative ecclesiastical and educational features of New England. Downing's treatises on rural cottages and the art of landscape gardening were especially influential in crystallizing the settlement ideal into a suburban vision. His 1850 plan for a "country village," in which detached houses on tree-lined streets surround a landscaped public park, appears remarkably like a center village, whereas Vaux's designs exhibited connection to the natural setting, much like a hilltop center village formed over a generation in the early nineteenth century. Olmsted, also a protégé of Dwight's student Bushnell, contrived naturalistic space. The center village served as an explicit model. Olmsted self-consciously sought a metaphor for the urban perfected in the suburban in the culturally constructed, loosely built center village seated around the open public space of the meetinghouse lot. Successors of the urban park tradition, like Horace W. S. Cleveland and Robert Morris Copeland, had also grown up in this pastoral-urban nineteenth-century New England landscape.[55]

Nineteenth-century social reformers and landscape architects had good reason for utopian thinking. Challenged by the perceived ills of the industrial city, they sought to replicate landscapes they believed had worked in the past to foster domesticity and community in the present. They collectively fabricated a socially conscious, aesthetically appealing landscape of residential communities that were separate from the city geographically, socially, politically, and attitudinally. Much of this Romantic urban landscape failed to materialize, however, as the grid captured the attention of less idealistic city builders. Moreover, the imaginative and complex settlement ideal was popularly debased as sentimental pastoralism. Symbolically, however, the center village had come to serve as model for utopian settlement that would beneficially shape habits of human interaction. Places where one might try to "have both" suggested a vision of what a suburb could be.

Suburban Vision

England, of course, invented the modern residential suburb and no doubt influenced the American Romantic suburban vision.[56] Emerson took much delight in both London and the English countryside during visits in 1833 and 1847, noting approvingly that "England is a huge phalanstery."[57] Catharine Beecher, Downing, and Vaux were especially taken with "English Evangelical domestic ideology" and the "picturesque tradition of design."[58] All had rediscovered England once the living memory of the American Revolution had passed. What degree of influence English expressions of domestic ideology and picturesque landscape may have had, however, can only be interpreted in context. Certainly incipient suburbs—often overdressed villages enveloped by the "morphological advance of the city"[59]—had developed by 1820 around New York, Philadelphia, and Boston. In the case of Boston, nearby villages had, by the 1820s, come to offer an advantageous mix of local self-sufficiency, political autonomy, and adequate external linkage for suburban commuting.

Dwight had noted in the 1790s a set of road-centered villages well connected commercially to Boston that would eventually become, Henry Binford argues, "the first suburbs." Urban-fringe communities in Cambridge and Charleston offered residential options for those who chose to commute to Boston before the age of mass transportation.[60] Villagers in the urban fringe themselves originated residential suburbs and passionately defended their political independence and cultural conformity. Emerson articulated the settlement ideal even as more and more countryside and center villages were enveloped by expanding Boston. Concord, a dozen miles farther removed from Boston than Cambridge and comfortably linked by rail in the 1840s, became part of the urban fringe. Center villages, by then, had become desirable alternatives to cities, excluding all but those who shared social, economic, ethnic, and religious affinity. Social reformers and landscape architects, both preaching exclusive community and detached, single-family dwelling, articulated the Romantic imagery of the New England village at the very time some center villages had come to serve as suburban refuges. Center villages provided substance if not source for a new American suburban vision.

The suburban impulse came from both country and city. Picturesque scenery and mechanical means of transportation offered an opportunity to establish homogeneous communities and live a better life removed from the corrupting influences of the city. New England center villages already serving as residential satellites were ready American models for planned residential communities.[61] Suburban proponents were familiar with the few center villages that had existed in the late eighteenth century, like Litchfield and Concord. They were observers of or participants in the development of the new center villages that formed across New England in the early decades of the nineteenth century, when village and tradition were fused. But as suburbanization came to flourish in the later nineteenth century, urban expansion forced an accommodation of city and country not necessarily to the liking of idealists. What had been a vision for integrating city and country had become a means for retreating from the city.

Diffusing the Village Tradition

New England, of course, has long had a profound cultural influence on the remainder of the United States. This influence has most often been invoked in literary and cultural terms, and no doubt Romantic literature had much to do with diffusing New England-as-tradition nationally in the nineteenth

FIG. 6.8 Public Square, Mansfield, Ohio, c. 1845. The settlement landscape in the Western Reserve of Connecticut mirrors the "noble marks of moral improvement" attributed to New Englanders. (Howe 1847, p. 431. Courtesy, American Antiquarian Society.)

century. The landscape influence has been great as well. The tradition of employing towns as instruments of land division and community formation served as both figurative and functional model for trans-Appalachian settlement. Formal land companies modeled community after New England towns, and systematic land subdivision owes much to New England antecedents of replicative settlement by rectangular town grants. New Englanders carried New England ways and traditions across New York, into the Old Northwest, and beyond, town and village serving as inchoate settlement models there as well: "Wherever they have penetrated into the interior of this continent, they have exhibited . . . the implements of husbandry and the arts, the axe, the plough, the forge and the loom, and still noble marks of moral improvement, the school house, and the tall spire directing the head to the skies."[62] One cannot mistake the New England landscape influence in the Connecticut Western Reserve, for instance, where the maturing settlement landscape was contemporaneous with the rise of center villages in New England itself (FIG. 6.8).

Certain enduring geographical habits reflecting the New England village ideal were expressed widely outside the westward yankee migration belt as well. New England has no unique claim to originality. Other parts of the United States had nucleated settlement traditions, and the Pennsylvania town was another important geographical model for the American small town.[63] Commercial blocks appeared simultaneously in many regions of the country, and railroads appreciably altered main street form where and when they arrived. Likewise, villages about New York, Philadelphia, and a host of other commercial and industrial cities had also served as "first suburbs." But elite New Englanders articulated for other Americans in word and deed how to build their own worlds. New Englanders imbued other places with a characteristic village ideology reflected in landscape compositions of widely spaced, single-family houses fronting on broad lawns along tree-shaded residential streets.[64] New Englanders contributed the settlement ideal, now reflected in residential landscapes across an urbanized and corporatized America.

Conclusion

Romantic New Englanders built their own worlds. Simultaneously they constructed center villages from colonial town and village landscapes of dispersed settlement and they invented a Romantic New England tradition of village life. They manipulated a geographical image to fuse New England-as-tradition with village-as-setting and to create an enduring settlement ideal. Emerson and his contemporaries articulated that ideal while seeking both country and city in a suburban borderland. Emerson was transcendental in Concord and urbane in Boston, commuting between the two on the Fitchburg Railroad.

The settlement ideal endures in villages, real and imagined, across the United States. Relict center villages like Lenox and Litchfield embody idealized pasts and contrived landscape elements reflective of a persistent gentried ideology of exclusivity and elitism.[65] Woodstock, Vermont, proclaims its Chamber of Commerce, is "a town with the spiritual flavor and old fashioned values of an earlier day"; yet in Woodstock one can also "discover the pleasures and treasures of today"—a place, Robert Sack would argue, where one can consume geography.[66] Many a center village of the nineteenth century, and industrial village as well, has become a cultural amenity, a retreat from the city. Quite literally such places failed in the nineteenth century to become cities and were Romantically reconfigured as symbols of an idealized past.

Nor has the settlement ideal been lost to present-day suburbia, where it has been manipulated in a succession of historical and aesthetic contexts.

The composite landscape of America's enduring affluent suburbs most closely reflects the nineteenth-century settlement ideal as suburban vision.[67] An excursion about contemporary borderlands of hundreds of American cities, however, is adequate to reveal how overt place-makers and geographical imagineers have manipulated the Emersonian settlement ideal into both modernist and postmodernist versions of the suburban vision (FIG. 6.9). In the past few years, a new traditionalism for contemporary design of suburban communities has self-consciously harkened to the village tradition.[68] Avant-garde landscape architects have brought the nineteenth-century settlement ideal into sharp focus once more. They propose that Americans wish to live and work in exclusive, aesthetically controlled, self-governed, mixed-use settlements, elitist constructions like Concord's center village, rather than the monotonous residential subdivisions that have been served up for the past half century. Indeed, few Americans have ever achieved what even Emerson found to his chagrin he could not have. When suburbanization was democratized in the late industrial era, the settlement ideal lost much of its promise. The ideal of integrating country with city had devolved into an imperative to withdraw from the city.

In gaining a settlement ideal, albeit neither universally accepted nor commonly realized, we have lost another—a sense of place-seated community. Place-seated community may never have been more than a Romantic literary conceit.[69] True, colonial New Englanders formed a social web, the configuration of which structured the settlement space of the New England town. Nathaniel Hawthorne, however, causes one to wonder about efficacy of such a thing as "village community." A community ideal is much with us, metaphorically perpetuated by the village tradition, but experience teaches us that people, not places, create communal relationships. Landscapes are reflections, not causes, of the human condition, a notion reformers, planners, and developers who fabricate place to contrive community in contemporary subdivisions have yet to discover.[70] Community has become less place-bound than ever, as we communicate and commute in functional space increasingly difficult to define in Euclidean terms. Our place-images of where we live have become more important to our daily lives than the places where we live. Place-images, as simple as zip codes for some, tell marketers who we are. They tell us as well how much we have built worlds to achieve a settlement ideal.

What of the worlds we have built? How has the elitist construction of Emerson or Olmsted devolved into our contemporary settlement model for

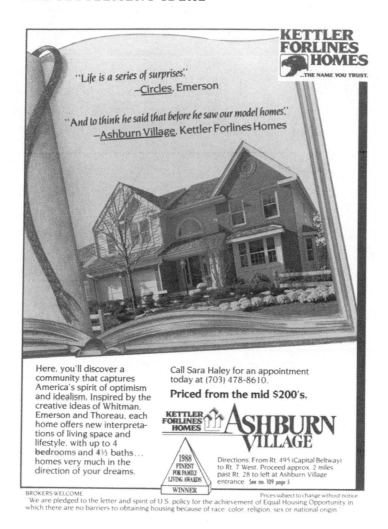

FIG. 6.9 Ashburn Village. The Emersonian settlement ideal endures in suburban Northern Virginia in 1989. (Courtesy, Robert L. Simmons, Kettler Forlines Homes.)

the urban fringe? Barbara Rubin asks a similar question: How does an operationally coherent and efficient urban commerce exist in a modern urban landscape idiom popularly characterized as dysfunctional? The answer, she suggests, is that aesthetic ideology serves to reinforce corporate ideology.[71] Since the loss of the nineteenth-century urban vision of integrating country with city, place-making, like aesthetic ideology, has fallen into new hands. The settlement ideal and suburban vision, like aesthetic ideology, reflected an elitist construction. Today the settlement ideal, like aesthetic ideology, has become the province of those for whom materialist concerns and preoccupation with symbolic, often historicist, images influence design. The settlement ideal serves a corporate culture instrumental in making taste and imagineering place.[72] America's subdivision "villagers" inhabit a landscape of corporate construction modeled on the elitist construction of the nineteenth century.

A most vexing question remains. How have scholars formalized and perpetuated the confounding of Romantic tradition with cultural landscape? How have scholars contributed to the invention and manipulation of place-images, justifying the past and legitimating the present? Are scholars as ingenuous as Romantic New Englanders, building their own worlds as art and artifact? If so, explaining the invention of tradition lies in assessment of neither objective nor impressionistic space. It lies, as Rubin has noted about aesthetic ideology, in *terra incognita* separating real and ideal, where New Englanders built their own worlds and where Americans, in designing, constructing, and living in suburbs, elaborate on others' geographies in the contemporary landscape.[73]

7 · *A World We Have Gained*

~: In this final chapter we recast the argument of the previous chapters in the context of the invention of tradition, while simultaneously summarizing the argument of the book. Tradition and history are not the same concepts. Traditions are conventions that evolve. Traditions are the pasts we make in the present. The New England tradition of large colonial houses encircling town commons to form puritan villages was invented in the nineteenth century, and Michael Steinitz and I here employ a four-stage model to explain how. Colonial images of hard-bitten puritans shaping garden out of wilderness became nineteenth-century myths played out in contemporary village ensembles. Village-improvement, architectural-preservation, and local-historical societies self-consciously carved out a landscape of relict features to stand for the whole, and thereby completed invention of tradition during the 1870s and following decades, a period of great flowering of tradition in England as well. Finally, colonial-revival architects reinterpreted colonial form to contrive a universalized historical landscape tradition, which scholars of town origins and of the roots of vernacular building traditions converted to conventional scholarly wisdom. :~

~: THE ENSEMBLE OF SUBSTANTIAL HOUSE, TOWN COMMON, AND CENTER village encountered in New England reflects an invented tradition: New England's towns were planted and perpetuated as puritan villages composed of two-story houses surrounding common pastures or decorative town plots. "The fruits of this policy are seen in the villages which are today so attractive and characteristic a feature of New England life."[1] The puritan-village tradition embodies covenanted community, cultural enlightenment, and democratic self-government. Universalized, this tradition persists in popular and scholarly imagination as a simplified geography of associated objects representing a natural and inevitable process of regional development. This tradition—prosperous colonial yeomen inhabiting substantial houses encircling open commons to form rock-ribbed villages majestically sited on New England hilltops—especially exemplifies the formative role of New England in the creation of American religious and national orthodoxy (FIG. 7.1). The news reports and photographs of United States Supreme Court Justice-designate David Souter attending church services in the meetinghouse of Hopkinton, New Hampshire, prior to his 1990 confirmation by the United States Senate, were hardly unintentional. The Anglo-Saxon heritage and individualistic yet communitarian ethic of the patriotic yeomen who once lived in the fine houses and pastured cattle on the commons of these once steadfast agricultural villages was clear.

Invention of this puritan-village and New England landscape tradition occurred in the nineteenth century.[2] Erasure of the memory of a rude, pre-Revolutionary landscape of dispersed farms and cramped cottage dwellings reflected a self-conscious need for a New England tradition during a period of national development, when the New England influence on national culture and political economy was beginning to fade and an industrial economy was displacing an agricultural one. The tradition links New England unambiguously and uncompromisingly to its colonial heritage but is embodied largely in nineteenth-century landmarks, in substantial houses, town commons, and center villages that are contrived symbols of a glorious past. We assess development of this puritan-village ensemble in the context of the historiographical conception of tradition. We relate our understanding of the construction of the New England settlement landscape from initial colonization through the nineteenth century. We then develop the argument for invention of the New England landscape tradition within a framework suggested by Martyn Bowden.[3] We discuss as well the popularizing of New

FIG. 7.1 Colburn Park and the Meetinghouse, Lebanon, New Hampshire, c. 1852. The painter captures both some of the cultural iconography of the New England village ensemble and of the self-consciousness of center village builders. Even so, not all houses were large or stylish. See FIG. 3.1 for comparison. (Painting by Ulysses D. Tenny. Courtesy, Lebanon Public Library.)

England landmarks and landscape and comment on the scholarly elaboration of the New England tradition as embodied in the village ensemble.

The Invention of Tradition

Tradition has a powerful effect on interpretation of the past. British social historians Eric Hobsbawm and Terence Ranger, concerned with notions of national identity and legitimacy, were especially struck by the number of nineteenth-century expressions of a need to establish some aspect of social life as continuous and unchanging in the face of innovation and change in the modern world. Romantic elites of the late eighteenth and early nineteenth centuries had conceived of tradition as a property of organic nature. Tradition in Enlightenment understanding had been the opposite of change and modernity. It had constrained rational thought. But Romantics restored tradition by removing it from history and locating it in organic processes and visible landscapes. There, tradition could produce an uncomplicated narrative of social development that stretched from the past to the present. Tradition obscured historical disorder and discontinuity. It reduced both diachronic complexity and synchronic richness. It produced a comprehensible ensemble of a few key elements, a tableau that became a historical image of selected elements of the past. Tradition thus implied a particular and definitive heritage. As Lévi-Strauss has noted, "modern societies interiorize history, as it were, and turn it into the motive power of their development." The ideological effect of interiorized history was a critical inheritance that legitimated the present. Tradition thus emerged from modernity as a self-conscious reflection on the past. Tradition here is not opposed to modernity as much as it is a vehicle for modernity.[4]

Reconstruction of centrally symbolic landmarks has been a typical means of identifying critical inheritance, inventing tradition, and thereby articulating cultural, political, and economic power. The iconographic significance of urban architectural forms as powerful generators of invented traditions is well established.[5] Yet widespread and pervasive vernacular processes of tradition-making may simultaneously operate across a regional cultural landscape. Martyn Bowden has offered a framework for analysis of the invention of such cultural landscape tradition in the American context. He has noted four stages. *Image formation* begins with the very creation of the landscape itself, in which a significant erasure of memory of past reality occurs. Image gains credence and memory fades still more with *myth creation*, as one is removed further in time from the past reality. *Invention of tradition* follows self-conscious generalizing from relict features of the landscape associated with the image and the myth. *Universalization* is the elaboration of the tradition, including the wholesale popular and scholarly acceptance of the tradition as conventional wisdom.[6]

The lines between image, myth, and tradition are fuzzy at best, but the framework provokes an understanding of the world of house, common, and village we have gained in New England. The tradition of the puritan-village ensemble is intertwined with those of an "ignoble savage" in a *vacuum domicilium* and of a "desart [sic] wilderness," but its particular context is nineteenth-century sentimental pastoralism, the vehicle for modernity which, Leo Marx has noted, "enabled the nation to continue defining its purpose as the pursuit of rural happiness while devoting itself to productivity, wealth, and power."[7]

Colonial ministers had formed an image of New England as wilderness converted to garden. Nineteenth-century Romantic elites fashioned a corresponding myth of puritan antecedence, democratic society, and patriotic fervor, which became tradition in the powerfully nostalgic search for national and local identity during the centennial years of the 1870s. The tradition is the consequence of quite deliberate attempts to create a mythical landscape at both the local level (by families and communities) and the national level (by the influential, self-conscious promoters of a new, literary, aesthetic, and historical ideology). The tradition was particularly expressed in an architectural vision that selected particular houses and places of New England as representative of the whole. Scholars seeking the origins of American democracy in the New England town meeting and the roots of American vernacular building traditions further elaborated on this past and linked New England to a larger Anglo-Saxon tradition. Center villages, town commons, and substantial dwelling houses became the historic landmarks and monumental constructions that served as the contrived symbols of shared perceptions and imaginative conceptions of the colonial past.

Constructing the New England Landscape

As we have seen in previous chapters, colonial New Englanders employed English ways to mold a new English landscape. To New England they brought a varied set of regional English agricultural ways, building practices and house forms, and settlement traditions, many of which they wished to perpetuate and others they wished to forget. Puritans among the settlers consciously left behind what of late Renaissance England and Anglicanism they resented or which repelled them. The movement was an opportunity to create a new England, one in which freemen and their families could own land. In staking out their farms, as most settlers did, colonists thus created a new geography of English cultural subregions and constructed a complex domestic landscape that reflected the different construction traditions and local patterns of settlement and land use that had developed in the subregions of England.[8]

Colonial housewrights and carpenters represented several distinct vernacular building traditions. Those from the upland north and west knew small, single-story houses. They replicated modest forms of housing when they came to New England. Immigrants from the lowland eastern and southern parts of England had experienced a great housing revolution in the late

sixteenth and early seventeenth centuries. There, prosperous yeomen had replaced earlier generations of housing stock with larger, more comfortable
houses. In Massachusetts Bay, where these immigrants of southern and eastern England predominated, the best-built houses reflected both the attitudes
and favored forms of the English housing revolution: heavy timber-framed,
multiroom houses two stories in height, built around a massive central interior chimney that heated several rooms. Nevertheless, documentary and archaeological evidence suggests that most New England colonists in the seventeenth century lived in rather modest, single-story, one- or two-room houses.
The substantial multiroom houses of local elites that survive show a selective
modification and elaboration of English building techniques in the new
world by the end of the first century of settlement.[9]

New England settlers experimented as well with a variety of settlement
forms with various English antecedents. New England was a commercial
venture; entrepreneurs constructed large houses and lived in commercial
places. Inland concentrations of farmers in wide alluvial river valleys were
not uncharacteristic in the seventeenth century. The long, linear clusters of
affluent farms with large houses in the Connecticut River Valley persisted
throughout the colonial period, but were uncharacteristic of other regions of
New England. In eastern Massachusetts, however, the inhabitants of the few,
famous, largely ephemeral nucleated settlements, such as Sudbury, Dedham,
and Andover, had dispersed at the first opportunity to build small houses on
their detached freehold farms. Hundreds of other towns and villages from
the first years of settlement framed settlements of single-family farms at
most confined in loose clusters on arable land. Villages were secondary forms
of towns, usually ecclesiastical parishes. Towns and villages alike had a center,
where settlers located their meetinghouse, burying ground, nooning sheds,
and Sabbath Day houses about the meetinghouse lot, the land reserved or
designated for the ecclesiastical society in each town or village grant. A tavern
sometimes was the sole public building on the site, serving as the place for
town governance until eighteenth-century town houses formalized this function. Social and political activity thus focused on the town or village center,
the place that symbolized the community.[10]

At the end of the colonial period, then, dispersed farmsteads, predominantly of small houses, dominated the landscape. In the last quarter of the
eighteenth century, two-thirds of the houses of the central uplands of Massachusetts were still only one story in height. In southeastern Massachusetts
and the western Massachusetts hill towns, over 90 percent of the houses

standing at the end of the eighteenth century were modest, one-story affairs. In only a few rural areas, like Essex County, Massachusetts, one of the oldest, wealthiest, and most densely populated regions of the eastern seaboard, did substantial, two-story houses predominate. From the mid-eighteenth century onward, prosperous yeoman families in well-favored agricultural zones of the Connecticut Valley and Middlesex County began to build the types of larger, two-story dwellings most often associated with the colonial New England countryside. Here, two-story, two-room-deep houses typically proclaimed the generational accumulation of wealth by families located on especially prime farmland. The appearance of these substantial houses reflected the aspirations of these families for a fashionably symmetrical and controlled architecture. Yet large houses were never dominant regionally, and they became significant in numbers in most locations only very late in the eighteenth century. Elsewhere in the hinterland, the occasional country estate stood out amidst the one-story regional landscape of dispersed farms that characterized town and village settlement landscapes across most of New England throughout the colonial period.[11]

Stylish, substantial Georgian houses were most concentrated in the coastal ports. Newburyport, Newport, and Norwich, like Boston, Salem, and New Haven, exemplified this pattern of wealthy mercantile places distinct from the hundreds of inland agricultural towns. Likewise, a handful of eighteenth-century nucleated places inland from tidewater and away from the Connecticut Valley, like Worcester, Massachusetts, and Windham, Connecticut, were shire towns (county seats). Here urban places had formed about meetinghouse lots, the church land at town centers, sustained by a few score individuals employed in government and related economic services. The Georgian houses of these wealthy merchants, self-styled gentry, and colonial patronage elite signaled power, status, and self-conscious separation from New England's dispersed yeoman majority living in capes and cottages on the eve of the Revolutionary War.

Remaking the Landscape

New England experienced a commercial and cultural flowering in the years following the American Revolution. Members of a new middle class of prosperous farmers, merchants, artisans, and professionals remade the New England landscape in the form we recognize today. Increasing extralocal exchange drew previously dispersed, nonfarm activities to the town centers,

FIG. 7.2 East View of the Village of North Bridgewater, Massachusetts, c. 1845. This lithograph captures the Romantic village in a formal, classical garden landscape. (Lithograph by A. Conant. Courtesy, American Antiquarian Society.)

where the meetinghouse and tavern were already located. Town roads had long converged at the center, focusing there social and economic intercourse. Increased trade, transportation, and communication facilitated growth and development of an interwoven and commercialized settlement landscape of which town centers became hubs of activity. New Englanders built substantial dwellings in the countryside and about meetinghouse lots at these town centers, forming center villages with new shops, stores, schools, churches, and town buildings. They adopted the stylish aesthetics of classical formalism in architectural and village design—early on with delicately appointed, symmetrical facades, low-hip roofs, and elaborate entry surrounds; later through the use of gable-front forms and temple-like porticos. The building boom saw the increasing use of more expensive brick rather than wood as a construction material and, of course, more multistoried construction. The center village especially was a very self-conscious creation, and so were the tastefully fashionable Federal and Greek Revival style buildings of those who shaped it (FIG. 7.2; see FIG. 7.1).

Center village morphology resulted from adaptation to site conditions and elaboration of the road network that had been laid down for other reasons in an earlier time. Disestablishment of church and town produced town commons from public portions of residual meetinghouse lots. The remainder of the lots were retained by the congregation for a new church building and expansion of the burying ground. Rebuilt roads and new turnpikes intersected at town centers-cum-center villages, reinforcing the comparative situation locally and solidifying the morphology, as now stately homes dressed the main thoroughfares framing the town common and leading from the center village. But despite its early commercial lead, New England's relative agricultural productivity failed to keep pace with developments elsewhere. Marginal agricultural areas experienced significant farm abandonment by the second quarter of the nineteenth century. Industrialization drew much of the surplus agricultural labor and reconfigured the emerging urban system of New England as well. Business in many towns migrated literally downhill from center villages to industrial villages, leaving only a burying ground and a small, open remnant of the old meetinghouse lot at a hilltop intersection of roads. Center villages became romantic backwaters in a landscape that Alfred Kazin has characterized as "the most conceivably left-over place that rapidly transforming America could provide" in the nineteenth century.[12] Decline and decay became the material grist for invention of tradition.

Image Formation

The four-stage process of invention of the village ensemble as a New England landscape tradition began with the preparation for colonization. The rhetoric of puritan intellectuals attempting to justify New England settlement served as the basis for image formation. John Winthrop, Massachusetts Bay's first governor, wrote that in their errand in the wilderness, colonists would build a new England, a community that would stand as an ideal for others, "as a city upon a hill."[13] The New England village ensemble bears the burden of this prophecy today, substantial house, town common, and center village standing for community forbearance in a period of strict political, religious, and societal discipline and economic competence. As literary historian Bruce Tucker has argued, "Whatever else New England was, it was a story, a creation of mind that each generation of ministers retold in order to connect New England to a central purpose that transcended their own time and place."[14] Puritans had employed town and village to create an English garden from an imagined New England wilderness. Over a century and a half, introspective and self-contained colonial townspeople carved out their garden landscape, and, as in time out of mind, looked to the meetinghouse at their town centers as symbolizing community, perambulated their bounds, and warned off strangers to protect their exclusivity. In so doing, they erased evidence of the non-European humanized landscape they had first encountered and then the early-implanted English subregional differences exemplified in architectural form and building practice. Proclaimed Jedediah Morse in his popular *American Universal Geography*, "It may in truth be said, that in no part of the world are people happier, better furnished with the necessaries and conveniences of life, or more independent than the farmers of New England." Fellow minister Timothy Dwight, president of Yale University from 1795 to 1817, celebrated the millennialist importance of New England and its institutions, convinced that New England's towns and villages had achieved near perfection architecturally, culturally, and spiritually.[15] The landscape sustained continuity with its New England founders and their ideals. The image of a new England with a bold history and an exceptional cultural geography was formed.

Myth Creation

Nineteenth-century New Englanders, caught up in the transition to industrial capitalism and Romantic cultural expression simultaneously, elaborated on the image. They created a myth of puritan antecedence, democratic society, and yankee patriotic fervor with attendant symbolic forms. The generations of New Englanders who built the stylish houses that encircled meetinghouse lots to form center villages in the early nineteenth century saw traditional ways of life withdraw and New England's predominant economic role in national life eclipsed, as forest cover crept back across abandoned farms. New Englanders vigorously promoted their cultural influence. They formed academies and lyceums to celebrate and perpetuate their cultural awareness and sophistication. They contributed significantly to the national cultural marketplace, in which symbolism correlated directly with commodification of the landscape.[16] In place of lost English symbols of the colonial era, they provided a new revolutionary iconography to foster linkages and loyalties between region and nation. And they carried New England ways and forms beyond New England. Churches, schools, and colleges; social, political, and economic enterprise; architectural and settlement plans; an evangelical impulse—all gave a veneer of New England culture and institutions to the national landscape.

Romanticism fused categories of nature, history, and fiction. The Romantic literary imagination imposed significance upon the world of things in a period of growing symbolic apprehension and social reproduction.[17] Landscape poetry, regional prose, and commemorative discourse thus exploited local life and landscape. Rufus Choate characterized the period in his 1833 oration on "The Importance of Illustrating New England History by a Series of Romances Like the Waverly Novels." Ralph Waldo Emerson's Romantic *Historical Discourse* on Concord (1835) translated Dwight's millennialism to the here and now, where the potential for those who lived by their highest spiritual capabilities to attain a state of perfection had been realized in the social and political institutions of the town. Novels from Catherine Maria Sedgwick's *A New England Tale* (1822) to Harriet Beecher Stowe's *Oldtown Folks* (1869) and *Poganuc People* (1878) glorified rustic settings and celebrated conventional New England ways.[18] Such literary endeavors reduced diachronic complexity and synchronic richness to a simplified, comprehensible, and orthodox set of images, narratives, and objects. New Englanders created as cultural orthodoxy the settlement ideal epitomized in the village ensemble. Puritans had established social order, economic security, and local self-government, employing towns and villages to convert wilderness to garden and capping their success with fine houses. The village ensemble was the tableau upon which history had been played out in this Romantic myth. By formalizing and ritualizing puritanism, covenanted community, and patriotism, myth justified a pastoral ideal of place-seated community, domestic tranquility, yeoman virtue, and precapitalist commerce, for which the village ensemble served as legitimate historical-geographical symbol.[19] Despite the considerable erasure of the colonial artifacts in the landscape of the early nineteenth century, "colonial" had been loosely used well into the twentieth century to mean the period before about 1840.[20] The term gave credence to myth creation in the face of modernization.

The tangible, visible landscape was both context and embodiment of Romantic myth creation. In local folk memories, the stratified, complex settlement landscape of the eighteenth century had been replaced by a simplified countryside and village landscape of large houses, many of which were the selective survivals of the colonial landscape. Reconception of the landscape appeared in local oral traditions, many of which later found their way into written local histories, family histories, and genealogies. These reconceptions most typically extended back in time the date at which a surviving house was built to link a later building with an earlier era. Eighteenth-century houses were given seventeenth-century construction dates. Houses from the regional building boom of the late eighteenth and early nineteenth centuries were projected back to before the Revolutionary period. The first, insubstantial house on a site was often conveniently forgotten, and the substantial, rebuilt house of the second or third generation of a family was projected back to the earliest resident, making all the more remarkable the transformation of wilderness into a controlled, humanized new English landscape, and substantiating the prowess of the family in question from the beginning. In Deerfield, Massachusetts, successful efforts to save the Parson Williams House from demolition in 1877 hinged on its alleged association with one of the survivors of the Deerfield massacre of 1704, despite later admission that it was probably built by Williams' son in the mid-eighteenth century and had nothing to do with the earlier event in local history. For the most part, however, it was the successful farming and professional families of the late eighteenth and early nineteenth centuries, the families who rebuilt or who located in the emerging center villages, whose identity, lineage, and social status were remembered in local folk history, and whose substantial, historic houses validated their social position.[21]

Landscape ideal converged most closely with landscape reality in the mid-nineteenth century, by which time both the present-day village ensemble and the Romantic myth had been intertwined with landscape design. As the village ensemble became visual icon for New England town in the popular imagination of the nineteenth century, village improvement and Romantic reconstruction proceeded apace. Horace Bushnell's "The Age of Homespun" had aroused interest in improvement of village landscapes after midcentury, the movement for village improvement built upon notions of community pride and civic responsibility to produce an attractive, sanitized, and satisfying landscape.[22] Residents and summer people alike insisted upon prosperous appearance, urban amenity, and Victorian taste. They built their stylish houses in Gothic or Italianate to harmonize with the aesthetic of the period and the picturesque nature of the landscape. Romanticism's aesthetic molded both the geographical imagination of Americans and their landscape.

Although New Englanders lamented the passing of their rural landscape, they found the source of their cultural enlightenment and their commercial enterprise in their Anglo-Saxon heritage. Colonial fathers in Boston, Salem, and New Haven had successfully laid a foundation for the economic and cultural development of the nineteenth century, the "age of homespun" symbolizing a glorious past. Brahmin historians of the mid-nineteenth century formalized the literary saga of Anglo-Saxon cultural superiority and New England centrality in the formation of American nationhood. Romantic creation of the myth went to extraordinary lengths to justify a past in which the

FIG. 7.3 The Great Centennial Celebration at Litchfield, Connecticut, 1851. It was on the common in the center village that New Englanders celebrated their past. (Drawing by J. Busch. Courtesy, Old Print Shop, Inc.—Kenneth M. Newman.)

mainstream of American political and cultural development flowed from "Plymouth to the present."[23] Through the incorporation of towns, puritans had sustained their principles, formed the New England character, promoted their industry and economy, provided for their education, and secured independence for the country as a whole. When New Englanders celebrated town founding or Independence Day and their patriotic revolutionary exploits with marches on the town common and with orations, songs, and prayers, they celebrated a glorious past, but not a past for which they were necessarily nostalgic or to which they wished to revert (FIG. 7.3).

Invented Tradition

New Englanders quite self-consciously projected the puritan-village ensemble into a national cultural symbol in the nation's centennial decade. Discontented with industrialization, urbanization, and immigration, disillusioned with the Civil War and reconstruction, and dismayed by financial panic in 1873, Americans increasingly came to extol a less complicated past and exhibit a fresh historical consciousness.[24] Myth became tradition as architects reinterpreted forms associated with the created past to contrive a revived colonial landscape. The popular enthusiasm for things colonial and for tangible signs of the past led to the invention of a strong national image of a traditional colonial New England landscape that was celebrated in public and private building form and landscape design and institutionalized by historical societies and architectural preservationists.

Architecture most effectively embodied the centennial revival of things colonial. In the early 1870s, *Harpers Magazine* had promoted popular interest with a series of articles on New England's picturesque historic ports and seaside regions. Enthusiastic were the descriptions of "colonial" architecture—for the most part the high-style landmarks of the merchant elites of the region's Federal period commercial economy. Community-level folk mythologies that had projected selective survivals back to the colonial period were amplified. Practicing architects studied Georgian and Federal buildings through sketches, measured drawings, and photographs. These endeavors reinforced the national image of a region dominated by substantial, multistory, classical town houses and estates. All of these endeavors helped create a national taste for a Colonial Revival out of an architectural image of a region dominated by substantial, stylish houses clustered about town commons in village settings.

The ideology of the Colonial Revival was of a simple, rationally ordered, harmonic, and visually appealing past environment. The domestic houses of New England became the objects of what Richard Guy Wilson calls the "vernacular fetishism" of American Arts-and-Crafts and Colonial Revival architects, who were seeking the native historical equivalent of British medieval and Queen Anne models.[25] That search was quite localized, directed primarily toward the architecture of New England's picturesque backwater coastal ports and their surrounding colonial era agricultural neighborhoods, areas that in the late nineteenth century were developing as the stylish seaside resorts and suburban country estate districts where many of the leading architects were obtaining their commissions. These were areas, of course, that had indeed contained unusually high proportions of multistory, high-style eighteenth-century buildings. For example, Vincent Scully notes the efforts of the influential architect Charles F. McKim in search of vernacular forms in Newport, Rhode Island, and its immediate hinterland in the mid-1870s, a search that included the commissioning of documentary photographs of early buildings.[26] By the late 1870s, in New England's cultural capital, the

Boston Society of Architects and the Boston Chapter of the American Institute of Architects both began to sponsor competitions for the best measured drawings of colonial houses. Simultaneously, national architectural journals began publishing drawings and extolling the merits of Georgian and Federal buildings.[27]

Various architectural preservation societies and historical institutions collaborated in this invention of tradition, creating "a common fund of approved and communicable experience."[28] The rediscovery of the "colonial" architecture by elite architects in the postcentennial decades had coincided with a more broadly based appearance of these societies to preserve buildings with significant historical associations. The dramatic saving of the Old South Meetinghouse in Boston from demolition in 1877 marked the beginning of a sometimes militant regional movement to preserve buildings associated with the Revolutionary era, ancestral homesteads, or birthplaces of historic figures.[29] Local historical societies, chapters of the Daughters of the American Revolution, and family associations purchased and "restored" buildings to secure a physical link that perpetuated these groups' connections to an earlier era. In the context of the demographic changes happening in New England in the period, Rhoads has characterized these groups as "nativist organizations out to defend the relics of the old, pre-Irish, pre-Italian New England."[30]

The tradition extended throughout New England in the centennial period, initiating a new phase of village improvement, during which town commons became village greens. Commemorative "centennial" trees and monuments memorialized New England's contribution to the Revolution and the Civil War and enhanced the symbolic quality of village greens. Elms were especially popular because of their distinctive branching pattern and rapid growth. The fruits of village improvement, Victorian gazebos, bandstands, fountains, and sculptured flower beds, along with fences that kept traffic off the plantings, enabled townspeople and villagers to use greens for endless community activities, carnivals, auctions, fairs, and patriotic celebrations to elaborate the tradition.[31]

The effect of celebrating and institutionalizing the invented tradition was most clearly expressed in New England's elite landscape. Wealthy urbanites replicated the aesthetic of the Colonial Revival to further reshape the New England landscape and our subsequent conception of it. Fragments of the historic landscape were combined in picturesque suburban or seaside settings and gentrified locales for urbane living in the booming resort and exurban economy of the late nineteenth century. In interior New England, the

Fɪɢ. 7.4 Leicester, Massachusetts, from Mt. Pleasant. This late-nineteenth-century photograph celebrates the great cultural, if not economic, success of John Winthrop's dream of "a city upon a hill." (Courtesy, American Antiquarian Society.)

process typically involved the self-conscious transformation of the landscape of the late-eighteenth- and early-nineteenth-century elite into a utopian, suburban, resort landscape. The gentrification of places like Stockbridge, Deerfield, and Litchfield created a contrived, colonial-revival landscape out of the two-story, high-style houses of these quite unrepresentative center villages. New Englanders had successfully invented a selected past represented by the village ensemble of large houses, town commons, and center villages, an icon of puritan antecedence and yankee patriotism—Winthrop's "city upon a hill" (ꜰɪɢ. 7.4).

Universalization

Myth creation and tradition invention attached colonial geography to the nineteenth-century landscape. As the tradition became universalized—and intertwined—in popular and academic minds, so the landscape not only objectified the tradition but also proved it. Especially the concentration of studies in the first years of professional historiography and architectural history on colonial New England drew attention to that region—attention that continues today out of all proportion to the historical study of other periods and regions. Such attention, for a region which Meinig notes was "eccentric and contingent," reinforced the received scholarly tradition of the village ensemble in the present century.[32]

Contemporary historiography of the New England village ensemble begins with Herbert Baxter Adams. His theory that "the town and village life of New England is as truly the reproduction of Old English types as those again are reproductions of the village community system of the ancient Germans" was simple and plausible. It served as the working hypothesis for a generation of historians who produced an uncomplicated and tidy view of New England.[33] Anne Bush MacLear summarized the tradition in a widely circulated 1908 monograph:

> The New England town of the seventeenth century was a village community settled for purposes of good neighborhood and defense. Its most characteristic features resulted from the topography of the country, and from the ideas of the nature of a town which colonists brought from England. Forced by the geographical features of New England and by the necessity of protection, the colonists, already acquainted, settled in groups, and at once began organizing their settlements in accordance with the type familiar to them—the old English manor.[34]

One could then easily explain colonial garrison houses with second-story overhangs—constructed to pour boiling water on attacking Indians—and town commons—relict cow pastures. American scholars of the late nineteenth century, like their European counterparts, participated in the universalization of a previous generation's invented Romantic tradition and shaped conventional wisdom to this day.

Proliferation of architectural renderings in the early twentieth century helped further popularize what had become a scholarly tradition. Villagers in Litchfield, an eighteenth-century shire town, restored houses through exterior architectural change, enlarged actual colonial remnants, colonialized early-nineteenth-century structures, and divested Victorian houses of their Romantic and Gothic elements, dressing them with pilasters, balustrades, and black or dark green shutters. Or they built new, modern "colonial" houses.

They romanticized, sentimentalized, idealized, and refined "colonial" settings, and in 1913 undertook further extensive colonializing, renovating, restoring, and re-siting of structures to fit a set of architect-inspired "Colonial Plans for Litchfield." Today, Litchfield carries National Historic Landmark status, the *Report on the National Survey of Historic Sites and Buildings on Litchfield, Connecticut* noting that it is "probably New England's finest surviving example of a typical late eighteenth century New England town."[35]

Twentieth-century colonializing was not restricted to gentrified villages or backwater landscapes. Weyerhauser and other lumber interests promoted *The White Pine Series of Architectural Monographs* to stimulate use of wood construction. For two decades after 1915, the *White Pine Series* disseminated essays, photographs, and drawings of colonial and Federal era architecture. Winning design competition drawings of colonial-revival suburban residences and public buildings were interspersed with the historical documentation and promotional texts on the superior virtues of wood as a building material.[36] *The White Pine Series*, of course, drew on elite mansions with high-style details suitable for replication. The image of colonial New England that resulted was that of a wealthy region of urbane taste, where the massive, picturesque, shingle-clad arks of the seventeenth century were quickly followed by even larger, classical "Georgian" town houses and country seats. The series was unprecedented in its region-by-region approach. Part of its power came from its inclusion of all the New England states and many subregions. Its architectural catalog appeared sufficiently comprehensive that a later generation of scholars may have been tempted to equate lumber sales propaganda for vernacular documentation.[37] In fact, *The White Pine Series* followed the well-worn path of the standard itinerary of mythical New England established by *Harpers* in the 1870s, making the usual stops at the picturesque backwater ports of the New England coast, as well as at the inland centers of the Colonial Revival, like Litchfield, Stockbridge, Deerfield, and Concord, which epitomized the village ensemble.[38]

Historiographical debate in the twentieth century shifted from a focus on origins of town and village to religious declension among later generations of colonial New Englanders. The change affected understanding of settlement and architectural form. Settlement, it was argued, had challenged perpetuation of religious and social orthodoxy, the pillars of colonial New England conformity, and had caused dissolution of community life, increased commercialism, modification of architectural forms and styles, and dispersal of settlement from initial house lots and compact agricultural villages. Geog-

FIG. 7.5 Waitsfield, Vermont, c. 1900. Late-nineteenth-century villages, even in stark landscapes, retained tradition. Compare with FIG. I.1, Arlington, Vermont, in 1852, painted a half century before this photograph for a similar, if more picturesque, landscape portrayal. Compare as well with FIG. 7.4, Leicester in central Massachusetts, a contemporary if ostensibly more wealthy place than Waitsfield in central Vermont. (Courtesy, Erik A. Davis.)

raphers Edna Scofield and Glenn Trewartha built on declension theory and sociological theories of ideal-type settlement forms a model of progressive stages of colonial settlement form, from nucleated to linear to dispersed. Both Scofield and Trewartha, citing Anne Bush MacLear, published their research in *The Geographical Review*.[39] The convention was established with Ralph Brown in *The Historical Geography of the United States*, citing Scofield and Trewartha and many of their authorities.[40] Today, most contemporary texts in cultural geography that mention New England have come to confirm the convention in geographical thought.[41]

Similarly, students of domestic colonial architecture proposed models of progressive stages of house plan and form that implicitly paralleled social development from the pioneering through the commercial phases of New

England's history. Despite the detractors of J. Frederick Kelly's stage model of the 1920s, folklife scholars and geographers in the 1960s and 1970s adopted it to define New England as a dynamic and expanding culture region.[42] Henry Glassie called Kelly's book "the most important work on New England houses," while Fred Kniffen, Peirce Lewis, and others perpetuated an image of a region dominated by substantial, two-story "folk" and "vernacular" houses of the type promoted in the colonial revival catalogs.[43] The disappearance of much of the eighteenth-century landscape of small houses and town centers, the selective survival of the best-built, large houses of the period, and the rise of center villages in the early nineteenth century meant that the landscape itself confirmed both the popular image and the scholarly conception of house, common, and village.

Conclusion

Colonial New England was a land of modest, dispersed, one-story farmsteads. Nineteenth-century commercial elites remade the landscape, which Romantic elites then transformed into an imaginary colonial landscape of stylish houses encircling a town common in a puritan village. Like seventeenth-century English colonists before them, the imaginations of local folk, fiction writers, revivalist architects, genealogists, nativists, preservationists, and scholars all created colonial New Englands of the mind. The invention of tradition was a vehicle for modernization in the nineteenth century that operated on a variety of levels and in different contexts, with house, common, and village logical physical and symbolic entities through which multiple generations have played out their historical-geographical fantasies of a glorious past and a utopian present. The village ensemble, wherever one finds it across New England (FIG. 7.5), carries the burden of the tradition still today, a realized myth and essential ingredient in the social reproduction of our world.

Notes

PREFACE

1. Bumsted and Lemon 1968, p. 99. But see also E. Brown 1975, pp. 309–10, who argued that "we should stop trying to use amateur local histories for our scholarly purposes."
2. An exception is A. Hudson 1904.
3. See, for instance, Scofield 1938; Reps 1965; and Reps 1969.

INTRODUCTION

1. See, for instance, Bridenbaugh 1946; Haller 1951; Arensberg 1955; Reps 1969; and Sutter 1973. Powell 1963; Greven 1970; Lockridge 1970; and Stilgoe 1976b all recognized early breakdown of compact settlements in the seventeenth century. Rutman 1965a; Rutman 1965b; Rutman 1967; Bumsted and Lemon 1968; and Merrens 1975 all expressed misgivings with the pervasiveness of the tradition.
2. Marvin 1868, p. 389.

CHAPTER 1: THE COLONIAL ENCOUNTER WITH THE LAND

Originally published as J. Wood 1994.
1. See, among such works, Allen 1982; Cronon 1983; Cressy 1987; Greene 1988; Merchant 1989; Fischer 1989; Canup 1990; J. Martin 1991; and Anderson 1991.
2. See, for instance, Scofield 1938; Trewartha 1946; R. H. Brown 1948; Hart 1975; McManis 1975. I have previously challenged the conventional wisdom regarding form itself in J. Wood 1982a.
3. Individual town studies invariably address the unique environmental features that appealed to the town's first settlers, but systematic studies of the geographical distribution of settlements relative to agricultural resources are rare. McManis 1975, pp. 42–56, provided a concise summary of settlement expansion. See also Friis 1968. Meinig 1986 places settlement in the larger context of the Atlantic world.
Many have recognized a correlation between agricultural resources and settlement, but not adequately developed the argument, including Weeden 1891; Garvin 1951; McManis

1975; Russell 1976; and Anderson 1991. Daniels 1979, pp. 172, 188–90, comes closest to such a systematic study, employing an analysis of soil types relative to settlement chronology, but he fails adequately to distinguish among land types and local qualitative differences.

4. Jordan 1989.

5. Bowden 1992; J. Wood and Steinitz 1992; Earle 1992.

6. Cantor 1987, pp. 4–12, 49; Coones and Patten 1986, pp. 215–17; Garvin 1951, p. 60.

7. Cantor 1987, pp. 10–37, 45.

8. Ibid., pp. 4–12, 34–47; Coones and Patten 1986, p. 215.

9. Laslett 1965, pp. 53–80, may overstate the case.

10. Cantor 1987, pp. 65–69.

11. Ibid.; Blum 1971, pp. 157–67; Anderson 1991, pp. 28–30.

12. Some would argue that this was the Agricultural Revolution. Cantor 1987, pp. 34, 38; Greene 1988, pp. 30–35.

13. Cantor 1987, pp. 23–49; Cressy 1987, pp. 74–94; Greene 1988, pp. 31–34.

14. Anderson 1985, pp. 368–74; Anderson 1991, p. 35; Vickers 1990, p. 12.

15. Canup 1990, p. 4; Anderson 1985, pp. 372–74; Cressy 1987, pp. 86–94, 98.

16. Cantor 1987, p. 27; Anderson 1985, pp. 352–53, 358, 361–65, 367; Anderson 1991, p. 31; Cressy 1987, pp. 64–67.

17. Anderson 1985, p. 351; Cressy 1987, pp. 45, 52–63, 66; Courtwright 1987, p. 11.

18. Greene 1988, pp. 34, 196–97; Vickers 1990, p. 29.

19. Anderson 1985, p. 356; Fischer 1989, pp. 30–47.

20. Cressy 1987, pp. 87–98; Fischer 1989, pp. 189–90; Anderson 1991, pp. 17ff.; D. Hall 1989, pp. 18, 119; Greene 1988, p. 21. Parenthetically, D. Hall 1989, p. 4, n. 1, argues that puritanism lacks any real precision and may be best understood as referring to a tendency within the Church of England to practice strict discipline. Hence, Cressy 1987, p. viii, decapitalizes it, as I do, to deemphasize its uniqueness.

21. D. Hall 1989, p. 9; Anderson 1991, pp. 42–45; Greene 1988, pp. 21–22, 36–38; and Cressy 1987, p. 45. See also Innes 1991.

22. Kupperman 1982, pp. 1262–89; Earle 1992, p. 486.

23. Cronon 1983, 25.

24. On subregions in New England, see Bowden 1989; and Bowden 1992.

25. Cotton 1654, as quoted in Stilgoe 1976b, p. 7.

26. East 1944, p. 256.

27. Bradford 1921, p. 201.

28. W. Wood 1865, pp. 11–12.

29. Winthrop 1825–26, 1:160. See also Cronon 1983, p. 141.

30. On the nature of grasslands, see Cronon 1983, pp. 25–33; as well as Jorgenson 1971; and Thomson 1977.

31. Anderson 1991, p. 155.

32. Pruitt 1978, as cited by Merchant 1989, p. 277.

33. McManis 1975, pp. 42–56, provides a concise summary of settlement expansion. For case studies of a number of towns, see J. Wood 1978.

34. Garvin 1951, pp. 14–15.

35. W. Wood 1865, p. 49.

36. Winthrop, 1825–26, 1:132.

37. Ekwall 1960, pp. 213–14; Mawer 1924, 1:26, 32

38. See Meinig 1962, pp. 394–413.

39. J. Martin 1991, pp. 10–12, notes peripatetic pion

40. Anderson 1985, pp. 346–48; Anderson 1991, p.
found immigrants from common-field, enclosed-farm,
many traits left behind. See also Fischer 1989, pp. 56–6

41. Anderson 1991, pp. 127–30.

42. *Records of Massachusetts Bay* 1853–55, 1:179; Has
pp. 65–67; Allen 1982, pp. 223ff.; Fischer 1989, p. 198. S

43. Kishlansky 1980, p. 146.

44. Cantor 1987, p. 8; Vickers 1990; Fischer 1989, pp.

45. Haller 1951, pp. 53, 133; Egleston 1886, pp. 42, 47;

46. Akagi 1924, p. 294; J. Martin 1991.

47. Allen 1982, pp. 30–37, 121–31.

48. Allen 1982, pp. 205–22; Greene 1988, pp. 59–60.

49. See, for instance, Rutman 1965a, p. 9; Daniels 1979.
Cronon 1983, pp. 73–74; Fischer 1989, pp. 158–59, 184.

50. McManis 1975, pp. 95–96; Russell 1976, pp. 30–47;
1991, pp. 151–54.

51. Stilgoe 1983, p. 184; Cronon 1983, pp. 141–42.

52. Cressy 1987, pp. 178ff., 292.

53. Greene 1988, p. 197; Fischer 1989, pp. 72–73; Vance 19

54. J. Wood 1982a.

55. Found among the *Winthrop Papers*. Massachusetts His
and cited by Donnelly 1968, p. 17; and Stilgoe 1976b, p. 3.

56. Bradford 1921, pp. 201, 253.

57. *Records of Massachusetts Bay* 1853–55, 1:76.

58. Ibid., 1:159. The order was cited by Scofield 1938, p. 65;
Morris 1951, p. 221; and Stilgoe 1976b, p. 3, for instance.

59. Rutman 1965a, p. 78; Powell 1963, p. 81; and Breen and I

60. Carroll 1969, p. 142.

61. *Records of Massachusetts Bay* 1853–55, 1:181, 210, 227, 291

62. Carroll 1969, pp. 254–55.

63. *Records of Massachusetts Bay* 1853–55, 2:96–97.

64. Ibid., 5:66 (1675).

65. Rutman 1965a, pp. 69–70, 76, 89–90, 93–95. See the map
p. 71.

66. Carroll 1969, pp. 127–28, 144, details the tensions of cohes
the paradox of encouraging expansion with large grants of meado
defensive outposts in the 1630s.

67. J. Martin 1991.

68. Pillsbury 1987, pp. 37–54, provides a model for regional dev
graphical space.

Zuckerman 1977, pp. 183–214; Carroll 1969, pp. 127–28, 133, 140–47, 182–87; 1990, p. 29.

Cressy 1987, p. 14.

Vance 1990b, p. 206.

ER 2: VILLAGE AND COMMUNITY IN THE SEVENTEENTH CENTURY

ally published as J. Wood 1982a.

On settlement form, see Scofield 1938; Trewartha 1946; Morris 1951; and McManis On New England communities, see Powell 1963; Bushman 1967; Lockridge 1970; n 1970; and Daniels 1979.

Rutman 1973, p. 58.

Ibid., pp. 62–63; Bender 1978, p. 7 (including n. 4).

Tuan 1977, p. 3; see also Bender 1978, p. 61; Rutman 1973, pp. 62–63; and Kauf-1959.

Newton 1974.

Oxford English Dictionary 1933, s.v. "village."

Webster's New International Dictionary 1935, s.v. "village."

Demangeon 1927; Christaller 1967. As an objective measure, Martyn J. Bowden of University in personal communication has suggested that a nucleated settlement e in which more than four neighbors dwell purposefully within hailing distance of another, perhaps one hundred meters. Four houses located by chance at a crossroads not be considered a nucleated settlement.

Dickinson 1949; Pfeifer 1956.

o. Thirsk 1967a; Homans 1969.

1. See, for example, Powell 1963; Lockridge 1970; and Greven 1970.

2. Rutman 1973, p. 67, n. 29; Breen 1975, p. 20; Breen 1978, p. 9.

3. J. Wood 1978, pp. 58–202.

14. Allen 1981; Breen and Foster 1973a; Lemon 1980a, pp. 119–21.

15. Winthrop 1825–26, 2:263. See also *Records of Massachusetts Bay* 1853–55, 2:135.

16. Haller 1951; McCutcheon 1970.

17. A. Lewis and Newhall 1865, p. 131; R. Johnson 1973, p. 251.

18. *Records of Massachusetts Bay* 1853–55, 1:272; 3:7.

19. Dwight 1821–22, 1:216 (emphasis added).

20. Ibid. (emphasis added).

21. E. Johnson 1867, p. 46 (emphasis added).

22. *Records of Massachusetts Bay* 1853–55, 2:17.

23. Hazen 1883, pp. 24–26.

24. *Records of Massachusetts Bay* 1853–55, 5:247–48; Upham 1867; Perley 1916, . 177–91; Boyer and Nissenbaum 1974; Gildrie 1975. The use of the term *town* in this ntext suggests that, like *village*, it could be ambiguous in colonial New England. In New ngland, as in England, *town* could refer to a major market center, like Salem or Boston, well as an incorporated township. For additional comments, see Earle 1977.

25. On the classification of towns by order, see McCutcheon 1970.

26. *Records of Massachusetts Bay* 1853–55, 1:306, 319; 2:10–11, 17; Abbot 1829, pp. 12,

47, 74–76; Greven 1965, pp. 133–48; G. Chase 1861, pp. 42, 61. See also Powell 1963; and Lockridge 1970.

27. *Records of Massachusetts Bay* 1853–55, 2:11; pt. 2, 4:408–9; Lincoln 1837, pp. 6–7, 30–31, 43.

28. *Records of Massachusetts Bay* 1853–55, pt. 2, 4:528–29; Temple and Sheldon 1875, p. 165; *Public Records of Connecticut* 1850–90, 2:255; 3:1; Davis 1870, pp. 78–79.

29. J. Wood 1978, pp. 102–7, 117–36; Daniels 1979, p. 97; and Bender 1978, p. 72, n. 70.

30. Hughes 1908, pp. 67–75; Deming 1933, p. 68.

31. *Public Records of Connecticut* 1850–90, 4:15–16.

32. Ibid., 4:123–24.

33. Ibid., 5:63.

34. Ibid., 5:521.

35. Ibid., 3:190; *Records of Massachusetts Bay* 1853–55, 5:213–14, 311–12.

36. Scofield 1938; Trewartha 1946.

37. Thirsk 1967a; Homans 1969. See also Allen 1981 for detailed discussion of several distinct source communities.

38. A significant statement on this point is Allen 1981.

39. Laslett 1965, pp. 53–80, may overstate the case. See also Harris 1977, p. 471, esp. n. 6; Thirsk 1967b, p. 225.

40. Hill 1975; Thirsk 1967a, pp. 6–7; Russell 1976, pp. 26–27; Stilgoe 1976a.

41. Zuckerman 1977, pp. 183–214; see also Carroll 1969, pp. 133, 140–47, 182–87.

42. Allen 1981; Breen 1978, p. 5, n. 5; Warden 1978, pp. 687–88.

43. Harris 1977 elaborates on this process; but see also Mitchell 1979; Pollock 1979; and Harris 1979. Allen 1981, p. 222, argues that the trend away from open fields was faster in New England than was possible in England. On material culture, see Cummings 1979.

44. Allen 1981, pp. 231–32.

45. McManis 1975, pp. 92–102.

46. Murrin 1972, p. 231.

47. Bender 1978, pp. 63–68, provides a full summary of community in New England. See also Rutman 1973; Henretta 1978; Breen and Foster 1973b; Breen 1978.

48. *Public Records of Connecticut* 1850–90, 6:121; Davis 1870, p. 125; Gillespie 1906.

49. E. Johnson 1867, p. 44.

50. Tuan 1977, p. 166. Lemon 1978, pp. 198–99, argues that a critical difference between community in Pennsylvania and community in New England was the fixing of parish or town bounds to provide a strong sense of place for community groups.

51. McCutcheon 1970; and Daniels 1979 are good sources on the division of towns. The process of towns dividing into smaller units or sending out new villages, parishes, or towns has long been called "hiving off." The analogy is inappropriate because it suggests a nucleated settlement splitting to form another nucleated settlement, or hive.

52. Bender 1978, pp. 72–73; Rutman 1973, p. 68.

53. Zuckerman 1970. Bender 1978, pp. 3–13, 75–78, argues that a historically grounded concept of community is one that allows the alteration of its social structure—and by implication its spatial structure—to meet new conditions without necessarily breaking down.

54. See Daniels 1979, p. 173; and Lemon 1980a, pp. 129–30.

55. Lowenthal 1979.

56. J. Wood 1978, pp. 203–85.

CHAPTER 3: THE ARCHITECTURAL LANDSCAPE

Originally published as Steinitz 1989.

1. Sauer 1925.

2. See, for example, Sauer 1941.

3. Kniffen 1936.

4. Examples are Spencer 1945; Zelinsky 1953; and Zelinsky 1958.

5. A useful collection of citations to geographical publications from this period that made reference to housing can be found in Rickert 1967.

6. J. Jackson 1952; J. Jackson 1953; J. Jackson 1956–57; J. Jackson 1959–60.

7. Kniffen 1965; Glassie 1968.

8. See Zelinsky 1973, pp. 88–94; P. Lewis 1975.

9. Carson et al. 1981; Stone 1977.

10. Kniffen 1965, pp. 558–59; Glassie 1968, pp. 124–33.

11. Pillsbury and Kardos 1970; V. McAlester and L. McAlester 1984; Noble 1984.

12. This field assessment is supported by files on more than seven hundred Worcester County houses in Massachusetts Historical Commission's *Inventory of the Historic Assets of the Commonwealth of Massachusetts* n.d. For a general interpretation of the region's domestic architecture from this period, see Worsham 1985.

13. Brunskill 1978, pp. 26–29. The extent to which Brunskill's rule may apply to rural landscapes as recent as the late nineteenth century is suggested by King 1987.

14. My attention was initially drawn to the census through its use by Brooke 1982 and through discussions with Claire Dempsey.

15. See the Congressional Acts reprinted in Gorn 1979; also Soltow 1985.

16. Data on eleven towns were available on microfilm from the New England Historic Genealogical Society. Information on three additional towns was located in the manuscript collections of the American Antiquarian Society. For each house, six variables (town location, house-plan area, story height, number of windows, area of glass, and value) were entered and analyzed.

17. On the likely prevalence of small houses in the coastal lowlands in the seventeenth century, see Cummings 1979, pp. 22–24; and Candee 1969, pp. 105–11. For Cape Cod, see Connally 1960; and Dempsey 1987, pp. 163–68, 171–77.

18. Carson et al. 1981. For Virginia, see Glassie 1975, p. 65; but see also the critique of Glassie's interpretation, based on the evidence of the 1798 census for Maryland, in Stone 1977, pp. 45–53. For the Delaware Valley in New Jersey, Pennsylvania, and Maryland, see Herman 1987a. For Delaware, see Herman 1987b.

19. Brooke 1982, p. 527.

20. Hubka 1984, p. 37, has drawn similar conclusions on the social distinctions between dwellers of one-story houses and those of two-story houses in early-nineteenth-century Maine.

21. Latimer, R. Martin, and Lanphear 1927.

22. For the Connecticut Valley, my analysis of the 1798 census data essentially agrees

with the interpretation of Sweeney 1984, pp. 42–43. Although my calculations for South Hadley show only 40 percent of the houses there to have been of two stories, in nearby Granby and Easthampton, two-thirds of the houses were two stories high in 1798, as were half the houses in Southampton.

23. Pruitt 1984.

24. Carson et al. 1981, pp. 171–75.

25. Meinig 1986, p. 445.

CHAPTER 4: VILLAGES IN THE FEDERAL PERIOD

Originally published as J. Wood 1984.

1. Christaller 1967, pp. 14–20, 140–41; and Barton 1978, pp. 34–35.

2. Lemon 1972; McManis 1975; Cook 1976; Daniels 1979.

3. Christaller 1967, pp. 118–19; Vance 1970.

4. Barton 1978, p. 39; Christaller 1967, pp. 107ff.

5. McManis 1975, p. 74.

6. Christaller 1967, pp. 11, 122.

7. Ibid., pp. 16–19, 139–40; Barton 1978, pp. 40–44; Daniels 1979, p. 160.

8. Christaller 1967, pp. 17, 105, 152–55.

9. Newton 1974, p. 358. Also note Wheatley 1971, p. 225; Wagner 1972, pp. 45–49; and Rapoport 1982.

10. Dow 1893; Temple 1887, pp. 2, 107–8.

11. McManis 1975, pp. 72–84.

12. Sawtelle 1878, p. 145.

13. MacLear 1908, p. 31; Powell 1963; Greven 1970; McCutcheon 1970; Winslow 1952; Bushman 1967, pp. 60ff; Zuckerman 1970. Boyer and Nissenbaum 1974, pp. 39–45, described the process of division in Salem. Daniels 1979, pp. 34–43.

14. See Winthrop 1825–26, 2:254; Egleston 1886, pp. 32–33; Larned 1880, 1:65; Bushman 1967, p. 81; Gage 1840, pp. 360–66. Roy 1965, p. 56, referred to General Court records without citation. Sample data for Connecticut before 1776 were collected from the Connecticut State Library, Archives, Ecclesiastical Affairs, and provided by Christopher Collier, University of Connecticut. See also Daniels 1979, pp. 14, 24, 34, 41, 183–85; Haller 1951, p. 18.

15. McCutcheon 1970 provided a wealth of detail on the division process. On Connecticut, see Daniels 1979, pp. 8–44, 183–85.

16. Calculations are based on state, county, and town records for towns and parishes in 1800. The radius for a meetinghouse was thus about three miles or an hour's journey on foot or by cart. Doxiadis 1972, p. 80, argued that the basic underlying system of settlements everywhere was established on spacing of two hours' distance. Brush and Bracey 1955, p. 568, similarly suggested that places are generally four to six miles apart. The cultural tradition seems long-standing.

17. Akagi 1924, pp. 190ff.; Stackpole 1916, 1:365.

18. Daniels 1979, p. 162, argued that town centers in eighteenth-century Connecticut were more generally inhabited and, thus, the central-place system more fully developed; Barton 1978, p. 40, misconstrued the relatively insignificant extralocal role of the tavern in colonial times.

19. Cushing 1961; Staples 1890; Speare 1938, pp. 69, 147.

20. The changing character of the colonial rural economy, the causes of change, and the pace of change are elements in an ongoing argument. Henretta 1978 claims that commercialization began only after 1750. Lemon 1980b disagrees; for Lemon, far more continuity existed with early English ways. See also Lemon 1980a; Lemon 1981. A. Jones 1980 describes the relative wealth accumulated by New Englanders but does not provide a clear picture of market activity inland.

21. Carman 1939, p. 50, as cited by Bushman 1967, p. 108.

22. See especially H. Hall 1917; Schumacher 1948; Grant 1961; Stiverson 1976, pp. 37–44; A. Jones 1980, pp. 77–79, 111, 304; as well as Loehr 1952, pp. 37–41; A. Clark 1972; and Parks 1972. See also Dexter 1916, p. 409.

23. Rutman 1973; also see Henretta 1978, p. 19; and Lemon 1980a, p. 128.

24. For a general overview of agriculture in colonial New England, see Russell 1976.

25. Schumacher 1948, p. 88; A. Jones 1980, pp. 152, 201–2. See also J. Smith 1876, p. 46. Grant 1961, p. 69, noted that in the 1770s there was an average of twenty outstanding debts per adult male in Kent, Connecticut. Winterbotham 1795, 3:308–9. Temple 1887, p. 239, listed a large number of craftsmen in Framingham between 1710 and 1760, including at one time or another eight cordwainers, two weavers, two blacksmiths, two housewrights, a cabinetmaker, and a saddler.

26. D. Smith 1972, pp. 165, 171; Lockridge 1968, pp. 62–68; Greven 1970; Henretta 1971, p. 380; Rutman 1975, pp. 268–92; Waters 1982, pp. 64–68; Osterud and Fulton 1976, pp. 492–93; Easterlin 1976, p. 70; and Forster and Tucker 1972 address the demographic characteristics.

27. See Jensen 1968; J. Andrews 1955, pp. 99–110; Hooker 1936; Schumacher 1948; Bushman 1967, p. 135; Gross 1976, pp. 87, 172–73.

28. Newcomer 1953, pp. 109ff., 132; Saladino 1964, p. 43; Schlebecker 1976, pp. 35–36; Stiverson 1976; Bender 1978, pp. 78–79; Zuckerman 1970.

29. North 1961, p. 62; A. Jones 1980, pp. 82–84. See also Doherty 1977; Kendall 1809, 1:89; M. Martin 1938–39, p. 13; B. Labaree 1962; C. White 1947.

30. Winterbotham 1795, 3:304.

31. See, for instance, C. Clark 1979, pp. 169–89; Olson, 1935, pp. 9–10; Schumacher 1948, p. 144; McManis 1975, p. 101. See also Bidwell 1921, pp. 683–702; Purcell 1918, pp. 114, 158ff.; and Cahill 1970.

32. See Massachusetts Secretary of State 1836; Dodd 1954, pp. 196–97; O. Handlin and M. Handlin 1969; Kessler 1949, pp. 45–47; C. Clark 1979.

33. Old Sturbridge Village 1962, Appendixes I–IV. See also map in J. Wood 1978, p. 211.

34. See F. Wood 1919, esp. p. 63; Mead 1911, p. 186.

35. Parks 1966, p. 96; A. White 1920, pp. 94–95; Kendall 1809, 1:138–39; see also J. Smith 1876, p. 507; J. Wood 1978, p. 214.

36. A statistical account of the towns and parishes in the State of Connecticut 1811, p. 22; A. Jones 1980, p. 331. See also Schumacher 1948, p. 67; Saladino 1964, pp. 346–47; Davis 1870, p. 149; G. Wheeler and H. Wheeler 1878, p. 216; Temple 1887, p. 342; L. Brown 1968, p. 97.

37. Mead 1911, p. 185; L. Brown 1968, p. 97; Fox 1846, p. 193; Frizzell 1955, p. 257.

38. Winterbotham 1795, 2:14. See also M. Martin 1938–39, pp. 15–17; Brigham 1947; C. Clark 1979, p. 177; Rich 1924, pp. 182–83. See R. D. Brown 1974; Nelson 1975; Bushman 1967, p. 288; Saladino 1964, pp. 353–54; Massachusetts Secretary of State 1836.

39. Cochrane and G. Wood 1895, pp. 411–21; J. Smith 1869, p. 142; Temple 1887, pp. 351–53.

40. McLellan 1903, p. 262; Kendall 1809, 3:241, 243; Swift 1859, pp. 235ff.; Frizzell 1963, p. 569. J. Wood 1978, pp. 221–71, further documents graphically the rise of villages.

41. See Vance 1970; Polanyi 1944, pp. 56–60, for discussions of the "reach of trade" beyond the local community and its importance with respect to settlement patterns. Larned 1880, 2:240, 358. Newcomer 1953, p. 155, listed several newspaper advertisements for stores. See also J. Smith 1876, p. 46; Howes n.d., p. 48; Kellogg 1902, p. 70; E. Smith et al. 1924, pp. 94, 103; Stearns 1875, p. 375; Hubbard and Dartt 1895, p. 31; Lancaster 1845, p. 136; Annett and Lehtinen 1937, p. 398; Gilbert 1907, p. 362; Cole and Whitman 1915, p. 94; Williamson 1877, pp. 209, 639; French 1886, p. 80.

42. Because existing patterns determine subsequent patterns, Vance 1970, pp. 2–3, is correct that Christaller's 1967 central places are indeed a special regional case reflecting a system of medieval German villages. But Vance's model of an untouched world settled under European mercantilism (p. 148) is also a special case. Both of Vance's arguments bolster Christaller's point (pp. 47–48) that the prevailing pattern of interaction determines the resultant pattern of central places. Christaller (p. 191) also discussed reasons for differences in spacing between similar-order places.

43. Theoretically a hierarchy is based on a geometric progression determining a prescribed number of central places to be found in each order. The geometric progression reflects the interaction pattern upon which the system is built. Christaller 1967, pp. 60–80.

44. Bushnell 1846, p. 3.

45. Temple 1887, p. 156.

46. See Christaller 1967, p. 104, for elaboration.

47. Larned 1880, 2:358–59; Cochran and G. Wood 1895, p. 332; S. Wood 1908, p. 147. *Centennial Proceedings and Other Historical Facts and Incidents Relating to Newfane* 1877, pp. 25–28.

48. LeBlanc 1969, p. 18.

49. M. Jones 1909, pp. 54, 117; Foster and Streeter 1974, p. 346.

CHAPTER 5: THE VILLAGE AS A VERNACULAR FORM

Originally published as J. Wood 1986.

1. J. Wood 1982a; and J. Wood 1984.

2. J. Wood 1982b, p. 40; Dow 1893; J. Johnson 1917; Boyle 1945; C. Andrews 1889; Temple and Sheldon 1875; L. Labaree 1933; Wilcoxson 1939; Worthington 1827; Lockridge 1970; A. Hudson 1889; Powell 1963; R. Wheeler 1967; Abbot 1829; Greven 1970; G. Chase 1861.

3. McManis 1975, pp. 72–85; R. Wheeler 1967; Lincoln 1837; Larned 1880; A. White 1920.

4. J. Wood 1982a, pp. 339–40. Cummings 1979 argues for the simultaneous creolizing of architectural forms.

5. J. Wood 1984.

6. Levine 1971.

7. Larkin 1978.

8. Cochrane and G. Wood 1895; S. Wood 1908.

9. *Centennial Proceedings and Other Historical Facts and Incidents Relating to Newfane* 1877; M. Jones 1909; Foster and Streeter 1974; Kendall 1809, 3:33–34, 216; McDuffee 1892; G. Wheeler and H. Wheeler 1878; Lovering 1915; Sawtelle 1878; E. Parker 1851.

10. Hadfield 1933, p. 173; Larned 1880, 2:270.

11. Thomas 1955, p. 5. See Dwight 1821–22, 1:222; and Gowans 1964, p. 168; Larned 1880, 2:339, 359; J. Smith 1876, p. 9.

12. Bouton 1856, p. 515.

13. Anderson, Notter Associates 1974; P. White and D. Johnson 1973. See also Gowans 1964.

14. N. Chamberlain 1858, p. 11.

15. Donnelly 1968, pp. 79–80; Sinnott 1963, pp. 71–73; and Place 1922–23, p. 69.

16. Cushing 1961; Brodeur 1967; Meyer 1974.

17. Kurath 1939, p. 13; Meyer 1974.

18. N. Chamberlain 1858, p. 12.

19. Meinig 1979.

CHAPTER 6: THE SETTLEMENT IDEAL

Originally published as J. Wood 1991.

1. Leary 1980, p. 27; E. Emerson and Forbes 1910, p. 506; R. Emerson 1836, p. 94.

2. Cosgrove 1982.

3. Meinig 1979; Stilgoe 1983; Vance 1977.

4. P. Smith 1966, pp. 3, 13.

5. Everett 1824, p. 16.

6. Westbrook 1982; S. Chamberlain and Flynt 1957, p. 1.

7. Meinig 1979, p. 165.

8. Buell 1986, p. 305.

9. Meinig 1979, p. 188.

10. Hobsbawm and Ranger 1983.

11. Channing 1884; *Records of Massachusetts Bay* 1853–55; *Public Records of Connecticut* 1850–90; Stilgoe 1989, p. 79.

12. Ryan 1981; Gilmore 1989; Jaffee 1990.

13. J. Jackson 1972; Bell 1989.

14. R. Emerson 1835, p. 41; A. Hudson 1904, p. 4; Binford 1985.

15. Conron 1973, pp. 271–74; Buell 1986, pp. 208–9; Cosgrove 1982.

16. Buell 1986; Jaffee 1990.

17. Dwight 1794; Westbrook 1982, pp. 16, 21; Buell 1986, pp. 88, 92, 319; Stilgoe 1989, p. 78; Dwight 1821–22.

18. Sedgwick 1822; Westbrook 1982, pp. 57–64; M. Kelly 1984; Buell 1986, p. 4; D. Wood 1969.

19. Westbrook 1982, p. 66.

20. J. M. Duncan 1823, 1:93; Silliman 1824, p. 40; Royal 1826, p. 294.

21. Hawthorne 1897; Hawthorne 1900, 1:259.

22. Barber 1838; Barber 1839; Bartholomew 1858; R. Emerson 1836, p. 21.

23. Buell 1986, p. 261.

24. Kazin 1988, p. 48; Brooks 1936, p. 286.

25. R. Emerson 1836, pp. 10–11.

26. Thoreau 1854, pp. 87–88.

27. Brooks 1936, p. 283.

28. Dwight 1821–22, p. 109.

29. Westbrook 1982, pp. 78–81, 103–13; Buell 1986, pp. 206–7; Stowe 1869; Stowe 1878; M. Kelly 1984, p. 83.

30. H. Beecher 1868, p. 2.

31. Tolles 1973, pp. 17–18; Westbrook 1982, pp. 78–94; M. Kelly 1984, p. 2.

32. Butler 1985.

33. Thoreau 1906, 9:160.

34. Marx 1964, p. 226; Bender 1975, p. 14.

35. Buell 1986, pp. 193, 241.

36. Bushnell 1851; J. Jackson 1972, p. 37; D. Wood 1969.

37. J. Jackson 1972, pp. 101, 111, 113; Butler 1985.

38. Murphy 1985, p. 10.

39. Gowans 1964, pp. 287, 339.

40. Kazin 1988, p. 136.

41. Barber 1838; Barber 1839.

42. Tocqueville 1840; Buell 1986, p. 45; J. Parker 1866; Marsh 1843; H. Adams 1882; Porter 1883. The twentieth-century scholarly literature perpetuating the tradition of colonial village as nucleated form—transposing form and order—is voluminous, and I make no attempt to review or assess it here.

43. Hobsbawm and Ranger 1983.

44. Fries 1977.

45. Butler 1985; Vance 1977, p. 413.

46. Bender 1975, p. ix; Schuyler 1986.

47. Gross 1984.

48. E. Emerson and Forbes 1910, p. 506; Cowan 1967, p. 183. See also Marx 1964, p. 23.

49. Cowan 1967, p. 22; Porte 1982, p. 517.

50. Marx 1964, p. 231; Cowan 1967, pp. 6–7.

51. Bender 1975, pp. 89, 92; Stilgoe 1989, p. 98; Marx 1964, p. 23.

52. C. Beecher 1841; K. Jackson 1985, pp. 62–63; Fishman 1987, p. 122.

53. Bender 1975, pp. 129–57; Marx 1964, p. 101.

54. Stilgoe 1989; Schuyler 1986.

55. Downing 1853; Gowans 1964, pp. 313–14; Stern 1981, p. 6; K. Jackson 1985, p. 63; Fishman 1987, pp. 124–25; J. Jackson 1972, p. 111; Bender 1975, pp. 163–87; Schuyler 1986.

56. Vance 1977, p. 403; Archer 1983, p. 156; Fishman 1987.

57. R. Emerson 1856, p. 2. A phalanstery, here, is the dwelling of a Fourierite-like community of persons living cooperatively.

58. Fishman 1987, p. 121.

59. Vance 1977, p. 404.

60. Dwight 1821–22, 1:376; 3:80; Binford 1985.

61. Stern 1981, p. 5.
62. Kent 1831, p. 15.
63. Zelinsky 1977.
64. J. Jackson 1972, p. 37.
65. J. S. Duncan 1973.
66. Woodstock Chamber of Commerce 1986; Sack 1988.
67. Burns 1980.
68. Langdon 1988; Leccese 1988.
69. Hart 1983, p. 221.
70. Relph 1987, p. 267.
71. Rubin 1979, pp. 360–61.
72. Rubin 1979; Relph 1987.
73. Rubin 1979, p. 361.

CHAPTER 7: A WORLD WE HAVE GAINED

Originally published as J. Wood and Steinitz 1992.
1. Egleston 1886, p. 55.
2. J. Wood 1991.
3. Bowden 1992.
4. Our understanding of tradition has been informed by, among others, Charbonnier 1969, p. 3; Hobsbawm and Ranger 1983; Cosgrove 1984; Cosgrove and Daniels 1988; Lawson-Peebles 1988; Dorst 1989, pp. 128–29; Stock 1990, pp. 159–71.
5. See, for instance, Cosgrove 1982.
6. Bowden 1992.
7. Marx 1964, p. 226.
8. The most useful sources on the Great Migration are Allen 1982 and Cressy 1987; see also Bowden 1989.
9. Barley 1961; Mercer 1975; Cummings 1979; St. George 1982, pp. 159–201.
10. Despite Vance 1990a, p. 260, the example of the Boston common is the exception that proves the rule. Truly a common pasture, Boston's common was located in a peripheral site on the peninsula, not at the center of the community where the meetinghouse and statehouse stood. Cushing 1961, pp. 86–94; J. Wood 1982a.
11. Steinitz 1989.
12. Kazin 1988, p. 136. But see Bell 1989.
13. Winthrop 1629, 282–95. Also see P. Smith 1966.
14. Tucker 1986, p. 316. Cressy 1987 describes this process of rationalization and image formation in some detail.
15. Morse 1793, 1:316; Dwight 1821–22. See also Westbrook 1982, pp. 26–43.
16. Gilmore 1989, pp. 15–17.
17. Ibid., p. 16, citing Lukacs 1971.
18. Westbrook 1982; M. Kelly 1984; Buell 1986.
19. J. Wood 1991.
20. Ames 1985, pp. 11–12.
21. C. Hosmer 1965, p. 108; Yentsch 1988.
22. Bushnell 1851; J. Jackson 1972, p. 37; Meyer 1974; W. Wilson 1989, pp. 41–42.

23. Westbrook 1982, pp. 45–160; Buell 1986, p. 45. Greene 1988, p. 3, develops the argument.

24. Butler 1985, p. 19.

25. R. Wilson 1987.

26. Scully 1971.

27. R. Wilson 1987, p. 111; Rhoads 1977, pp. 606–7.

28. Scully 1971, p. 23.

29. C. Hosmer 1965, pp. 102–22.

30. Rhoads 1977, p. 517.

31. Cushing 1961; Meyer 1974; Butler 1985.

32. Meinig 1986, p. 403; Greene 1988.

33. H. Adams 1882, p. 52; Eisenstadt 1968; Westbrook 1982, pp. 147–60; Fischer 1989, p. 4. See such studies as Porter 1883; J. Hosmer 1884; Channing 1884; Aldrich 1884; Egleston 1886; and C. Adams 1892.

34. MacLear 1908, p. 13.

35. Butler 1985; Office of the National Register 1968.

36. Rhoads 1977, pp. 76–81. See, for instance, Rowlands 1917, pp. 15–16. Rowlands was vice president of the C. A. Goodyear Lumber Company of Chicago.

37. See, for example, Glassie 1968, pp. 125, 129.

38. A selection of articles from *The White Pine Series of Architectural Monographs* (1915–28) and *The Monograph Series* (1929–36), originally edited by R. F. Whitehead and F. C. Brown, has been collected in the *Architectural Treasures of America Series*. See, for instance, Mullins 1987, which includes original photographs of extant buildings, but not Colonial Revival building plans or lumber promotions.

39. Scofield 1938; Trewartha 1946; MacLear 1908.

40. R. H. Brown 1948.

41. Hart 1975; McManis 1975; Vance 1990a; or Jordan and Rowntree 1990. Jordan and Kaups 1989, p. 125, have revived the macro-Germanic-culture-region model of the origin of New England settlement patterns.

42. J. Kelly 1924. See the critique in Garvin 1951.

43. Glassie 1968, p. 125; Kniffen 1965; Pillsbury and Kardos 1970; and P. Lewis 1975. This scholarly misinterpretation remains alive in Noble 1984; and V. McAlester and L. McAlester 1984.

Bibliography

Abbot, Abiel. 1829. *History of Andover from Its Settlement to 1829*. Andover, Mass.: Flagg and Gould.

Adams, Charles F. 1892. "The Genesis of the Massachusetts Town and the Development of Town-Meeting Government." *Proceedings of the Massachusetts Historical Society* ser. 2, 7.

Adams, Herbert Baxter. 1882. *The Germanic Origin of New England Towns*. Johns Hopkins University Studies in Historical and Political Science, no. 2. Baltimore: Johns Hopkins University.

Akagi, Roy H. 1924. *The Town Proprietors of the New England Colonies: A Study of Their Development, Organization, Activities, and Controversies, 1620–1770*. Philadelphia: University of Pennsylvania Press.

Aldrich, D. E. 1884. "Origins of New England Towns; Their Powers and Duties." *Proceedings of the American Antiquarian Society* n.s. 3.

Allen, David Grayson. 1981. *In English Ways: The Movement of Societies and the Transferal of English Local Law and Custom to Massachusetts Bay in the Seventeenth Century*. Chapel Hill: University of North Carolina Press.

———. 1982. *In English Ways: The Movement of Societies and the Transferal of English Local Law and Custom to Massachusetts Bay in the Seventeenth Century*. New York: W. W. Norton.

Ames, Kenneth L. 1985. "Introduction." In *The Colonial Revival in America*. Alan Axelrod, ed. New York: W. W. Norton.

Anderson, Notter Associates. 1974. "Royalston Common and a Plan for Preservation." Offices of Notter, Finegold, and Alexander Research Report.

Anderson, Virginia DeJohn. 1985. "Migrants and Motives: Religion and the Settlement of New England, 1630–1640." *New England Quarterly* 68.

———. 1991. *New England's Generation: The Great Migration and the Formation of*

Society and Culture in the Seventeenth Century. Cambridge: Cambridge University Press.

Andrews, Charles M. 1889. *The River Towns of Connecticut: A Study of Wethersfield, Hartfield and Windsor.* Johns Hopkins University Studies in Historical and Political Science, ser. 7, nos. 7–9. Baltimore: Johns Hopkins University.

Andrews, John H. 1955. "Anglo-American Trade in the Early Eighteenth Century." *Geographical Review* 45.

Annett, Albert, and Alice E. E. Lehtinen. 1937. *The History of Jaffrey, New Hampshire.* Jaffrey, N.H.: By the Town.

Archer, John. 1983. "Country and City in the American Romantic Suburb." *Journal of the Society of Architectural Historians* 42.

Arensberg, Conrad. 1955. "American Communities." *American Anthropologist* 17.

A statistical account of the towns and parishes in the State of Connecticut. 1811. New Haven: State of Connecticut.

Barber, John Warner. 1838. *Historical Collections of Connecticut.* New Haven, Conn.: Durrie and Peck.

———. 1839. *Historical Collections of Massachusetts.* Worcester, Mass.: Dorr, Howland and Co.

———. 1841. *Historical Collections of the State of New York.* New York: S. Tuttle.

Barley, M. W. 1961. *The English Farmhouse and Cottage.* London: Routledge and Kegan Paul.

Bartholomew, William N. 1858. *Bartholomew's Sketches from Nature.* Boston: L. H. Bradford and Co.

Barton, Bonnie. 1978. "The Creation of Centrality." *Annals of the Association of American Geographers* 68.

Beecher, Catharine E. 1841. *A Treatise on Domestic Economy.* Boston: Marsh, Capen, Lynn, and Webb.

Beecher, Henry Ward. 1868. *Norwood; or, Village Life in New England.* New York: Charles Scribner and Co.

Bell, Michael M. 1989. "Did New England Go Downhill?" *Geographical Review* 79.

Bender, Thomas. 1975. *Toward an Urban Vision: Ideas and Institutions in Nineteenth Century America.* Baltimore: Johns Hopkins University Press.

———. 1978. *Community and Social Change in America.* New Brunswick, N.J.: Rutgers University Press.

Bidwell, Percy W. 1921. "The Agricultural Revolution in New England." *American Historical Review* 26.

Binford, Henry C. 1985. *The First Suburbs: Residential Communities on the Boston Periphery, 1815–1860.* Chicago: University of Chicago Press.

Blum, Jerome. 1971. "The European Village as Community: Origins and Functions." *Agricultural History* 45.

Bouton, Nathaniel. 1856. *The History of Concord, New Hampshire.* Concord, N.H.: Benning W. Sanborn.

Bowden, Martyn J. 1989. "The Subcultures of Colonial New England." Paper presented at the annual meeting of the Association of American Geographers.

———. 1992. "The Invention of Tradition in America." *Journal of Historical Geography* 18.

Boyer, Paul, and Stephen Nissenbaum. 1974. *Salem Possessed: The Social Origins of Witchcraft.* Cambridge, Mass.: Harvard University Press.

Boyle, John N. 1945. *Newtown, 1708–1758: Historical Notes and Maps.* Newtown, Conn.: Bee Publishing.

Bradford, William. 1921. *History of the Plymouth Plantation, 1606–1646.* W. T. Davis, ed. New York: Charles Scribner's Sons.

Breen, T. H. 1975. "Persistent Localism: English Social Change and the Shaping of New England Institutions." *William and Mary Quarterly* 3rd ser., 32.

———. 1978. "Transfer of Culture: Chance and Design in Shaping Massachusetts Bay, 1630–1660." *New England Historic Genealogical Register* 132.

Breen, T. H., and Stephen Foster. 1973a. "Moving to the New World: The Character of Early Massachusetts Immigration." *William and Mary Quarterly* 3rd ser., 30.

———. 1973b. "The Puritans' Greatest Achievement: A Study of Social Cohesion in Seventeenth-Century Massachusetts." *Journal of American History* 60.

Bridenbaugh, Carl. 1946. "The New England Town: A Way of Life." *Proceedings of the American Antiquarian Society* n.s. 56.

Brigham, C. S. 1947. *History and Bibliography of American Newspapers, 1690–1820.* Worcester, Mass.: American Antiquarian Society.

Brodeur, David D. 1967. "Evolution of the New England Town Common, 1630–1966." *The Professional Geographer* 19.

Brooke, John L. 1982. "Society, Revolution, and the Symbolic Use of the Dead: An Historical Ethnography of the Massachusetts Near Frontier, 1730–1820." Ph.D. dissertation, University of Pennsylvania.

Brooks, Van Wyck. 1936. *The Flowering of New England, 1815–1865.* New York: E. P. Dutton Co.

Brown, Elizabeth M. 1975. "Town Planning in Colonial New England." *Journal of the Society of Architectural Historians* 34.

Brown, Louis K. 1968. *Wilderness Town: The Story of Bedford, Massachusetts.* Bedford, Mass.: By the Author.

Brown, Ralph H. 1948. *Historical Geography of the United States.* New York: Harcourt, Brace, and World.

Brown, Richard D. 1974. "The Emergence of Urban Society in Rural Massachusetts, 1760–1820." *Journal of American History* 61.

Brunskill, R. W. 1978. *Illustrated Handbook of Vernacular Architecture.* Boston: Faber and Faber.

Brush, John E., and Howard E. Bracey. 1955. "Rural Service Centers in Southwestern Wisconsin and Southern England." *Geographical Review* 45.

Cronon, William. 1983. *Changes in the Land: Indians, Colonists, and the Ecology of New England.* New York: Hill and Wang.

Cummings, Abbott Lowell. 1979. *The Framed Houses of Massachusetts Bay, 1625–1725.* Cambridge, Mass.: Harvard University Press.

Cushing, John D. 1961. "Town Commons of New England, 1640–1840." *Old Time New England* 51.

Daniels, Bruce C. 1979. *The Connecticut Town: Growth and Development, 1635–1790.* Middletown, Conn.: Wesleyan University Press.

Davis, Charles H. S. 1870. *History of Wallingford, Connecticut, from its Settlement in 1670 to the Present Time.* Meriden, Conn.: By the Author.

"Dedham Village in 1795." 1903. *Dedham Historical Register* 14.

"Dedham Village in 1817." 1903. *Dedham Historical Register* 14.

Demangeon, Albert. 1927. "La geographie de l'habitat rural." *Annales de Geographie* 36.

Deming, Dorothy. 1933. *The Settlement of Connecticut Towns.* Connecticut Tercentenary Commission Publication, no. 6. New Haven, Conn.: Yale University Press.

Dempsey, Claire. 1987. "Architectural Development." In *Historic and Archeological Resources of Cape Cod and the Islands.* Peter Stott et al., eds. Boston: Massachusetts Historical Commission.

Dexter, Franklin B., ed. 1916. *Extracts from the Itineraries and Other Miscellanies of Ezra Stiles, D.D., LL.D., 1755–1794.* New Haven, Conn.: Yale University Press.

Dickinson, Robert E. 1949. "Rural Settlements in the German Lands." *Annals of the Association of American Geographers* 39.

Dodd, Edwin M. 1954. *American Business Corporations Until 1860 With Special References to Massachusetts.* Cambridge, Mass.: Harvard University Press.

Doherty, Robert. 1977. *Society and Power: Five New England Towns, 1800–1860.* Amherst, Mass.: University of Massachusetts Press.

Donnelly, Marion C. 1968. *New England Meeting Houses of the Seventeenth Century.* Middletown, Conn.: Wesleyan University Press.

Dorst, J. D. 1989. *The Written Suburb: An American Site, An Ethnographic Dilemma.* Philadelphia: University of Pennsylvania Press.

Dow, Joseph. 1893. *History of the Town of Hampton, New Hampshire.* Lucy E. Davis, ed. Salem, Mass.: By the Editor.

Downing, Andrew Jackson. 1853. *Rural Essays.* New York: George P. Putnam.

Doxiadis, C. A. 1972. "Ancient Greek Settlement: Second Annual Report." *Ekistics* 33.

Duncan, James S., Jr. 1973. "Landscape Taste as Symbol of Group Identity: A Westchester County Example." *Geographical Review* 63.

Duncan, John M. 1823. *Travels Through Parts of the United States and Canada in 1818 and 1819.* 2 vols. New York: W. B. Gilley.

Dwight, Timothy. 1794. *Greenfield Hill: A Poem in Seven Parts.* New Haven, Conn.: Childs and Swaine.

————. 1821–22. *Travels in New England and New York.* 4 vols. New Haven, Conn.: Timothy Dwight Jr.

Earle, Carville E. 1977. "The First English Towns in North America." *Geographical Review* 67.

———. 1992. "Pioneers of Providence: The Anglo-American Experience, 1492–1792." *Annals of the Association of American Geographers* 82.

East, Robert A. 1944. "Puritanism and New Settlement." *New England Quarterly* 17.

Easterlin, Richard A. 1976. "Population Change and Farm Settlement in the Northern United States." *Journal of Economic History* 36.

Egleston, Melville. 1886. *The Land System of the New England Colonies*. Johns Hopkins University Studies in Historical and Political Science, ser. 4, nos. 11–13. Baltimore: Johns Hopkins University.

Eisenstadt, Abraham S. 1968. *Charles McLean Andrews: A Study in American Historical Writing*. New York: AMS Press.

Ekwall, Eilert. 1960. *The Concise Oxford Dictionary of English Place-Names*. 4th ed. London: Oxford University Press.

Emerson, Edward Waldo, and Waldo Emerson Forbes, eds. 1910. *Journals of Ralph Waldo Emerson, 1820–1872*. Vol. 6. Cambridge, Mass.: Riverside Press.

Emerson, Ralph Waldo. 1835. *A Historical Discourse, Delivered Before the Citizens of Concord, 12th September, 1835, on the Second Centennial of the Incorporation of the Town*. Boston: W. B. Clark.

———. 1836. *Nature*. Boston: James Munroe and Co.

———. 1856. *English Traits*. New York: Hurst and Co.

Everett, Edward. 1824. *An Oration Pronounced at Cambridge*. Boston: By the Author.

Fischer, David Hackett. 1989. *Albion's Seed: Four British Folkways in America*. New York: Oxford University Press.

Fishman, Robert. 1987. *Bourgeois Utopias: The Rise and Fall of Suburbia*. New York: Basic Books.

Forster, Colin, and G. S. L. Tucker. 1972. *Economic Opportunity and White American Fertility Ratios, 1800–1860*. New Haven, Conn.: Yale University Press.

Foster, Helen N., and William W. Streeter. 1974. *Only One Cummington*. Cummington, Mass.: Cummington Historical Society.

Fox, Charles J. 1846. *History of the Old Township of Dunstable Including Nashua, New Hampshire*. Nashua, N.H.: Charles T. Gill.

French, W. R. 1886. *A History of Turner, Maine*. Portland, Maine: Hoyt, Fogg, and Donham.

Fries, Sylvia Doughty. 1977. *The Urban Ideal in Colonial America*. Philadelphia: Temple University Press.

Friis, Herman R. 1968. *A Series of Population Maps of the Colonies and the United States, 1625–1790*. New York: American Geographical Society.

Frizzell, Martha D. 1955. *Second History of Charlestown, New Hampshire: Old Number Four*. Charlestown, N.H.: By the Town.

———. 1963. *A History of Walpole, New Hampshire*. 3 vols. Walpole, N.H.: By the Walpole Historical Society and the Town.

Gage, Thomas. 1840. *The History of Rowley*. Boston: Ferdinand Andrews.

Garvin, Anthony N. B. 1951. *Architecture and Town Planning in Colonial Connecticut*. New Haven: Yale University Press.

Gilbert, Edward. 1907. *History of Salem, New Hampshire*. Concord, N.H.: Rumford Printing Co.

Gildrie, Richard P. 1975. *Salem, Massachusetts, 1628–1683: A Covenanted Community*. Charlottesville, Va.: University of Virginia Press.

Gillespie, C. Bancroft, comp. 1906. *A Century of Meriden*. Meriden, Conn.: Journal Publishing Co.

Gilmore, William J. 1989. *Reading Becomes a Necessity of Life: Material and Cultural Life in Rural New England, 1780–1835*. Knoxville: University of Tennessee Press.

Glassie, Henry. 1968. *Pattern in the Material Folk Culture of the Eastern United States*. Philadelphia: University of Pennsylvania Press.

———. 1975. *Folk Housing in Middle Virginia: A Structural Analysis of Historic Artifacts*. Knoxville: University of Tennessee Press.

Gorn, Michael H., ed. 1979. *An Index to the Microfilm Edition of the Massachusetts and Maine Direct Tax Census of 1798*. Boston: New England Historic Genealogical Society.

Gowans, Alan. 1964. *Images of American Living: Four Centuries of Architecture and Furniture as Cultural Expression*. Philadelphia: J. B. Lippincott Co.

Grant, Charles S. 1961. *Democracy in the Connecticut Frontier Town of Kent*. New York: Columbia University Press.

Greene, Jack P. 1988. *Pursuits of Happiness: The Social Development of Early Modern British Colonies and the Formation of American Culture*. Chapel Hill: University of North Carolina Press.

Greven, Philip J., Jr. 1965. "Old Patterns in the New World: The Distribution of Land in Seventeenth-Century Andover." *Essex Institute Historical Collections* 101.

———. 1970. *Four Generations: Population, Land, and Family Life in Colonial Andover Massachusetts*. Ithaca, N.Y.: Cornell University Press.

Gross, Robert A. 1976. *The Minutemen and Their World*. New York: Hill and Wang.

———. 1984. "Transcendentalism and Urbanism: Concord, Boston, and the Wider World." *Journal of American Studies* 18.

Hadfield, Joseph. 1933. *An Englishman in America, 1785, Being the Diary of Joseph Hadfield*. Douglas S. Robertson, ed. Toronto: Hunter-Ross.

Hall, David D. 1989. *Worlds of Wonder, Days of Judgement: Popular Religious Beliefs in Early New England*. New York: Alfred A. Knopf.

Hall, Henry B. 1917. "A Description of Rural Life and Labor in Massachusetts at Four Periods." Ph.D. dissertation, Harvard University.

Haller, William, Jr. 1951. *The Puritan Frontier: Town Planting in New England Colonial Development, 1630–1660*. New York: Columbia University Press.

Handlin, Oscar, and Mary F. Handlin. 1969. *Commonwealth: A Study of the Role of*

Government in the American Economy. Massachusetts, 1774–1861. Cambridge, Mass.: Harvard University Press.

Harris, R. Cole. 1977. "The Simplification of Europe Overseas." *Annals of the Association of American Geographers* 67.

———. 1979. "Comment in Reply." *Annals of the Association of American Geographers* 69.

Hart, John Fraser. 1975. *The Look of the Land*. Englewood Cliffs, N.J.: Prentice-Hall.

———. 1983. "The Bypass Strip as an Ideal Landscape." *Geographical Review* 73.

Haskins, George L. 1960. *Law and Authority in Early Massachusetts: A Study in Tradition and Design*. New York: Macmillan.

Hawthorne, Nathaniel. 1897. *Passages from the American Note-books*. Boston: Houghton Mifflin and Co.

———. 1900. "Sights from a Steeple." In *Twice Told Tales*. 2 vols. Boston: Houghton Mifflin Co.

Hazen, Henry A. 1883. *History of Billerica, Massachusetts*. Boston: A. Williams and Co.

Henretta, James A. 1971. "The Morphology of New England Society in the Colonial Period." *Journal of Interdisciplinary History* 2.

———. 1978. "Families and Farms: Mentalite in Pre-Industrial America." *William and Mary Quarterly* ser. 3, 35.

Herman, Bernard L. 1987a. "Rural Tenant Housing in the Late-Eighteenth Century Delaware Valley." Paper presented at the Middle Atlantic Archaeological Conference, Lancaster, Pa.

———. 1987b. "Delaware's Orphan Court Valuations and the Reconstruction of Historic Landscapes, 1785–1830." Paper presented at the Dublin Seminar, Deerfield, Mass.

Hill, Christopher. 1975. *Change and Continuity in Seventeenth-Century England*. Cambridge, Mass.: Harvard University Press.

Hobsbawm, Eric, and Terence Ranger, eds. 1983. *The Invention of Tradition*. New York: Cambridge University Press.

Homans, George C. 1969. "The Explanation of English Regional Differences." *Past and Present* 42.

Hooker, Roland M. 1936. *The Colonial Trade of Connecticut*. Connecticut Tercentenary Commission Publication, no. 50. New Haven, Conn.: Yale University Press.

Hosmer, Charles B., Jr. 1965. *Presence of the Past: A History of the Preservation Movement in the United States Before Williamsburg*. New York: Putnam.

Hosmer, J. K. 1884. *Samuel Adams: The Man of the Town-Meeting*. Johns Hopkins University Studies in Historical and Political Science, ser. 2, no. 4. Baltimore: Johns Hopkins University.

Howe, Henry. 1847. *Historical Collections of Ohio*. Cincinnati: Derby, Bradley and Co.

Howes, Frederick G. n.d. *The History of the Town of Ashfield, Franklin County, Massachusetts, 1742–1910*. Ashfield, Mass.: By the Author.

Hubbard, C. Horace, and Justus Dartt. 1895. *History of the Town of Springfield, Vermont, 1752–1895*. Boston: George H. Wacker and Co.

Hubka, Thomas C. 1984. *Big House, Little House, Back House, Barn: The Connected Farm Buildings of New England*. Hanover, N.H.: University Press of New England.

Hudson, Alfred S. 1889. *The History of Sudbury, Massachusetts, 1638–1889*. Sudbury, Mass.: By the Town.

———. 1904. *The History of Concord, Massachusetts*. 2 vols. Concord, Mass.: Erudite Press.

Hudson, Charles. 1868. *History of the Town of Lexington*. Boston: Wiggin and Lunt.

Hughes, Sarah E. 1908. *History of East Haven*. New Haven, Conn.: Tuttle, Morehouse, and Taylor Press.

Innes, Stephen. 1991. "Puritanism and Capitalism: Early Massachusetts as a Test Case." Paper presented at the Washington Area Seminar in Early American History, University of Maryland.

"Inventory of the Historic Assets of the Commonwealth of Massachusetts." n.d. Boston: Massachusetts Historical Commission.

Jackson, John Brinkerhoff. 1952. "Human, All Too Human Geography." *Landscape* 2.

———. 1953. "The Westward Moving House." *Landscape* 2.

———. 1956–57. "The Other Directed House." *Landscape* 6.

———. 1959–60. "First Comes the House." *Landscape* 9.

———. 1972. *American Space: The Centennial Years, 1865–1876*. New York: W. W. Norton.

Jackson, Kenneth C. 1985. *The Crabgrass Frontier: The Suburbanization of the United States*. New York: Oxford University Press.

Jaffee, David. 1990. "Humble Authors and Rural Readers: The Village Enlightenment in New England, 1760–1820." *William and Mary Quarterly* 47.

Jameson, E. O. 1886. *The History of Medway, Massachusetts, 1713–1885*. Medway, Mass.: By the Town.

Jensen, Merrill. 1968. *The Founding of a Nation: A History of the American Revolution, 1763–1776*. New York: Oxford University Press.

Jewett, Amos E., and Emily M. A. Jewett. 1946. *Rowley, Massachusetts, 1639–1850*. Rowley, Mass.: The Jewett Family of America.

Johnson, Edward. 1867. *Wonder-Working Providence of Sion's Saviour in New England*. (1654) reprint ed. Andover, Mass.: Warren F. Draper.

Johnson, Jane E., comp. 1917. *Newtown's History*. Newtown, Conn.: By the Compiler.

Johnson, Richard Brigham. 1973. "Swampscott, Massachusetts, in the Seventeenth Century." *Essex Institute Historical Collections* 109.

Jones, Alice H. 1980. *Wealth of a Nation to Be: The American Colonies on the Eve of the Revolution*. New York: Columbia University Press.

Jones, Matt B. 1909. *History of the Town of Waitsfield, Vermont, 1782–1908*. Boston: George E. Littlefield.

Jordan, Terry G. 1989. "Preadaptation and European Colonization in Rural North

America." *Annals of the Association of American Geographers* 79.

Jordan, Terry G., and Matti Kaups. 1989. *The American Backwoods Frontier: An Ethnic and Ecological Interpretation*. Baltimore: Johns Hopkins University Press.

Jordan, Terry G., and Lester Rowntree. 1990. *The Human Mosaic: An Introduction to Cultural Geography*. 5th ed. New York: Harper and Row.

Jorgenson, Neil. 1971. *A Guide to New England's Landscape*. Barre, Mass.: Barre Publishers.

Kaufmann, Harold R. 1959. "Toward an Interactional Conception of Community." *Social Forces* 38.

Kazin, Alfred. 1988. *A Writer's America: Landscape in Literature*. New York: Alfred A. Knopf.

Kellogg, Lucy C. 1902. *History of the Town of Bernardston, 1736–1900*. Greenfield, Mass.: By the Author.

Kelly, J. Frederick. 1924. *Early Domestic Architecture of Connecticut*. New Haven, Conn.: Yale University Press.

Kelly, Mary. 1984. *Private Woman, Public Stage: Literary Domesticity in Nineteenth-Century America*. New York: Oxford University Press.

Kendall, Edward A. 1809. *Travels Through the Northern Parts of the United States in the Years 1807 and 1808*. 3 vols. New York: Isaac Riley.

Kent, James. 1831. *An Address Delivered at New Haven*. New Haven, Conn.: By the Author.

Kessler, William C. 1949. "Incorporation in New England: A Statistical Study, 1800–1875." *Journal of Economic History* 8.

King, Deborah Phillips. 1987. "Here Today, Gone Tomorrow: Determining the Disappearance Rate of Agricultural Structures in Pike County, Ohio." Paper presented at the annual meeting of the Association of American Geographers.

Kishlansky, Mark A. 1980. "Community and Continuity: A Review of Selected Works on English Local History." *William and Mary Quarterly* ser. 3, 37.

Kniffen, Fred. 1936. "Louisiana House Types." *Annals of the Association of American Geographers* 26.

————. 1965. "Folk Housing: Key to Diffusion." *Annals of the Association of American Geographers* 55.

Kupperman, Karen O. 1982. "The Puzzle of the American Climate in the Early Colonial Period." *American Historical Review* 87.

Kurath, Hans, ed. 1939. *Linguistic Atlas of New England*. Providence, R.I.: Brown University Press.

Labaree, Benjamin W. 1962. *Patriots and Partisans: The Merchants of Newburyport, 1764–1815*. Cambridge, Mass.: Harvard University Press.

Labaree, Leonard W. 1933. *Milford, Connecticut: The Early Development of a Town as Shown in Its Land Records*. Connecticut Tercentenary Commission Publication, no. 13. New Haven, Conn.: Yale University Press.

Lancaster, Daniel. 1845. *The History of Gilmanton*. Gilmanton, N.H.: By the Author.

Langdon, Philip. 1988. "A Good Place to Live." *Atlantic Monthly*.

Larkin, Jack. 1978. "Interim Center Village Research Report." Old Sturbridge Village Research Report.

Larned, Ellen D. 1880. *History of Windham County, Connecticut*. 2 vols. Thompson, Conn.: By the Author.

Laslett, Peter. 1965. *The World We Have Lost*. New York: Scribner.

Latimer, W. J., R. F. R. Martin, and M. O. Lanphear. 1927. *Soil Survey of Worcester County Massachusetts*. Washington, D.C.: U.S. Department of Agriculture, Bureau of Soils.

Lawson-Peebles, Robert. 1988. *Landscape and Written Expression in Revolutionary America: The World Turned Upside Down*. Cambridge: Cambridge University Press.

Leary, Lewis. 1980. *Ralph Waldo Emerson: An Interpretive Essay*. Boston: Twayne Publications.

LeBlanc, Robert. 1969. *Location of Manufacturing in New England in the Nineteenth Century*. Dartmouth Publications in Geography, no. 7. Hanover, N.H.: Dartmouth College.

Leccese, Michael. 1988. "Brave Old World." *Landscape Architecture 78*.

Lemon, James T. 1972. *The Best Poor Man's Country: A Geographical Study of Early Southeastern Pennsylvania*. Baltimore: Johns Hopkins University Press.

———. 1978. "The Weakness of Place and Community in Early Pennsylvania." In *European Settlement and Development in North America: Essays in Honour and Memory of A. H. Clark*. J. R. Gibson, ed. Toronto: University of Toronto Press.

———. 1980a. "Early Americans and Their Social Environment." *Journal of Historical Geography* 6.

———. 1980b. "Comment on James A. Henretta's 'Families and Farms: Mentalite in Pre-Industrial America' (and Henretta's Reply)." *William and Mary Quarterly* ser. 3, 37.

———. 1981. "Spatial Organization in Early America: Local, Regional and Household." Paper presented at the Oxford Conference on Anglo-American Colonial History, Oxford University.

Levine, Herbert. 1971. "In Pursuit of the Nucleated Village." Old Sturbridge Village Research Report.

Lewis, Alonzo, and John R. Newhall. 1865. *History of Lynn, Essex County, Massachusetts*. Boston.

Lewis, Peirce. 1975. "Common Houses, Cultural Spoor." *Landscape* 19.

Lincoln, William. 1837. *History of Worcester, Massachusetts*. Worcester, Mass.: Moses D. Phillips and Co.

Lockridge, Kenneth A. 1968. "Land, Population and the Evolution of New England Society, 1630–1790." *Past and Present* 39.

———. 1970. *A New England Town: The First Hundred Years. Dedham, Massachusetts, 1636–1736*. New York: W. W. Norton.

Loehr, Rodney C. 1952. "Self-Sufficiency on the Farm, 1759–1819." *Agricultural History* 26.

Lovering, Martin. 1915. *History of the Town of Holland, Massachusetts*. Rutland, Vt.: Tuttle Company.

Lowenthal, David. 1979. "Age and Artifact: Dilemmas of Appreciation." In *The Interpretation of Ordinary Landscapes*. Donald W. Meinig, ed. New York: Oxford University Press.

Lukacs, Gyorgy. 1971. *The Theory of the Novel*. Anna Bostwick, trans. Cambridge, Mass.: MIT Press.

MacLear, Anne B. 1908. *Early New England Towns: A Comparative Study of Their Development*. Columbia University Studies in History, Economics, and Public Law, no. 29. New York: Columbia University.

Main, Jackson Turner. 1985. *Society and Economy in Colonial Connecticut*. Princeton, N.J.: Princeton University Press.

Marsh, George Perkins. 1843. *The Goths in New England*. Middlebury, Vt.: J. Cobb.

Martin, John Frederick. 1991. *Profits in the Wilderness: Entrepreneurs and the Founding of New England Towns*. Chapel Hill: University of North Carolina Press.

Martin, Margaret E. 1938–39. *Merchants and Trade of the Connecticut River Valley, 1750–1820*. Smith College Studies in History, no. 24. Northampton, Mass.: Smith College.

Marvin, Abijah P. 1868. *History of the Town of Winchendon, Massachusetts*. Winchendon, Mass.: By the Author.

Marx, Leo. 1964. *The Machine in the Garden: Technology and the Pastoral Ideal in America*. New York: Oxford University Press.

Massachusetts Secretary of State. 1836. *Report of the List of Incorporations and Their Capitals, Granted by the Legislature of Massachusetts, from the Adoption of the Constitution in 1780 to 1836*. Boston: State of Massachusetts.

Mawer, Allen, ed. 1924. *The Survey of English Place Names*. 2 vols. Cambridge: Cambridge University Press.

McAlester, Virginia, and Lee McAlester. 1984. *A Field Guide to American Houses*. New York: Alfred A. Knopf.

McCutcheon, Henry R. 1970. "Town Formation in Eastern Massachusetts, 1630–1802: A Case Study in Political Area Organization." Ph.D. dissertation, Clark University.

McDuffee, Franklin. 1892. *History of Rochester, New Hampshire from 1722–1890*. Sylvanus Hayward, rev. and ed. Manchester, N.H.: By the Editor.

McLellan, Hugh D. 1903. *History of Gorham, Maine*. Katherine B. Lewis, comp. and ed. Portland, Maine.: By the Editor.

McManis, Douglas R. 1975. *Colonial New England: A Historical Geography*. New York: Oxford University Press.

Mead, Spencer P. 1911. *Ye Historie of Ye Town of Greenwich*. New York: Knickerbocker Press.

Meinig, Donald W. 1962. "A Comparative Historical Geography of Two Railnets: Columbia Basin and South Australia." *Annals of the Association of American Geographers 52.*

———. 1979. "Symbolic Landscapes." In *The Interpretation of Ordinary Landscapes: Geographical Essays.* Donald W. Meinig, ed. New York: Oxford University Press.

———. 1986. *The Shaping of America: A Geographical Perspective on 500 Years of History,* vol. 1, *Atlantic America, 1492–1800.* New Haven, Conn.: Yale University Press.

Mercer, Eric. 1975. *English Vernacular Houses.* London: H.M. Stationary Office.

Merchant, Carolyn. 1989. *Ecological Revolutions: Nature, Gender, and Science in New England.* Chapel Hill: University of North Carolina Press.

Merrens, Roy H. 1975. "Settlement of the Colonial Atlantic Seaboard." In *Pattern and Process: Research in Historical Geography.* Ralph E. Ehrenberg, ed. Washington, D.C.: Howard University Press.

Meyer, John B. 1974. "The Village Green Ensemble in Northern Vermont." Master's thesis, University of Vermont.

Mitchell, Robert D. 1979. "Comment on the Simplification of Europe Overseas." *Annals of the Association of American Geographers 69.*

Morris, F. Grave. 1951. "Some Aspects of the Rural Settlement of New England in Colonial Times." In *London Essays in Geography.* L. Dudley Stamp and S. E. Woldridge, eds. London: London School of Economics.

Morse, Jedidiah. 1793. *The American Universal Geography.* Boston: Isaiah Thomas and the Author.

Mullins. Lisa C., ed. 1987. *Village Architecture of Early New England.* Harrisburg, Pa.: National Historical Society.

Murphy, Kevin Dean. 1985. "'A Stroll Thro' the Past': Three Architects of the Colonial Revival." Master's thesis, Boston University.

Murrin, John. 1972. "Review Essay." *Historical Theory 11.*

Nelson, William E. 1975. *The Americanization of the Common Law: The Impact of Legal Change on Massachusetts Society, 1760–1830.* Cambridge, Mass.: Harvard University Press.

Newcomer, Lee N. 1953. *The Embattled Farmers: The Massachusetts Countryside in the American Revolution.* New York: King's Crown Press.

Newton, Milton B., Jr. 1974. "Settlement Patterns as Artifacts of Social Structure." In *The Human Mirror: Material and Spatial Images of Man.* Miles Richardson, ed. Baton Rouge, La.: LSU Press.

Noble, Allen. 1984. *Wood, Brick and Stone: The North American Settlement Landscape,* vol. 1, *Houses.* Amherst, Mass.: University of Massachusetts Press.

North, Douglas C. 1961. *The Economic Growth of the United States.* Englewood Cliffs, N.J.: Prentice-Hall.

Office of the National Register. 1968. *Report of the National Survey of Historic Sites and Buildings on Litchfield, Connecticut.* Washington, D.C.: National Park Service.

Old Sturbridge Village. 1962. "Banks and Banking in New England, 1784–1840." Old Sturbridge Village Research Report.

Olson, Albert L. 1935. *Agricultural Economy and the Population of Eighteenth-Century Connecticut.* Connecticut Tercentenary Commission Publication, no. 40. New Haven, Conn.: Yale University Press.

Osterud, Nancy, and John Fulton. 1976. "Family Limitation and Age at Marriage: Fertility Decline in Sturbridge, Massachusetts, 1730–1850." *Population Studies* 30.

Oxford English Dictionary. 1933. Oxford: Clarendon.

Parker, Edward L. 1851. *The History of Londonderry, New Hampshire.* Boston: Perkins and Whipple.

Parker, Joel. 1866. "The Origin, Organization, and Influence of the Towns of New England." *Proceedings of the Massachusetts Historical Society* 9.

Parks, Roger N. 1966. "The Roads of New England." Ph.D. dissertation, Michigan State University.

———. 1972. "Comments on Change in Agriculture, 1790–1840." In *Farming in the New Nation: Interpreting American Agriculture, 1790–1840.* Darwin P. Kelsey, ed. Washington, D.C.: Agricultural History Society.

Perley, Sidney. 1916. "Part of Salem Village in 1700." *Essex Institute Historical Collections* 52.

Pfeifer, Gottfried. 1956. "The Quality of Peasant Living in Central Europe." In *Man's Role in Changing the Face of the Earth.* William L. Thomas, ed. Chicago: University of Chicago Press.

Pillsbury, Richard. 1987. "The Pennsylvania Culture Area: A Reappraisal." *North American Culture* 3.

Pillsbury, Richard, and Andrew Kardos. 1970. *A Field Guide to the Folk Architecture of the Northeastern United States.* Geography Publications at Dartmouth, no. 8. Hanover, N.H.: Dartmouth College.

Place, Charles A. 1922–23. "From Meetinghouse to Church in New England." *Old Time New England* 13.

Polanyi, Karl. 1944. *The Great Transformation: The Political and Economic Origin of Our Time.* New York: Farrar and Rinehart.

Pollock, Adrian. 1979. "Commentary—Europe Simplified." *Annals of the Association of American Geographers* 69.

Porte, Joel, ed. 1982. *Emerson in His Journals.* Cambridge, Mass.: Belknap Press.

Porter, Noah. 1883. "The New England Meetinghouse." *The New Englander* o.s. 42.

Powell, Sumner Chilton. 1963. *Puritan Village: The Formation of a New England Town.* Middletown, Conn.: Wesleyan University Press.

Pruitt, Bettye Hobbs, ed. 1978. *The Massachusetts Tax Valuation List of 1771.* Boston: G. K. Hall.

———. 1984. "Self-Sufficiency and the Agricultural Economy of Eighteenth Century Massachusetts." *William and Mary Quarterly* 3rd ser., 41.

Public Records of the Colony of Connecticut, 1636–1776. 1850–90. Hartford: State of Connecticut.

Purcell, Richard J. 1918. *Connecticut in Transition, 1775–1818.* Washington, D.C.: American Historical Association.

Rapoport, Amos. 1982. *The Meaning of the Built Environment.* Beverly Hills, Calif.: Wadsworth.

Records of the Governor and Company of the Massachusetts Bay in New England, 1628–1686. 1853–55. Boston: Commonwealth of Massachusetts.

Relph, Edward. 1987. *The Modern Urban Landscape.* Baltimore: Johns Hopkins University Press.

Reps, John W. 1965. *The Making of Urban America: A History of City Planning in the United States.* Princeton, N.J.: Princeton University Press.

———. 1969. *Town Planning in Frontier America.* Princeton, N.J.: Princeton University Press.

Rhoads, William B. 1977. *The Colonial Revival.* New York: Garland Press.

Rice, Howard C., Jr., and Anne Brown, eds. 1972. *The American Campaigns of Rochambeau's Army, 1780–1783.* 2 vols. Princeton, N.J.: Princeton University Press; Providence, R.I.: Brown University Press.

Rich, Wesley E. 1924. *The History of the United States Post Office to the Year 1829.* Cambridge, Mass.: Harvard University Press.

Rickert, John E. 1967. "House Facades of the Northeastern United States: A Tool of Geographic Analysis." *Annals of the Association of American Geographers* 57.

Rowlands, Lamont. 1917. "The Civilization of Colonial New England Reflected in White Pine." *The White Pine Series of Architectural Monographs,* no. 3.

Roy, Louis E. 1965. *Quabog Plantation Alias Brookfield: A Seventeenth-Century New England Town.* West Brookfield, Mass.: By the Author.

Royal, Anne. 1826. *Sketches of History, Life, and Manners in the United States.* New Haven, Conn.: By the Author.

Rubin, Barbara. 1979. "Aesthetic Ideology and Urban Design." *Annals of the Association of American Geographers* 69.

Russell, Howard S. 1976. *A Long Deep Furrow: Three Centuries of Farming in New England.* Hanover, N.H.: University Press of New England.

Rutman, Darrett B. 1965a. *Winthrop's Boston: Portrait of a Puritan Town: 1630–1649.* Chapel Hill: University of North Carolina Press.

———. 1965b. "Mirror of Puritan Authority." In *Law and Authority in Colonial America: Selected Essays.* George A. Billias, ed. Barre, Mass.: Barre Publishers.

———. 1967. *Husbandmen of Plymouth: Farms and Villages in the Old Colony, 1620–1692.* Boston: Plimouth Plantation.

———. 1973. "The Social Web: A Prospectus for the Study of the Early American Community." In *Insights and Parallels: Problems and Issues of American Social History.* William L. O'Neill, ed. Minneapolis, Minn.: Burgess Publishing Co.

————. 1975. "People in Process: The New Hampshire Towns in the Eighteenth Century." *Journal of Urban History* 1.

————. 1986. "Assessing the Little Communities of Early America." *William and Mary Quarterly* 43.

Ryan, Mary P. 1981. *Cradle of the Middle Class: The Family in Oneida County, New York, 1790–1865*. New York: Cambridge University Press.

Sack, Robert D. 1988. "The Consumer's World: Place as Context." *Annals of the Association of American Geographers* 78.

St. George, Robert Blair. 1982. "'Set Thyne House in Order': The Domestication of the Yeomanry in Seventeenth-Century New England." In *New England Begins: The Seventeenth Century*. Jonathan L. Fairbanks and Robert Trent, eds. Boston: Museum of Fine Arts.

Saladino, Gaspare J. 1964. "The Economic Revolution in Late Eighteenth-Century Connecticut." Ph.D. dissertation, University of Wisconsin.

Sauer, Carl. 1925. "The Morphology of Landscape." *University of California Publications in Geography* 2.

————. 1941. "Foreword to Historical Geography." *Annals of the Association of American Geographers* 31.

Sawtelle, Ithamar B. 1878. *History of the Town of Townshend, Massachusetts, 1676–1878*. Townshend, Mass.: By the Author.

Schlebecker, John T. 1976. "Agricultural Markets and Marketing in the North: 1744–1777." *Agricultural History* 50.

Schumacher, Max G. 1948. "The Northern Farmer and His Markets During the Late Colonial Period." Ph.D. dissertation, University of California.

Schuyler, David. 1986. *The New Urban Landscape: The Redefinition of Urban Form in Nineteenth Century America*. Baltimore: Johns Hopkins University Press.

Scofield, Edna. 1938. "The Origin of Settlement Patterns in Rural New England." *Geographical Review* 28.

Scully, Vincent J., Jr. 1971. *The Shingle Style and the Stick Style: Architectural Theory and Design from Richardson to the Origins of Wright*. Rev. ed. New Haven, Conn.: Yale University Press.

Sedgwick, Catherine Maria. 1822. *A New England Tale; Or, Sketches of New England Character and Manners*. New York: S. Bliss and E. White.

Silliman, Benjamin. 1824. *Remarks Made on a Short Tour, Between Hartford and Quebec in the Autumn of 1819*. 2nd ed. New Haven, Conn.: S. Converse.

Sinnott, Edward W. 1963. *Meetinghouse and Church in Early New England*. New York: McGraw-Hill.

Smith, Daniel S. 1972. "The Demographic History of Colonial New England." *Journal of Economic History* 32.

Smith, Edward C., et al. 1924. *A History of the Town of Middlefield, Massachusetts*. Middlefield, Mass.: By the Authors.

Smith, J. E. A. 1869. *The History of Pittsfield, Massachusetts, 1734 to 1800*. Boston: Lee and Shepard.

———. 1876. *The History of Pittsfield, Massachusetts, 1800–1876*. Springfield, Mass.: C. W. Bryan and Co.

Smith, Page. 1966. *As a City Upon a Hill: The Town in American History*. Cambridge, Mass.: MIT Press.

Soltow, Lee. 1985. "Egalitarian America and Its Inegalitarian Housing in the Federal Period." *Social Science History* 9.

Some Old Houses of Westborough, Massachusetts, and Their Occupants. 1906. Westborough, Mass.: Westborough Historical Society.

Speare, Eva A. 1938. *Colonial Meetinghouses of New Hampshire*. Littleton, N.H.: Daughters of Colonial Wars.

Spencer, Joseph E. 1945. "House Types of Southern Utah." *Geographical Review* 35.

Stackpole, Everett S. 1916. *History of New Hampshire*. 2 vols. New York: American Historical Society.

Staples, C. A. 1890. "A Sketch of the History of Lexington Common." *Proceedings of the Lexington Historical Society* 1.

Stearns, Ezra S. 1875. *History of the Town of Rindge, New Hampshire, 1736–1874*. Rindge, N.H.: By the Author.

Steinitz, Michael. 1989. "Rethinking Geographical Approaches to The Common House: The Evidence from Eighteenth-Century Massachusetts." In *Perspectives in Vernacular Architecture, III*. Thomas Carter and Bernard Herman, eds. Columbia: University of Missouri Press.

Stern, Robert A. M. 1981. "La Ville Bourgeoise." In *The Anglo-American Suburb*. Robert A. M. Stern and John M. Massengale, eds. London: Architectural Design.

Stilgoe, John R. 1976a. "Pattern on the Land: The Making of a Colonial Landscape, 1633–1800." Ph.D. dissertation, Harvard University.

———. 1976b. "The Puritan Townscape: Ideal and Reality." *Landscape* 20.

———. 1983. *Common Landscape of America, 1580–1845*. New Haven, Conn.: Yale University Press.

———. 1989. *Borderland: Origins of the American Suburb, 1820–1939*. New Haven, Conn.: Yale University Press.

Stiverson, Gregory A. 1976. "Early American Farming: A Comment." *Agricultural History* 50.

Stock, Brian. 1990. *Listening for the Text: On the Uses of the Past*. Baltimore: Johns Hopkins University Press.

Stone, Garry Wheeler. 1977. "Artifacts Are Not Enough." In *The Conference on Historic Site Archeology Papers*, vol. 2. Stanley South, ed. Columbia: Institute of Archeology and Anthropology, University of South Carolina.

Stowe, Harriet Beecher. 1869. *Oldtown Folks*. Boston: Fields, Osgood and Co.

———. 1878. *Poganuc People*. New York: Fords, Howard and Hulbert.

Sutter, Ruth E. 1973. *The Next Place You Come To: A Historical Introduction to Communities in North America*. Englewood Cliffs, N.J.: Prentice-Hall.

Sweeney, Kevin M. 1984. "Mansion People: Kinship, Class and Architecture in Western Massachusetts in the Mid-Eighteenth Century." *Winterthur Portfolio* 19.

Swift, Samuel. 1859. *History of the Town of Middlebury, Vermont*. Middlebury, Vt.: A. H. Copeland.

Temple, Josiah H. 1887. *History of Framingham, Massachusetts, 1640–1880*. Framingham, Mass.: By the Town.

Temple, Josiah H., and George Sheldon. 1875. *A History of the Town of Northfield, Massachusetts*. Albany, N.Y.: Joel Munsell.

Thirsk, Joan. 1967a. "The Farming Regions of England." In *The Agrarian History of England and Wales, 1500–1640*. Vol. 4. Joan Thirsk, ed. Cambridge: Cambridge University Press.

———. 1967b. "Enclosing and Engrossing." In *The Agrarian History of England and Wales, 1500–1640*. Vol. 4. Joan Thirsk, ed. Cambridge: Cambridge University Press.

Thomas, Milton H., ed. 1955. *Elias Boudinot's Journey to Boston in 1809*. Princeton, N.J.: Princeton University Press.

Thomson, Betty Flanders. 1977. *The Changing Face of New England*. Boston: Houghton Mifflin Co.

Thoreau, Henry David. 1854. *Walden; Or, Life in the Woods*. Boston: Ticknor and Fields.

———. 1906. *The Writings of Henry David Thoreau*. Vol. 6. Bradford Torrey, ed. Boston: Houghton Mifflin and Co.

Tocqueville, Alexis de. 1840. *Democracy in America*. 2 vols. Henry Reeve, trans. New York: J. and H. G. Langley.

Tolles, Bryant Franklin, Jr. 1973. *Norwood: The Centennial History of a Massachusetts Town*. Norwood, Mass.: Centennial Committee.

Trewartha, Glenn T. 1946. "Types of Rural Settlement in Colonial America." *Geographical Review* 36.

Tuan, Yi-Fu. 1977. *Space and Place: The Perspective of Experience*. Minneapolis: University of Minnesota Press.

Tucker, Bruce. 1986. "The Reinvention of New England, 1601–1770." *New England Quarterly* 59.

Upham, Charles W. 1867. *Salem Witchcraft*. Boston: By the Author.

Vance, James E., Jr. 1970. *The Merchant's World: The Geography of Wholesaling*. Englewood Cliffs, N.J.: Prentice-Hall.

———. 1977. *This Scene of Man: The Role and Structure of the City in the Geography of Western Civilization*. New York: Harper's College Press.

———. 1990a. *The Continuing City: Urban Morphology in Western Civilization*. Baltimore: Johns Hopkins University Press.

———. 1990b. "Democratic Utopia in the American Landscape." In *The Making of the American Landscape.* Michael P. Conzen, ed. Boston: Unwin Hyman.

Vickers, Daniel. 1990. "Competency and Competition: Economic Culture in Early New England." *William and Mary Quarterly* ser. 3, 47.

Wagner, Phillip L. 1972. *Environments and Peoples.* Englewood Cliffs, N.J.: Prentice-Hall.

Warden, G. B. 1978. "Law Reform in England and New England." *William and Mary Quarterly* ser. 3, 35.

Waters, J. J. 1982. "Family, Inheritance, and Migration in Colonial New England: The Evidence from Guilford, Connecticut." *William and Mary Quarterly* ser. 3, 39.

Webster's New International Dictionary. 1935. 2nd ed. Springfield, Mass.: G. and C. Merriam.

Weeden, William B. 1891. *Economic and Social History of New England, 1620–1789.* 2 vols. Boston: Houghton Mifflin Co.

Westbrook, Perry D. 1982. *The New England Town in Fact and Fiction.* East Brunswick, N.J.: Associated University Presses.

Wheatley, Paul. 1971. *The Pivot of the Four Quarters: A Preliminary Inquiry into the Origins and Character of the Ancient Chinese City.* Chicago: Aldine.

Wheeler, George A., and Henry W. Wheeler. 1878. *History of Brunswick, Topsham and Harpwell, Maine.* Boston: Alfred Mudge and Sons.

Wheeler, Ruth R. 1967. *Concord: Climate for Freedom.* Concord, Mass.: Concord Antiquarian Society.

White, Alain C., comp. 1920. *The History of the Town of Litchfield, Connecticut, 1720–1920.* Litchfield, Conn.: Litchfield Historical Society.

White, C. Hunter. 1947. *Wickford and Its Old Houses.* Wickford, R.I.: The Main Street Association of Wickford.

White, Philip A., and Dana D. Johnson. 1973. *Early Houses of Norwich, Vermont.* 2nd rev. ed. Norwich, Vt.: Norwich Historical Society.

Wilcoxson, William H. 1939. *History of Stratford, Connecticut, 1639–1939.* Stratford: Stratford Tercentenary Commission.

Williamson, Joseph. 1877. *History of the City of Belfast In the State of Maine, 1770–1875.* Portland, Maine: Loving, Short, and Harmon.

Wilson, R. G. 1987. "American Arts and Crafts Architecture: Radical Though Dedicated to the Cause Conservative." In *"The Art That Is Life": The Arts and Crafts Movement in America, 1875–1920.* Wendy Kaplan, ed. Boston: Museum of Fine Arts.

Wilson, William W. 1989. *The City Beautiful Movement.* Baltimore: Johns Hopkins University Press.

Winslow, Ola E. 1952. *Meetinghouse Hill: 1630–1783.* New York: Macmillan.

Winterbotham, William. 1795. *An Historical, Geographical, Commercial, and Philosophical View of the American United States.* 4 vols. J. Ridgeway, ed. London: By the Editor.

Winthrop, John. 1629. "A Model of Christian Charity Written on Board the Arra-
bella on the Atlantic Ocean." Winthrop Papers, II.

———. 1825–26. *The History of New England From 1630–1649.* 2 vols. James Savage,
ed. New York: Little, Brown and Co.

Wood, David H. 1969. *Lenox: Massachusetts Shiretown.* Lenox, Mass.: Town of Lenox.

Wood, Frederick J. 1919. *The Turnpikes of New England and Evolution of the Same
Through England, Virginia, and Maryland.* Boston: Marshall Jones Co.

Wood, Joseph S. 1978. "The Origin of the New England Village." Ph.D. dissertation, Pennsylvania State University.

———. 1982a. "Village and Community in Early Colonial New England." *Journal of
Historical Geography* 8.

———. 1982b. "Agricultural Villages, Circa 1780." In *This Remarkable Continent: An
Atlas of United States and Canadian Society and Cultures.* John F. Rooney, Jr., Wilbur
Zelinsky, and Dean Louder, eds. College Station: Texas A&M University Press.

———. 1984. "Elaboration of a Settlement System: The New England Village in
the Federal Period." *Journal of Historical Geography* 10.

———. 1986. "The New England Village as an American Vernacular Form." In *Perspectives on Vernacular Architecture, II.* Camille Wells, ed. Columbia: University of
Missouri Press.

———. 1991. "'Build, Therefore, Your Own World': The New England Village as
Settlement Ideal." *Annals of the Association of American Geographers* 81.

———. 1994. "New England's Exceptionalist Tradition: Rethinking the Colonial
Encounter with the Land." *Connecticut History* 35.

Wood, Joseph S., and Michael Steinitz. 1992. "A World We Have Gained: House,
Common, and Village in New England." *Journal of Historical Geography* 18.

Wood, Sumner G. 1908. *The Taverns and Turnpikes of Blandford 1733–1833.* Blandford,
Mass.: By the Author.

Wood, William. 1865. *New England's Prospect: A True, Lively, and Experimental Description.* London: John Bellamie, 1634. Reprint ed. Boston: The Prince Society.

Woodstock Area Chamber of Commerce. 1986. *Window on Woodstock.* Woodstock, Vt.

Worsham, Charlotte. 1985. "Architectural Development." In *The Historic and Archeological Resources of Central Massachusetts.* Michael Steinitz et al., eds. Boston:
Massachusetts Historical Commission.

Worthington, Erastus. 1827. *The History of Dedham.* Boston: Dutton and Wentworth.

Yentsch, Anne. 1988. "Legends, Houses, Families and Myths: Relationships Between Material Culture and American Ideology." In *Documentary Archaeology in
the New World.* Mary C. Beaudry, ed. New York: Cambridge University Press.

Zelinsky, Wilbur. 1953. "The Log House in Georgia." *Geographical Review* 43.

———. 1958. "The New England Connecting Barn." *Geographical Review* 48.

———. 1973. *The Cultural Geography of the United States.* Englewood Cliffs, N.J.:
Prentice-Hall.

———. 1977. "The Pennsylvania Town: An Overdue Geographical Account." *Geographical Review* 67.

Zuckerman, Michael. 1970. *Peaceable Kingdoms: New England Towns in the Eighteenth Century.* New York: Alfred A. Knopf.

———. 1977. "The Fabrication of Identity in Early America." *William and Mary Quarterly* ser. 3, 34.

Index

Page references to illustrations are printed in italic type.

Related Books in the Series